Perspectives on Connoisseurship of Chinese Painting

Perspectives on Connoisseurship of Chinese Painting

Edited with an Introduction
by Jason C. Kuo

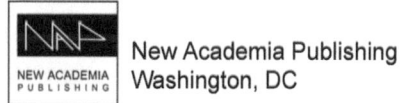

New Academia Publishing
Washington, DC

Library of Congress Control Number: 2008923009
ISBN 978-0-9800814-7-3 hardcover (alk. paper)

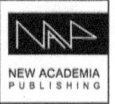

New Academia Publishing
P.O. Box 24720, Washington, DC 20038-7420
info@newacademia.com - www.newacademia.com

To

Yuli
Linda
Leo

Contents

Illustrations

Acknowledgments

I am most grateful to the Henry Luce Foundation for its generous support of the three-year Summer Institute of Connoisseurship of Chinese Calligraphy and Painting at the University of Maryland and the publication of this book. I would like to thank all of the participants in the Institute for their contribution. I am very grateful to many of the visiting instructors of the Institute, including Marilyn Wong-Gleysteen; Joseph Chang, John Wang, and Jan Stuart of the Freer Gallery of Art and the Arthur M. Sackler Gallery; Lo Ch'ing-che of the National Taiwan Normal University; Yu Hui of the Palace Museum in Beijing; and Wang Yao-t'ing and Lin Po-t'ing of the National Palace Museum in Taipei. Several institutions and individuals generously made their collections available to the participants for firsthand examination, including the Freer Gallery of Art and the Arthur M. Sackler Gallery, the National Palace Museum in Taipei, Professor Lo Ch'ing-che of the National Taiwan Normal University, and Professor Yang Ju-pin of the National Tsing Hua University in Hsinchu. The support of James Harris, Dean of the College of Arts and Humanities, and my colleagues in the Department of Art History and Archaeology at the University of Maryland was indispensable to the success of the Institute. The Institute for Global Chinese Affairs at the University of Maryland provided all necessary logistical assistance and I am most grateful to Rebecca McGinnis for her assistance.

I would also like to express my sincere gratitude to all of the contributors to the book for sharing their insights; to Wen Jingen, who twice participated in the Institute, for his generous assistance in preparing the book; to Quint Gregory, for his assistance in preparing the illustrations; and to Joel Kalvesmaki, for his patient and careful copyediting.

Jason C. Kuo

Note on Transcriptions

In general, the pinyin system of transcribing Chinese names and terms is used in this book. Exceptions include self-chosen names of modern Chinese scholars and artists (such as Chang Dai-chien, Wen C. Fong, Wai-kam Ho, C. C. Wang, Ju-hsi Chou, and Shen C. Y. Fu), names and terms in titles of publications using different systems of transcription (such as the Wade-Giles system), and a few names in Southern Chinese dialects. Japanese names and terms are transcribed according to the modified Hepburn system.

Introduction

Jason C. Kuo

The book has grown out of material presented at the Summer Institute of Connoisseurship of Chinese Calligraphy and Painting at the University of Maryland, funded by a generous three-year grant from the Henry Luce Foundation. The Institute, which I directed, was held from 2001 to 2003. It was attended by scholars from Harvard University, Princeton University, The Ohio State University, the University of California at San Diego, the University of California at Los Angeles, the University of California at Santa Barbara, the University of California at Berkeley, the University of Pennsylvania, and the University of Maryland, as well as the Palace Museum in Beijing and the National Palace Museum in Taipei. The institute was established to provide intensive training in connoisseurship through firsthand experience with works of art in the Washington, D.C. area. The goal of the institute was to promote the study both of original works of art and of the fundamental problems in the connoisseurship of Chinese calligraphy and painting, and to enhance the quality of art-historical research and teaching.

As John Walsh, former director of the Getty Center, aptly put it in his convocation speech at the 1999 annual meeting of the College Art Association, one of the most important challenges facing art historians and museum professionals today is that graduate schools have produced art historians with serious weaknesses, particularly a lack of direct firsthand experience with original works of art. Indeed, in *The Art of Art History: A Critical Anthology*, edited by Donald Preziosi and published in 1998, which was called by Norman Bryson of Harvard University "definitely the best introduction to art history currently available," there is very little, if any, attention to connoisseurship.[1] Walsh called for closer cooperation between art history programs and museums in rectifying this deficiency in our education of both future art historians and museum professionals.

In this country, graduate programs in Chinese art in general and in Chinese calligraphy and painting in particular have not escaped this problem. In fact, many of our advanced graduate students and recent Ph.D.s in Chinese art have received very little, if any, formal training in connoisseurship; many of them could not decipher the cursive- and seal-script calligraphy of the inscriptions or colophons that accompany Chinese paintings, or of the legends of seals used by calligraphers, painters, and collectors, that are found on almost every Chinese painting. Thus, in many cases, they could not even identify important information about the works of art, let alone make a sound judgment about their quality or authenticity. As to the nature of brushwork in Chinese calligraphy and painting, because new scholars rarely possess experience in creating calligraphy and painting with the pliant brush employed by Chinese calligraphers and painters, they often fail to see patterns in how Chinese calligraphers and painters make decisions and to connect these patterns to the art of the past. It is no surprise that connoisseurship in Chinese calligraphy and painting is often avoided not only by professors in art history but also by graduate students. It goes without saying that to construct art history out of artworks unproven as to their authorship and dates of production tends to produce a "history" without foundation and of little value. If we base our construction of art history on works of calligraphy and painting and on the inscriptions, colophons, and seal impressions that accompany them, we must first make sure of their authorship and identity.

Although the literature on connoisseurship written in Chinese is extensive, so far there is no publication, in any language, in which connoisseurship in Chinese painting and in European painting are discussed together. The only substantial publication in English on connoisseurship of Chinese painting, *Chinese Pictorial Art as Viewed by the Connoisseur* by Robert Hans van Gulik, was published in 1958 in Rome; the book was quite useful when first published but is now considered outdated by most scholars.[2] The other two publications, *Studies in Connoisseurship: Chinese Paintings from the Arthur M. Sackler Collection*, a catalog of an exhibition organized by Marilyn W. Fu and Shen C. Y. Fu (1976), and *Issues of Authenticity in Chinese Painting*, edited by Judith G. Smith and Wen C. Fong (1999), are limited to either works in the collection of a collector (Sackler) or a single painting (*Riverbank* attributed to Dong Yuan of the tenth century in The Metropolitan Museum of Art).[3]

In Chapter 1 ("Reflections on Connoisseurship of Chinese Calligraphy and Painting"), I review traditional Chinese connoisseurship in recent decades to provide the background for subsequent chapters. It is clear, from the rich array of recent Chinese publications on the subject, that scholars in China are acutely aware of the tradition of Chinese connoisseurship as well as the challenges facing today's scholars, both within and without China. The essay by Cahill (Chapter 2: "Chinese Art and Authenticity") opens the discussion with wide-ranging reflections on his lifelong experience as a curator, collector, and art historian of Chinese painting. He discusses various factors that bring into question the authenticity of some of the works ascribed to noted Chinese artists. His essay compares the Chinese attitude toward authenticity and forgery with that of Western scholars of Chinese painting and highlights the fundamental issues in constructing the history of Chinese painting. Silbergeld's essay (Chapter 3: "Three Paradigms for the Consideration of Authenticity in Chinese Art") is, in part, an expansive response to Cahill's piece. Silbergeld addresses the problems inherent in authentication and in trying to understand important and complex art-historical puzzles.

The essay by Richard Spear (Chapter 4: "What Is an Original?") explores the various aspects of the meaning of an "original" work of art in the field of Baroque art. In response to the essays by Cahill and Silbergeld, he provides fascinating comparisons between the Chinese and European traditions of art-historical scholarship. The essay by John Brown (Chapter 5: "Connoisseurship: Conceptual and Epistemological Fundamentals") provides readers with a philosopher's perspective on the basic epistemological concepts in the practice of connoisseurship, with comments on the essays by Cahill and Silbergeld. In her "Afterword: Chinese Brushwork and the Well-Informed Eye" (Chapter 6), Karen Lang comments on all of the essays, exploring the historiography of art history as an academic discipline and the intellectual and philosophical implications of the essays.

These essays, except Lang's "Afterword," were either presented or discussed extensively at the Summer Institute of Connoisseurship of Chinese Calligraphy and Painting at the University of Maryland. It is my hope that this book will encourage reasoned discussion among scholars, art historians, and curators in Chinese art in particular and those in the history of world art in general about fundamental issues in the study of art connoisseurship.

Notes

[1] Donald Preziosi, ed., *The Art of Art History: A Critical Anthology* (Oxford and New York: Oxford University Press, 1998).

[2] R. H. van Gulik, *Chinese Pictorial Art as Viewed by the Connoisseur* (Rome: Istituto italiano per il Medio ed Estremo Oriente, 1958).

[3] Marilyn Fu and Shen Fu, *Studies in Connoisseurship: Chinese Paintings from the Arthur M. Sackler Collection in New York and Princeton* (Princeton: The Art Museum, Princeton University, 1973); Judith Smith and Wen C. Fong, eds., *Issues of Authenticity in Chinese Painting* (New York: The Metropolitan Museum of Art, 1999).

1

Reflections on Connoisseurship of Chinese Calligraphy and Painting

Jason C. Kuo

In Chinese art history, the examination of painting and calligraphy is of great importance, because dating and authenticating specimens is a precondition for accurately rebuilding the history of Chinese painting and calligraphy, just as historical documents must be examined before they can be used to rewrite history. In subfields of Chinese art history that deal with epigraphy, identifying forged ancient inscriptions on bones and tortoise shells can make historians use them more cautiously. For example, Zhang Guangyu's *Wei zuo xian Qin yiqi mingwen shu yao* [Commentaries on forged inscriptions on pre-Qin sacrificial vessels] published in 1974 and Luo Fuyi's *Shang Zhou Qin Han qingtong qi bian wei lu* [Records on distinguishing genuine and forged bronze objects of Shang, Zhou, Qin, and Han dynasties] published in 1981 are works that all researchers on China's ancient history must consult.[1] From a certain angle, judging paintings and calligraphic works may be more difficult than judging counterfeit inscriptions on bones, forged pre-Qin sacrificial vessels, and even faked Tang-dynasty tricolor glazed pottery. This is chiefly because painting and calligraphic forgery has a long history and the forging techniques have become rather sophisticated. Some-times even first-rate artists make counterfeits. But, precisely because of the difficulties in connoisseurship, researchers must be even more careful and cautious in their study.

Owing to the uniqueness of its materials and its own de-velopment, art history has become over the last century a not-ed branch of humanities in the West. As a branch of Chinese art history the historical study of painting and calligraphy treats a wide range of subjects, such as the media and materi-als used, execution techniques, verification of works, iconol-ogy, biography (including psychology and psychoanalysis), geistesgeschichte, and so on. However, as stated above, con-noisseurship belongs to the fundamentals of art history. Zhu Shengzhai has gone into details in his essay "Lun shu hua shang jian zhi bu yi — gu jin zhong wai shi li ju zheng [On the difficulties of calligraphy and painting connoisseurship — old and new cases in Chinese and non-Chinese art historical stud-ies]," and there is no need for me to repeat the cases here. Citing the cases of Zhang Taijie (ca. 1633), Gao Shiqi (1645–1704), Du Ruilian (ca. 1881), Kang Youwei (1858–1927) and Dong Zuobin (1895–1964), he proves, by quoting Deng Chun (ca. 1167) from *Hua ji* (written as a sequel to *Tuhua jianwen zhi* [Records on seen and heard-of paintings] by Guo Ruoxu, ca. 1080), that "they are mainly literary persons. Though some of them may know painting, such persons are few." He also gives a precise interpretation of the heart of the matter in painting and calligraphy connoisseurship, quoting the preface by Yu Enrong (1808–1893) to his unpublished *Cang zhuo xuan zhen shang mu* [Catalogue of rare artworks viewed in the Studio of Hiding Incompetence; preface dated 1872] which is worth citing at length:

> The jade from Jingshan Mountain was not recognised as a treasure before Bian He presented it [to the king of State Chu, who twice dismissed it as a common stone]

three times. The steed from Jibei was not valued before Bole caught sight of it and recommended it. Since ancient times there have been a lot of fine jade and good horses, but Bian He and Bole do not emerge in all ages. For this I cannot help feeling sorry for the difficulty to become keen-eyed connoisseurs. Furthermore, paintings have been handed down from ancient times. Through the Jin, Tang, Song, Yuan to Ming dynasties there have been no lack of specialists and reputed masters in each era. Usually a foot-long piece of silk or paper [with such masters' painting or handwriting on it] is valued as highly as ancient jade, and can be priced at a thousand teals of silver in market. So profiteers compete with each other to imitate such works, and as a result the genuine and the forged become indistinguishable. Without reliable evidence for authenticity, those who are fond of ancient works judge them by the inscriptions they bear. Those people do not know that during the Yuan dynasty, Li Wenjian [Li Kan, ca. 1312] saw a dozen paintings of bamboo executed in ink, attributed to [the Song-dynasty painter] Wen Tong (1019–1079), and that accordingly, he profusely inscribed them all. None of those paintings turned out to be genuine. Shen Shitian [Shen Zhou, 1427–1509] produces a small painting in the morning and by noon a duplicate comes up. The forgers who forge by impressing counterfeit seals have several seals after his, and those who forge by imitating his colophons write exactly his hand. Another example is Dong Wenmin [Dong Qichang, 1555–1636], who was reserved and who seldom produced paintings for others. When entreated, he would ask other painters to oblige. When his servants proffered a forged piece in place of his genuine one and asked him to put a colophon on it, he would gladly grant the request. So are inscriptions reliable evidence of authenticity of a piece? Recently art dealers adopt numerous new artifices. When they get a famous painting, they divide the painting proper from the inscription. Often a false inscription is added to the genuine painting, and so the authenticity of the painting covers up the spuriousness of the forged inscription; on the other hand, when a genuine inscription is juxtaposed with a forged painting, the inscription lends credence to the painting forgery. On paintings of unknown artist of former times, false signatures are added. Since collectors tend to take seal imprints and colophons as evidence of authenticity, some forgers carve seals after those of artists of former times, and copy their colophons. The side margins of a vertical scroll and the matting to the right and the left of the painting proper on a horizontal scroll are full of such matters—counterfeit seal imprints of former times and celebrities' colophons put on spurious pieces. However, the vulgar [untrained] eyes cannot discern them, and as a result, crude rock from the Yan region is taken as a fine jade and a nag passes for a steed, and they are expected to be sold at a high price. Generally, this practice does little harm to ancient people. What is regrettable is that while through dynasties many ancient genuine works have been examined by noted connoisseurs, not a few works have been closely guarded in private collections and have not been shown to other people, hence not judged or inscribed. Once in the hand of a profiteer, impressions of private seals and comments will be added to those unexamined works. In case they are not elaborately mounted, nitpickers will call it a flaw, and consequently genuine ancient pieces are cast away without further investigation. This is really deplorable![2]

The last part of Yu Enrong's preface deserves particular attention. Some researchers may be overcautious and take genuine paintings for forgeries, and ancient paintings for paintings by later artists. This is as wrong as arbitrarily labeling paintings and calligraphies with famous artists' names. Being unduly careful is as bad as being careless. Neither excessive nor inadequate care keeps with the principle that truth must be based on finding out facts. Counterfeiting artworks has a long history, both in China and in other countries. Apart from commercial profit pursued by merchants, the other motivations or purposes of forgers are worth investigation. Notorious art forgers include Reinhold Vasters (1827–1909), who counterfeited medieval and Renaissance gold ware, Hans van Meegeren (1889–1947), who faked Johannes Vermeer's paintings, and Chang Dai-chien (Zhang Daqian, 1899–1983), who forged paintings of Bada Shanren (Zhu Da; 1626–1705), Shitao (Daoji; 1641–ca. 1720), Mei Qing (1623–1697), Hongren, Shixi (Kuncan; active 1657–1674) and many other artists from various dynasties.[3] It is important to note that there are also a large number of forgeries of calligraphic works and paintings purported to be by Zhang Daqian in both private and public collections.[4]

One of the best ways to review recent scholarship in con-noisseurship of Chinese painting and calligraphy would be to begin with the essay titled "Gu jiu zi hua jianbie fa [Methods of judging old paintings and calligraphic works]" by Li Zhichao (1900–1978). Less than thirty pages long and published post-humously, it is a concise introduction to traditional Chinese connoisseurship. In Section 4, "Bian wei [Distinguishing gen-uine works from the forged]," forty-three methods of forgery are concisely discussed to make students of connoisseurship more vigilant. The range of these methods is indeed mind-boggling:[5]

(1) Some works are copies, made by tracing on paper or silk the outline of the original work underneath.
(2) Some works, chiefly calligraphic, are traced on transparent waxed paper called *ying huang* (literally,

"stiff and yellow," the effect of the bee wax on the paper).

(3) Some works are duplicates executed by superimposing a sheet of paper or silk over the original work set against a light source and tracing the outline.

(4) There are works that have been executed by the ascribed artist's father, who was an established artist and who was eager to boost his son's reputation.

(5) There are works that have been created by persons other than the ascribed artists.

(6) Genuine paintings may have segments executed by artists other than the ascribed creator.

(7) Some calligraphic works and paintings are forged by the artist's contemporaries, and others by later artists. Forgeries done by an artist's contemporary who is himself or herself a well-trained artist are difficult to identify.

(8) Some forgers fabricate obscure artists' paintings.

(9) Some artists who resent being ignored by the public counterfeit celebrated artists' works to ridicule snobbery.

(10) Some forged or ghosted paintings bear genuine colophons of famous artists.

(11) Some paintings allegedly from the Song-dynasty imperial academy of painting have been created by artists who did not work in the academy.

(12) Some forgers remove the original colophons from artworks and add to them forged colophons of renowned artists, or falsified new colophons.

(13) Sometimes a personage or connoisseur is asked to inscribe paintings or calligraphic works and, as he/she finds it hard to decline the request, he/she has to oblige; usually such inscriptions do not touch on authenticity of the inscribed work.

(14) In the past, students of calligraphy used to copy model calligraphic works together with the original colophons and then put their own names underneath; forgers cut down the copier's colophon but keep the calligrapher's; they also impressed forged seals on the copy and thereby passed it off as an original ancient work.

(15) Some counterfeit paintings have colophons copied from other works.

(16) Sometimes a genuine colophon may lurk in an unnoticed place of a painting.

(17) Absence of half or two thirds of the inscription and seal imprints may be a sign either of the ravages of time or of a forger's handiwork.

(18) Inscriptions attributed to the Emperor Qianlong (r. 1736–1795) dating to the 64th year of his reign (1799, four years after he abdicted) could have been done by the emperor himself, because after abdicating his throne, he lived in his palace and continued to use the reign title Qianlong.

(19) In imperial China if one's name contained a character that is used in the name of the emperor on the throne, one must write that character with one stroke missing; also, one who paid tribute to the emperor with an artwork might remove one stroke from the artist's colophon in case the creator of the painting had a character coinciding with one in the emperor's name.

(20) Some paintings bear the inscription of a poem that is written by a much later poet.

(21) Wrongly written and misused characters may indicate forgery.

(22) An artist's name miswritten is a sign of forgery.

(23) Some inscriptions are physically transferred from other artworks.

(24) Forgers cut down part of a (landscape) painting along the outline of the mountains on the background and add a new background.

(25) Some worn-out paintings have patches from other worn-out paintings or touches added by other artists to make up the missing strokes or to link the patches.

(26) A large worn-out painting or calligraphic work may be reduced in size to pass for a new one.

(27) A handscroll may be destroyed (for instance, one may cut off a round fan-shaped piece from a handscroll and pass off the piece for an independent painting).

(28) A long scroll may be cut into two, one with the original colophon and seal imprints, and the other with falsified ones.

(29) Leaves from different albums, even of different times, may be remounted into one album.

(30) An album should have an even number of leaves. In case an album has an odd number of leaves, one tries to add leaves from other albums or ask an artist to create new leaves so as to make an even number.

(31) A set of hanging scrolls, sometimes bearing linked images, may have one or more scrolls missing.

(32) Paintings were forged in large quantities in Suzhou since the Ming dynasty at the latest.

(33) Paintings used in Buddhist or Daoist ceremonies to redeem the souls of the deceased may be remounted by merchants and pass for Song-dynasty works.

(34) Pictures of the 18 arhats (*luohan*) did not exist before the era of the Emperor Shenzong (r. 1068–1085) of the Song dynasty; be cautious of early paintings with this theme.

(35) Some artworks are anachronistic (for example, painting on folding fans first appeared during the reign of Chenghua [1465–1487] of the Ming dynasty, initially

on gold-foiled fans; fan paintings earlier than this time may be spurious).

(36) Paintings jointly created by more than one artist may bear false colophons.

(37) Some forgers counterfeit a painting and ascribe it to artists who lived at different times.

(38) Some paintings are actually collotype prints.

(39) A painting without imprints from an artist's seal is not necessarily a forgery.

(40) Genuine seal imprints and colophons may be transferred onto a forged painting, and vice versa.

(41) Inscriptions on the "poetry hall" (a blank space above the painting proper for inscription on the matting of a hanging scroll), on the sides, or on the right or left end of the matting, or the title labels, may be forged.

(42) Aged paper or silk is not reliable verification for the authenticity of the painting or calligraphic work it bears (paper and silk may be antiqued).

(43) Not all catalogues of art collections are reliable; they must be used with caution. Examples of catalogues in which forgeries are published include Zhang Taijie's *Bao hui lu* [Records of treasure paintings; preface dated 1633], Du Ruilian's *Gu Fen Ge shu hua ji* [Records of calligraphy and painting in the Pavilion of Antique Fragrance; preface dated 1881] and Yang Enshou's *Yan fu bian* [Records of feasts for my eyes; preface dated 1885].[6]

Compared with Li Zhichao's essay, Li Tiejiang's essay "Ping Zhai shu hua zha [Notes on calligraphy and painting in the Duckweed Studio]" and Li Dichen's book *Jianbie hua kaozheng yao lan* [Main points on judging paintings] not only are brief, but they repeat many views of former authors.[7] So they are less informative. Wang Yikun's book *Shu hua jianding jian shu* [A short introduction to connoisseurship in painting and calligraphy] is more substantial.[8] It has five chapters and an appended bibliography of records of important paintings and calligraphic works through dynasties. Based on his own experience as a curator for fifty years at the Palace Museum in Beijing, the author cites many cases to illustrate the principles that the main basis for judging the authenticity of paintings and calligraphic works are the spirit of the artists' times and their personal style as manifested in the works in question (Chapter 1), and that the accessory references may include seal imprints on artworks, silk or paper as the medium used, colophons and title labels, related recordings in catalogues and historical documents, the mountings of the artworks, and their decorations (Chapter 2). The third chapter expounds related knowledge about verifying painting and calligraphy, introducing many artists' alternative names (*zi*), style names (*hao*), and birthplaces and dates of birth and death. The fourth chapter of this book exposes different methods of counterfeiting paintings and calligraphic works, and finally, the fifth chapter presents the whole procedure of connoisseurship and offers points for attention. The third part of the third chapter, "Forgery with local features," and the fifth chapter merit special attention. The former lists characteristics of counterfeit paintings and calligraphic works produced in Suzhou, Henan, Hunan, Guangdong, the "back gate" (Di'anmen) of Beijing, Yangzhou (where faked paintings with the false colophon of Shitao are noted for the brushstrokes in the shape of a cobbler's knife, hence the name *pijiang dao* "cobbler's knife"), and the forgers' group in Shanghai. The fifth chapter illustrates the whole procedure of examining painting and calligraphy with real cases. The author points out, "The paintings and calligraphic works we are verifying are of various kinds. Each piece is in its own condition. We must analyze different types of real painting and calligraphic works in line with their own state of existence." On the basis of his experience over the years in connoisseurship, the author cites artworks from the collections of many museums, so that readers can corroborate the author's judgment by themselves. This makes the book worth perusing. Its appendix "Li dai shu hua zhu lu yao mu [Main catalogues of calligraphic works and paintings through dynasties]" is worth reading but seems a bit too short. So the reader should also consult the following works: *Shu hua shu lu jie ti* [Abstracts of painting and calligraphy catalogues] by Yu Shaosong, *Gu shu hua za ji* [Miscellaneous notes on old paintings and calligraphic works] by Huang Miaozi, *An Annotated Bibliography of Chinese Painting Catalogues and Related Texts* by Hin-cheung Lovell, and *Si bu zong lu yishu bian* [A reference book on art compiled from the complete works of the four branches of learning] edited by Ding Fubao and Zhou Yunqing.[9]

Of all works on connoisseurship published in recent years, Xu Bangda's *Gu shu hua jianding gailun* [An introduction to connoisseurship in ancient painting and calligraphy] may be regarded as the most systematic treatise.[10] The book has five chapters: "Zong lun [Introduction]," "Ge dai zhuyao shu-hua jia he liupai jianshu [Outline of major calligraphers and painters and the schools through dynasties]," "Jianbie gu shu hua ying zhuyi de ge dian [Points for attention in judging ancient calligraphy and painting]," "Gu shu hua jianding de fuzhu ziliao [Accessory matters consultable for examination of ancient painting and calligraphy]," and "Zuowei he wuding de shi kuang [Cases of forgery and misidentifications]." Xu Bangda is also the author of *Li dai shu hua jia zhuanji kaobian* [Studies in biographies of calligraphers and painters through dynasties], with studies in the lives of 27 ancient Chinese artists.[11] The most enlightening are the chapters "Shu-huajia mingzi xiangtong huo xiangjin zhi er ren wu hun wei yi kaobian [Studies in misidentification of two artists as one due to identical or similar names]" and "Jiang shu-huajia ming yu zi fenkai yizhi wu ding wei er ren kaobian [Studies in recognizing one artist as two due to separation of his/her *ming* (given name) and *zi* (alternative/courtesy name)]." The chapter "Gong Xian shengping ji kaoding [Studies in Gong Xian's life and art]," which compares styles of Gong Xian (1619?–1689) and his students Zong Yan, Guan Quan, the monk Julai and Gong Zhu (active 1696), is also instructive. A number of his articles published in the journal *Shu Pu* [Treatise on calligraphy] in Hong Kong and other periodicals in recent years are also noteworthy. "Song Huizong Zhao Ji qinbi yu daibi hua kaobian [Examination and identification of paintings executed by Zhao Ji the Emperor Huizong (r. 1101–1125) of the Song dynasty, and paintings created by other artists and ascribed to him]" and "Gu shu hua bian wei shi zhen (3)—Dong Qichang (1555–1636), Wang Shimin, Wang Jian zuopin kaobian [Identifying the counterfeit and recognizing the genuine, part 3: Studies in authentic and forged paintings of Dong Qichang, Wang Shimin (1592–1680), and Wang Jian (1588–1677)]" are consummate discourses on ghosting in the history of ancient Chinese painting. Xu Bangda's most monumental work so far, however, must be the four-volume set titled *Gu shuhua wei e kaobian* [Examination and identification of the forging of ancient calligraphy and painting].[12] In a sympathetic review of the book, Thomas Lawton, former Director of the Freer Gallery of Art and the Arthur M. Sackler Gallery of Art in Washington, D.C., summarizes the importance of this work: "There is no better guide for young scholars who want to learn more about the connoisseurship of Chinese calligraphy and painting than the writings of Xu Bangda. His keen observations make them not only an invaluable reference work, but also extraordinarily instructive. Serious consideration should be given to using *Gu shuhua wei e kaobian*, together with *Gu shu hua jianding gailun*, as textbooks for seminars on Chinese connoisseurship. Older, more opinionated specialists should appreciate the rare

opportunity of being able to match wits—and convictions—
with one of China's most distinguished specialists."[13]

It is important to mention here the contributions made by
other senior Chinese scholars (such as Xie Zhiliu, Qi Gong,
Liu Jiu'an, Yang Renkai, and Fu Xinian) who, like Xu Bangda,
served on the Committee on the Authentication of Ancient
Chinese Calligraphy and Painting from 1984 to 1992.[14] In contrast to Xu Bangda's *Gu shuhua wei e kaobian* and *Gu shu hua
jianding gailun*, Xie Zhiliu's *Jian yu za gao* [Miscellaneous notes
written after examining artworks] is a collection of essays covering a wide range of topics.[15] The concluding essay, "Lun shu
hua jianbie [On painting and calligraphy connoisseurship],"
provides general principles regarding connoisseurship of
painting and calligraphy. It provides an easy approach to
connoisseurship and should be read in tandem with an older
treatise entitled *Zenyang jianding shu hua* [How to authenticate calligraphy and painting] by Zhang Heng.[16] Xie Zhiliu's
other major articles in this book are also worth perusing; they
treat the Jin-dynasty calligrapher Wang Xizhi's (303?–361?)
Shan yu tie, Tang-dynasty painter Zhou Fang's (late 8th to
early 9th century) *Zhan hua shi nü tu* [Ladies with flowers in
their hair] and the spirit of the artist's time, the Tang-dynasty
calligrapher Liu Gongquan's (778–865) *Meng zhao tie* [model
calligraphic book on "by his majesty's edict..."] and *Zi si sa tie*
[model calligraphic book on "purple silk sandals"], and the
Song-dynasty artist Li Cheng's (919–967) *Mao lin yuan xiu tu*
[Dense forest and distant peaks]. As to Xie Zhiliu's achievement
in connoisseurship, the contemporary critic Zheng Zhong provides a special analysis. So I will not dwell on it here.[17]

Qi Gong cong gao [Collected works of Qi Gong] by Qi Gong
(1912–2005) collects the author's finest articles, published
over decades, on identifying painting and calligraphic works.
In the article "Dong Qichang shu hua daibi ren kao [Studies
in artists who created calligraphies and paintings and gave
authorship to Dong Qichang]," he holds that the so-called

album *Xiao zhong jian da* [Seeing the great from the small] now in the collection of the National Palace Museum in Taipei was produced by Chen Mingqing and not by Dong Qichang or Wang Shimin. There are also articles on the forged albums attributed to Bada Shanren (Zhu Da) and Wu Li (1632–1718), and the faked handscroll *Xi yuan ya ji tu* [Refined meeting in the western garden] attributed to Qiu Ying (1494?–1552?).[18] The essays in this book make it clear that to be a connoisseur of ancient Chinese calligraphy and painting requires not only artistic sensibility but also immense erudition.

Former director of the Liaoning Provincial Museum at Shenyang, Yang Renkai's best-known publication is perhaps his 1991 book, *Guobao chenfou lu: Gugong sanyi shuhua jianwen kaolue* [Record of the vicissitudes of national treasures: investigation of the dispersed and lost calligraphies and paintings from the former palace that I have seen and heard about].[19] Apart from the high drama about the dispersal and recovery of a large number of important Chinese works of art during the twentieth century, Yang Renkai also discusses the fascinating history of systematic making of forgeries in Suzhou; his discussion of *Suzhou pian* should be read in conjunction with Ellen Johnston Laing's article on *Suzhou pian* and the problem of Qiu Ying.[20] Yang Renkai's other important contribution to the study of connoisseurship can be seen in his more systematic treatise titled *Zhongguo shuhua jianding xue gao* [A preliminary study on the connoisseurship of Chinese calligraphy and painting].[21] Perhaps the most fascinating aspects of this work are Yang Renkai's discussion on the disagreements among Chinese and non-Chinese experts on the dating and authenticity of key extant monuments in the history of Chinese calligraphy and painting. It is instructive and mind-boggling to peruse his list, Appendix 1 to the book, of the different and often contradictory judgments given by the members of the Committee on the Authentication of Ancient Chinese Calligraphy and Painting on a large number of Yuan and pre-Yuan calligraphies and paintings. In 1998, he organized a special exhibition, at the Shanghai Museum, of major paintings and calligraphic works from the Liaoning Provincial Musuem; one of the highlights of the exhibition was the display of several pairs of genuine and forged calligraphies and paintings, both to intrigue and to instruct general museum-goers and students of connoisseurship.[22] In 2006, he published a fine selection of his essays on connoisseurship in a book titled *Zhongguo shuhua yanjiu* [Studies on Chinese calligraphy and painting].[23] Yang Renkai's intellectual honesty is admirable and we are made acutely aware of the challenges in our enterprise in connoisseurship.

One of the most educational and fascinating exhibitions that I have seen was the "Exhibition of Important Forgeries of Calligraphies and Paintings in the Nation" held in the fall of 1994 at the Palace Museum in Beijing. According to Yang Xin, then Deputy Director of the Palace Museum, who wrote the preface to the exhibition catalog titled *Zhongguo lidai shuhua jianbei tulu* [An illustrated catalog of authenticated Chinese calligraphies and paintings through the ages] edited by Liu Jiu'an, such an exhibition had been first proposed by Zhang Heng more than thirty years earlier and was initiated by Liu Jiu'an and realized with the support of the Bureau of Cultural Relics of the Ministry of Culture.[24] Liu Jiu'an's essay titled "Tan Zhongguo gudai shuhua jianding [On the authentication of ancient Chinese calligraphy and painting]" provides students with one of the most concise contemporary treatises on various methods of forgeries. But the most useful and instructive aspect of the exhibition and the accompanying catalog is the large number of side-by-side comparisons of genuine and forged works and the clear and convincing demonstration of how the authentication was achieved by means of visual and textual evidence. Liu Jiu'an also published his methodological essays and several case studies on connoisseurship in an important book titled *Liu Jiu'an shuhua jianding ji* [Liu Jiu'an on the connoisseurship of calligraphy and painting]; these essays, when read in conjunction with his comments on specific works illustrated in *Zhongguo lidai shuhua jianbei tulu*, will certainly enable students to become more acutely aware of the pitfalls as well as the challenges in looking at Chinese calligraphy and painting.[25]

Fu Xinian is one of China's most eminent archaeologists and scholars of Chinese architecture. It is therefore not surprising that he often looks at Chinese painting through the perspectives of archaeology and history of architecture. His essay on the dating of the handscroll *You chun tu* ["Spring Outing"], attributed to Zhan Ziqian (ca. late sixth century) and now in the Place Museum in Beijing, is a good example of using archaeological evidence in authenticating ancient Chinese painting.[26]

Lu Wuya's *Zhongguo gu hua jian bian zhishi* [Introduction to the authentication of ancient Chinese paintings] is a collection of essays, and not a systematic treatise. However, his vivid and easy style has its merits.[27] In the preface the author points out, "It is true that one should see genuine works. But one must see forgeries as well. From comparison of a large number of genuine and counterfeit pieces one will acquire experience and sharpen one's eyes" (p. 3). His other viewpoints are enlightening too. For example, he insists, "better have a small collection of fine works than a large collection of poor works" (p. 10); "I'd rather buy a sketch from life executed by Huang Binhong (1865–1955) at a low price than buy a complete scroll of landscape at a high price. The reason is simple: I prefer genuine works to works of suspect authorship" (p. 65). The author succinctly explains the characteristics of horses painted by Xu Beihong (1895–1953) and how to authenticate them (p. 59). When discussing a landscape after ancient works done by Qi Baishi (1863–1957) in 1922, the author points out that one cannot condemn Qi Baishi's works executed prior to his age of seventy as fakes on the ground that they lack for Qi

Baishi's "traditional" vigor (evident in works done from age seventy to ninety). Therefore, he notes, "It is paramount to realize that with passage of time, an artist's brushwork and ink application changes" (p. 35). All in all, this essayistic book offers valuable suggestions to beginners. Lu Wuya's discussion of forgeries purported to be from the hands of twentieth-century masters is a reminder that, as long as there is a market for art, there will be forgeries of both ancient, modern, and contemporary art.

Use of seal imprints is a feature of Chinese calligraphy and painting. Seal imprints play a significant role in the examination of artworks. Unfortunately there exist not only counterfeit paintings and calligraphic works, but also counterfeit seals and seal imprints on both genuine and forged calligraphies and paintings. For examination and authentication of seals imprints, Luo Fuyi's article "Cong yinzhang shang jianbie gu shu hua [Judging ancient paintings and calligraphic works by examining seal imprints]" is illuminating.[28] As for earlier seals, Xu Bangda's "Song Jin nei fu shu hua de zhuanghuang biaoti cang yin he kao [Studies in titles and collectors' seal imprints on paintings and calligraphic works in imperial collections of the Song and Jin dynasties]" is also a good reference.[29] Zhuang Shen's essay "Gugong shu hua suo jian ming dai ban guan yin kao" [Studies in truncated imprints of a Ming-dynasty official seal on paintings and calligraphic works in the collection of the National Palace Museum in Taipei]" is very helpful for dating artworks.[30] The author authenticates and lists truncated imprints of a Ming-dynasty official seal found on artworks in public and private collections, including those in the collection of the National Palace Museum; the essay is thus beneficial to would-be connoisseurs, because the imprint was made by an office that was in operation only between 1374 and 1384 in the Ming court and therefore a genuine imprint on a work of art indicates that such a work was in the imperial collection before 1384. The challenge, of course, is how to distinguish between imprints made from genuine seals and those from forged ones.[31]

The important role of authenticated seal imprints in determining the authenticity and date of Chinese calligraphic works and painting brings us to the necessity of studying calligraphy for any aspiring connoisseur of Chinese painting; this is one of the reasons that there is often a department of calligraphy and painting, not merely a department of painting, in major museums in China. In other words, the connoisseurship of Chinese painting cannot be separated from that of Chinese calligraphy. One of the most important events in the academic study of Chinese calligraphy in the postwar period in the United States was the publication of *Traces of the Brush: Studies in Chinese Calligraphy* by Shen C. Y. Fu in collaboration with Marilyn W. Fu, Mary G. Neill, and Mary Jane Clark; it was published as the catalogue of a special exhibition of calligraphy held at the Yale University Art Gallery and the University Art Museum at the University of California, Berkeley in 1977.[32] Shen Fu, the organizer of the exhibition was trained in Taiwan as a calligrapher-painter and art historian in Taiwan before embarking on further study at Princeton University; he later taught at Yale University and served as curator at the Freer Gallery of Art and the Arthur M. Sackler Gallery in Washington, D.C. Since he has returned to Taiwan to live and teach and since the revised edition of the catalog has been translated into Chinese and published in China, it is appropriate to consider his scholarship in the present essay.[33] Noticeable is the catalog's first chapter, in which the authors elaborate on basic terms in connoisseurship of Chinese calligraphy—*linmo*, copy (which has three subcategories: *ying huang*, copy on transparent waxed paper; *xiangta*, copy done by putting paper or silk over the original and tracing the outline of the original against a light source; and *goutian*, copy done by tracing the outline of strokes of the original and filling the outline with ink); *fang*, imitation;

zao, fakes; as well as *ke tie*, rubbing from stone inscriptions. Then the author lists some copies, including that of Wang Xizhi's *Xing rang tie* on transparent waxed paper done by Tang-dynasty artists, in the collection of Princeton University; copy of Chu Suiliang's (596–658) *Ai ce* [Funeral oration] done by the Ming-dynasty artist Yang Cheng (1540–1600) by tracing the outline of the original and filling the outline with ink strokes, in the collection of Weng Wange (Wan-go H. C. Weng); the copy of Huang Tingjian's (1045–1105) *Han Shan Pang Yun shi* [Poems of Han Shan and Pang Yun as transcribed by Huang Tingjian] on a handscroll executed during the late Ming dynasty, in the collection of John M. Crawford, Jr.; the handscroll *Shuang song ping yuan tu* [Two pines against a flat vista] by Zhao Mengfu (1254–1322) now in The Metropolitan Museum of Art in comparison with a tracing copy of the painting now in Cincinnati Art Museum; the handscroll of Xianyu Shu's (1257?–1302) *Yu shi zhen* [Admonitions to the imperial censors] in large regular-running script, in the Art Museum of Princeton University and its copy (an anonymous loan to the exhibition) done by tracing the outline of the original and filling the outline with ink; the handscroll of Shitao's *Song Ren'an shi* [Farewell poem to Ren'an] in large running script in the Museum of Fine Arts in Boston; Wen Tonghe's (1830–1904) couplet (each line in seven characters), and a copy of the couplet done by elaborating on the backing paper separated from the original piece, both in the author's own collection. Through these case studies, the author and his collaborators meticulously illustrate different methods and procedures of painting and calligraphy connoisseurship; they also demonstrate that studying calligraphy and painting together is all part and parcel of being a connoisseur.

Of books published in recent years on examination of rubbings (*bei* or "ink squeezes") from calligraphy carved on the surfaces of either stone or wood and autographic calligraphy (*tie*), Wang Zhuanghong's *Bei tie jianbie changshi*

[An introduction to examining rubbings and autographic calligraphy] is a most succinct and practical guide to aspiring connoisseurs who are keen acquiring a firsthand knowledge of Chinese calligraphy as part of their training in connoisseurship.[34] Its appendix "Yingyin ben li dai moji zhen wei biao [A list of photo-offset copies of genuine and counterfeit ancient calligraphic works (prior to the Yuan dynasty 1206–1368)]" is particularly helpful. Due to the advance of photographic technology in modern times, an immense amount of photo-offset copies of calligraphic works are being produced. Those copies are a mixture of the genuine and counterfeit. If one is not careful enough, one tends to take counterfeit copies as genuine models. For example, *Chu shi song* [On military expedition] attributed to Suo Jing (239–303) and published by the Commercial Press in Shanghai, *Liu yi xu* [On the six arts] in cursive script attributed to Liu Xin (d. 23) and published by the Yi yuan zhen shang she [Publishing house for genuine appreciation in art] in Shanghai, *Qian zi wen* [Thousand-character essay] in regular and cursive scripts attributed to the monk Zhiyong (6th century) and published jointly by the eminent scholar Luo Zhenyu (1866–1940) and the Japanese publisher Hakubundō, and *Gui qu lai ci* [Poem on homeward journey] in regular-running script attributed to Su Shi and published by Tokyōdō in Japan, are all counterfeits. This is a reminder that one must exercise extreme caution in utilizing any text or visual material to authenticate Chinese calligraphy and painting.

A further example of the tremendous demands on being a connoisseur is the amount of sinological training required in disciplines such as philology, history, and literature. Fangyu Wang's many essays, including the essay titled "Bada Shanren's Methods on Inscribing Dates on His Works," clearly demonstrate that, to decipher the artist's inscriptions (including poems, dates, and signatures) and seals correctly, one has to be knowledgeable about sometimes arcane literary allusions, diverse methods of dating, and archaic inscriptions. Ignorance about Bada Shanren's use of dating methods based, not on the more common system of "heavenly stems and earthly branches [*tiangan dizhi*]," but on the ancient text *Er Ya* and the "Li shu [Book of calendars]" section of the *Shi Ji* by Sima Qian (ca. 145–86 BC) of the Western Han dynasty, has led some scholars to misidentify the dates of his works.[35] On the other hand, classical learning alone does not necessarily qualify a scholar to be a connoisseur. For example, Xu Fuguan, one of the most eminent modern scholars of the Confucian classics, could not see the difference between the two versions of the fourteenth-century masterpiece, *Dwelling in the Fuchun Mountains* by Huang Gongwang (1269–1354), both in the National Palace Museum.[36]

In recent years exhibitions focusing on individual artists and art schools have been held and their catalogues are of academic value. Such exhibitions include the exhibition of Shitao's paintings curated by Richard Edwards in 1967 at the University of Michigan Museum of Art, the special exhibition of Wen Zhengming's works also organized by Richard Edwards in 1976 at the University of Michigan Museum of Art, the exhibition of Shitao's works curated by Shen C. Y. Fu with Marilyn W. Fu in 1973 at the Art Museum of Princeton University, the three consecutive exhibitions of the Wu School (Suzhou School) paintings curated by Jiang Zhaoshen in 1973–1974 at the National Palace Museum in Taipei, the special exhibition of Huangshan School (Anhui School) paintings organized by James Cahill in 1981 at the University Art Museum in Berkeley, the exhibition of nineteenth-century painting organized by Claudia Brown and Ju-hsi Chou in 1992–1993 at the Phoenix Art Museum, and the exhibition on the Zhe School organized by Richard Barnhart in 1993 at the Dallas Art Museum, to name just a few examples.[37] Such exhibitions often gave rise to disputes concerning authenticity of certain works. For example, Shen C. Y. Fu gave his opinions concerning some works in Edwards's exhibition of Shitao; Ju-hsi Chou raised questions about authenticity of Shen C. Y. Fu's exhibition of Shitao's paintings.[38] Perhaps one of the most contentious events in the field in recent years was the exhibition and the accompanying catalog and international symposium devoted to a single work of art, *Riverbank*, attributed to Dong Yuan and now in The Metropolitan Museum of Art.[39] These debates among scholars trained in both the Chinese and non-Chinese traditions have undoubtedly advanced the connoisseurship of Chinese painting and calligraphy.

In the words of Wai-kam Ho, "In the past twenty years or so, connoisseurship has been at the center of a cultural and intellectual dilemma which has divided the field of art history into bitterly opposing groups: those who are for connoisseurship, and those who are against it. Those who are opposed to traditional connoisseurship denounce it as one of the true signs of cultural elitism, which, in my opinion, is a misplaced criticism—an arbitrary separation of 'object' and 'theory,' and the kind of moral distortion remarked upon by the poet Su Shi almost a thousand years ago when he said: 'Every time a unified field of study is forced to split, the opportunists become more and more clever in disguising their falsehoods.'"[40] Shitao, the great seventeenth-century painter, called his method of painting the "Method of No-method (*wufa er fa*)."[41] In view of the intellectually challenging issues discussed in my brief review of recent scholarship, it is important that we do not limit our approaches to the study of Chinese calligraphy and painting to any particular tradition but must always be open to new perspectives.[42]

Notes

[1] Zhang Guangyu, *Wei zuo xian Qin yiqi mingwen shu yao* [Commentaries on forged inscriptions on pre-Qin sacrificial vessels] (Hong Kong: Xianggang shuju, 1974); Luo Fuyi, *Shang Zhou Qin Han qingtong qi bian wei lu* [Records

on distinguishing genuine and forged bronze objects of Shang, Zhou, Qin, and Han dynasties] (Hong Kong: Xianggang zhongwen daxue Zhongguo wenhua yanjiusuo Wu Duotai Zhongguo yuwen yanjiu zhongxin, 1981).

[2] Zhu Xingzhai, *Huaren huashi* (Hong Kong: Zhongguo shuha chubanshe, 1961), 234–55; the quote from Yu Enrong appears on 244–45.

[3] See, for example, Theodore Rousseau, "The Stylistic Detection of Forgeries," *The Metropolitan Museum of Art Bulletin* 26, no. 6 (February 1968): 247–52; James Cahill, "The Case Against *Riverbank*: An Indictment in Fourteen Counts," in *Issues of Authenticity in Chinese Painting*, ed. Judith Smith and Wen C. Fong (New York: The Metropolitan Museum of Art, 1999): 13–63; Maxwell K. Hearn, "A Comparative Physical Analysis of *Riverbank* and Two Zhang Daqian Forgeries," in the same volume, 95–113; Shen Fu with Jan Stuart, *Challenging the Past: The Paintings of Chang Dai-chien* (Washington, D.C.: Arthur M. Sackler Gallery, Smithsonian Institution, 1991): 189–92; Shen Fu, "Chang Dai-chien's *The Three Worthies of Wu* and His Practice of Forging Ancient Art," *Orientations* 20, no. 9 (September 1989): 56–72.

[4] See, for example, Yang Xin and Pan Shengliang, *Zhongguo jinxiandai shuhua zhenwei jianbei: Zhang Daqian juan* [Authenticating modern Chinese calligraphy and painting: Zhang Daqian] (Beijing: Daxiang chubanshe, 2005).

[5] Li Zhichao, "Gu jiu zi hua jianbie fa [Methods of judging old paintings and calligraphic works]," in *Meishu lunj: di yi ji*, ed. Shen Peng and Linghu Biao (Beijing: Renmin meishu chubanshe, 1982), 195–224.

[6] For an illuminating essay on Zhang Taijie's *Bao hui lu* [Records of treasure paintings] in which every painting listed is a forgery, see Zheng Qian, "Zhang Taijie *Bao hui lu* cai wei," in *Wenxue shixue zhexue: Shi Youzhong xiansheng bashi shouchenjinian lunwenji*, ed. Zhang Cuo and Chen Huihua (Taipei: Shibao wenhua chuban shiye youxian gongsi, 1982), 51–69.

[7] Li Tiejiang, "Ping Zhai shu hua zha [Notes on calligraphy and painting in the Duckweed Studio]," in *Xuelin manlu* (Beijing: Zhonghua shuju, 1982), 215–24; Li Dichen, *Jianbie hua kaozheng yao lan* [Main points on judging paintings] (Nan'ning: Guangxi renmin chubanshe, 1982).

[8] Wang Yikun, *Shu hua jianding jian shu* [A short introduction to connoisseurship in painting and calligraphy] ([Nanjing]: Jiangsu renmin chubanshe, 1982).

[9] Yu Shaosong, *Shu hua shu lu jie ti* [Abstracts of painting and calligraphy catalogues] (Beiping [Beijing]: Guoli Beiping tushuguan, 1931); Huang Miaozi, *Gu shu hua za ji* [Miscellaneous notes on old paintings and calligraphic works] (Hong Kong: Daguang chubanshe, 1982); Hin-cheung Lovell, *An Annotated Bibliography of Chinese Painting Catalogues and Related Texts* (Ann Arbor: Center for Chinese Studies, University of Michigan, 1973); Ding Fubao and Zhou Yunqing, eds., *Si bu zong lu yishu bian* [A reference book on art

compiled from the complete works of the four branches of learning] (Shang-hai: Shangwu yinsuguan, 1957; Beijing: Wenwu chubanshe, 1984).

[10] Xu Bangda, *Gu shu hua jianding gailun* [An introduction to connois-seurship in ancient painting and calligraphy] (Beijing: Wenwu chubanshe, 1981); it was revised and published in Shanghai by the Shanghai renmin meishu chubanshe in 2000 and revised again and published in Beijing by the Zijincheng chubanshe in 2005. The fact that this book has been published by three different publishers over a period of 14 years and each version contains different illustrations suggests its usefulness and popularity among students of Chinese calligraphy and painting.

[11] Xu Bangda, *Li dai shu hua jia zhuanji kaobian* [Studies in biographies of calligraphers and painters through dynasties] (Shanghai: Shanghai renmin meishu chuabanshe, 1983).

[12] Xu Bangda, *Gu shuhua wei e kaobian* [Examination and identification of the forging of ancient calligraphy and painting] (Nanjing: Jiangsu guji chu-banshe, 1984).

[13] Thomas Lawton, review of *Gu shuhua wei e kaobian* by Xu Bangda, *Ars Orientalis* 17 (1987): 184–87, at 187.

[14] The Committee, also known as the Group for Authentication of An-cient Calligraphy and Painting, has published its work in two major publica-tions: *Zhongguo gudai shuhua mulu* [Catalog of ancient Chinese calligraphy and painting] (1984–1993) and *Zhongguo gudai shuhua tulu* [Illustrated catalog of selected works of ancient Chinese calligraphy and painting] (1986–1995); both were published under the auspices of the Cultural Relics Research Pro-tection Bureau.

[15] Xie Zhiliu, *Jian yu za gao* [Miscellaneous notes written after examining artworks] (Shanghai: Shanghai renmin meishu chubanshe, 1979).

[16] Zhang Heng, *Zenyang jianding shu hua* [How to authenticate calligra-phy and painting] (Beijing: Wenwu chubanshe, 1966).

[17] Zheng Zhong, "Huajia lilunjia Xie Zhiliu," *Duoyun* 6 (May 1984): 130–42.

[18] Qi Gong, *Qi Gong cong gao* (Beijing: Zhonghua shuju, 1981).

[19] Yang Renkai, *Guobao chenfou lu: Gugong sanyi shuhua jianwen kaolue* [Re-cord of the vicissitudes of national treasures: investigation of the dispersed and lost calligraphies and paintings from the former palace that I have seen and heard about] (Shanghai: Shanghai renmin chubanshe, 1991).

[20] Thomas Lawton, review of Yang Renkai, *Guobao chenfou lu: Gugong sanyi shuhua jianwen kaolue* [Record of the vicissitudes of national treasures: investigation of the dispersed and lost calligraphies and paintings from the former palace that I have seen and heard about] in *Artibus Asiae* 54, nos. 3–4 (1994): 378–80. For *Suzhou pian*, see Ellen Johnston Laing, "'Suzhou Pian' and Other Dubious Paintings in the Received 'Oeuvre' of Qiu Ying," *Artibus Asiae* 59, nos. 3–4 (2000): 265–95 and Liu Jianlong, "Shitan 'Suzhou pian' de

lailong qumo [Art counterfeiting in the Suzhou region]," *Jianshangjia* 7 (January 1998): 56–59.

[21] Yang Renkai, *Zhongguo shuhua jianding xue gao* [A preliminary study on the connoisseurship of Chinese calligraphy and painting] (Shenyang: Liaohai chubanshe, 2000).

[22] See the special issue on connoisseurship in *Jianshangjia* 7 (January 1998).

[23] Yang Renkai, *Zhongguo shuhua yanjiu* [Studies on Chinese calligraphy and painting] (Shanghai: Shanghai guji chubanshe, 2006).

[24] Yang Xin, preface to Liu Jiu'an, ed., *Zhongguo lidai shuhua jianbei tulu* [An illustrated catalog of authenticated Chinese calligraphies and paintings through the ages] (Beijing: Zijincheng chubanshe, 1999).

[25] Liu Jiu'an, *Liu Jiu'an shuhua jianding ji* [Liu Jiu'an on the connoisseurship of calligraphy and painting] ([Zhengzhou]: Henan meishu chubanshe, 1999).

[26] Fu Xinian, "Guanyu Zhan Ziqian 'You chun tu' niandai de tantao [On the date of *Spring Outing* by Zhan Ziqian]," in *Wenwu jianshang conglu: shuhua (yi)* [An anthology of essays on connoisseurship of cultural relics: calligraphy and painting, part one], ed. Guojia wenwu jianding weiyuan wei (National Committee on the Authentication of Cultural Relics) (Beijing: Wenwu chubanshe, 1994): 136–67.

[27] Lu Wuya, *Zhongguo gu hua jian bian zhishi* [Introduction to the authentication of ancient Chinese paintings], ed. Mai Feng (Hong Kong: Sheying huabao youxian gongsi, 1983).

[28] Luo Fuyi, "Cong yinzhang shang jianbie gu shu hua [Judging ancient paintings and calligraphic works by examining seal imprints]," in Xie Zhiliu, Zhang Heng, and Luo Fuyi, *Zhongguo shuhua jianding yanjiu* (Hong Kong: Nantong tushu gongsi, 1974), 115–29.

[29] Xu Bangda, "Song Jin nei fu shu hua de zhuanghuang biaoti cang yin he kao [Studies in titles and collectors' seal imprints on paintings and calligraphic works in imperial collections of the Song and Jin dynasties]," *Meishu yanjiu* 1 (1981): 83–85.

[30] Zhuang Shen, "Gugong shu hua suo jian ming dai ban guan yin kao [Studies in truncated imprints of Ming-dynasty official seals on paintings and calligraphic works in the collection of the National Palace Museum in Taipei]," in *Zhongguo huashi yanjiu xuji* (Taipei: Zhengzhong shuju, 1972), 1–46.

[31] Thus, one must be cautious in using a reference work such as Victoria Contag and Wang Chi-ch'ien, *Seals of Chinese Painters of the Ming and Ch'ing Periods*, revised ed. (Hong Kong: Hong Kong University Press, 1966).

[32] Shen C. Y. Fu in collaboration with Marilyn W. Fu, Mary G. Neill, and Mary Jane Clark, *Traces of the Brush: Studies in Chinese Calligraphy* (New Haven: Yale University Art Gallery, 1977).

[33] Fu Shen, *Haiwai shuji yanjiu*, trans. Ge Hongchen (Beijing: Zijincheng chubashe, 1987).

[34] Wang Zhuanghong, *Bei tie jianbie changshi* [An introduction to examining rubbings and autographic calligraphy] (Shanghai: Shanghai shuhua chubanshe, 1979).

[35] Fangyu Wang, "Bada Shanren's Methods on Inscribing Dates on His Works," *The Bulletin of the Museum of Far Eastern Antiquities* 53 (1981): 257–89.

[36] Compare Xu Fuguan, *Huang Dachi liang shanshui changjuan de zhenwei wenti* (Taipei: Taiwan xueshen shuju, 1977) and Rao Zongyi, *Huang Gongwang ji "Fuchun shanju tu" linben* (Hong Kong: Chinese University of Hong Kong, 1976).

[37] Richard Edwards and others, *The Paintings of Tao-chi* (Ann Arbor: The University of Michigan Museum of Art, 1967); Richard Edwards and others, *The Art of Wen Cheng-ming* (Ann Arbor: The University of Michigan Museum of Art, 1976); Marilyn W. Fu and Shen C. Y. Fu, *Studies in Connoisseurship: Chinese Paintings from the Arthur M. Sackler Collection* (Princeton: The Art Museum, Princeton University, 1973); Jiang Zhaoshen, *Wu pai hua jiushinian zhan* (Taipei: Guoli gugong bowuyuan, 1975); James Cahill, ed., *Shadows of Mt. Huang: Chinese Painting and Printing of the Anhui School* (Berkeley: University Art Museum, 1981); Claudia Brown and Ju-hsi Chou, *Transcending Turmoil: Painting at the Close of China's Empire, 1796–1911* (Phoenix: Phoenix Art Museum, 1992); Richard Barnhart and others, *Painters of the Great Ming: The Imperial Court and the Zhe School* (Dallas: Dallas Museum of Art, 1993).

[38] Shen Fu, "Ming Qing zhiji de kebi goule fengshang yu Shitao de zaoqi zuopin [The dry-brush painting style during the Ming-Qing transition and Shitao's early work]," *The Journal of the Institute of Chinese Studies of the Chinese University of Hong Kong* 8, no. 2 (1976): 579–615; Ju-hsi Chou, "Are We Ready for Shih-t'ao?" *Phoebus* 2 (1979): 75–87.

[39] Judith Smith and Wen C. Fong, eds., *Issues of Authenticity in Chinese Painting* (New York: The Metropolitan Museum of Art, 1999); Maxwell K. Hearn and Wen C. Fong, *Along the Riverbank: Chinese Paintings from the C. C. Wang Family Collection* (New York: The Metropolitan Museum of Art, 1999); Lu Fusheng and Shu Shijun, eds., *Jiedu "Xi an tu"* [Analyzing *Riverbank*] (Shanghai: Shanghai shuhua chubanshe, 2003).

[40] Wai-kam Ho, "The Eye in a Storm: Charting the Paths of Connoisseurship," *Orientations* 35, no. 8 (Nov.–Dec. 2004): 89–90.

[41] Shi Daoji (Shitao), *Kugua heshanghuayulu*, in *Hualun congkan*, ed. Yu Anlan (Beijing: Renmin meishu chubanshe, 1960), 147.

[42] In addition to various issues raised in the essays in this volume, I have in mind the philosophical, social, institutional, and ethical issues related to connoisseurship; see, for example, Alex Neill and Aaron Ridley, eds., *Arguing About Art: Contemporary Philosophical Debates*, second ed. (London and New York: Routledge, 2002): 81–111.

2

Chinese Art and Authenticity

James Cahill

Chinese Art and Authenticity

The problem of authenticity in Chinese art can be considered from two points of view, theirs and ours: how the Chinese thought about the problem, that is, and how we can and should grapple with it.

Regarding the Chinese attitude toward forgery, there is a widespread belief outside China that the Chinese do not really care about authenticity, that is, distinguishing the real thing from the copy or imitation. A 1998 *New Yorker* article, for instance, adduces the Chinese practice of making replicas of archaeological objects and other artifacts so convincing that they can send them abroad in exhibitions, in place of the original objects—as well as rebuilding old buildings instead of preserving or restoring them, duplicating old artifacts with modern materials, and using conservation techniques that do not permit the original parts to be clearly distinguished from the restorations. All these convince the writer that the Chinese have a very different concept of authenticity from ours, and he comes to this conclusion: "Recognizing the importance of the original hand of the artist places a value on individualism that is foreign to Chinese culture."[1]

But that statement is much too broad, and is true for some of the Chinese arts but quite false for others. To be sure, the identity of "the original hand of the artist" plays no part in evaluations of architecture, sculpture, bronzes, ceramics, and others that correspond, for the Chinese, with what we would call the applied arts. But for those that correspond roughly to our concept of "fine arts," primarily painting and calligraphy, the hand of the maker and his or her original style are absolutely central to appreciating them. Works by the artist are not to be conflated with copies or imitations. And these two categories of art, whatever we call them—Nelson Goodman uses the terms *autographic* and *allographic*—cannot be lumped together when we consider problems of authenticity.[2]

I will address myself chiefly to Chinese painting because it presents, I think, the most interesting authenticity problems. Since it would be dull simply to sum up accepted views on the matter, I will try to offer some less accepted, even controversial ones—trusting (and knowing from previous occasions of this kind) that my colleague Jerome Silbergeld will not let them slip by unchallenged. But before turning to painting I want to note a few implications of the common Chinese practice of replicating or forging (the distinction isn't always clear) archaeological finds.

In the 1940s, small grey-pottery figurines with burnished black surfaces and sculpturally interesting shapes, said to date from the late Zhou period (ca. 4th cent. BC) and to have come from tombs at a place called Huixian (after which they were named), began to appear on the market in Luoyang and elsewhere. They were bought by collectors and museums all over the world. As time went on, examples appeared that were even more excitingly expressionist-looking. But eventually the bubble burst: forgers in Luoyang were making them in quantities to supply the market, and prices dropped dramatically. Some of the Huixian figurines, however, appear to have been genuinely antique. But to my knowledge no examples have turned up in controlled excavations to date, and the thermoluminescence technique of dating ceramics can be used to sort them out from the forgeries.

The forgers' practice of supplying a demand when archaeology or genuine tomb looting falls short continues today. In 1992–93 attractively slim figurines of young men and women were uncovered in an early Han imperial tomb near Yangling, and they have appeared on the market since then in greater numbers than clandestine excavation and smuggling can account for. Antique stores in Hong Kong are filled with replicas of tomb objects purportedly smuggled from excavations on the mainland; most of them are in fact made for the trade. The majority of tomb figurines were mass produced to begin with, and one could almost argue that for most types there are enough to go around. One-of-a-kind objects present a different kind of ethical issue: every new catalog from the dealers who specialize in smuggled early Chinese art is likely to evoke in specialist scholars twinges of dismay along with excitement as they encounter for the first time great and unique pieces that should have stayed in China, with their archaeological contexts intact.

On the other hand, even in this area the forgers remain one step ahead of us. A painted marble relief of a guardian figure, said to have been removed improperly from the tenth-century tomb of Wang Chuzhi in Hebei province, now famous for the reliefs and paintings later found there in a controlled excavation, was put up for auction last year but withdrawn when Chinese authorities demanded its return.[3] Reports from those who have been in the tomb, however, indicate that there is nowhere it can have come from, and to my eyes it looks quite spurious. There have been other examples of purportedly smuggled objects that in fact were made probably to supply this already morally clouded demand; one is unsure just what principled stance is proper to such cases. The one observation we can make is that fooling the foreigners has always been regarded in China as a perfectly honorable enterprise.

But so, for that matter, has fooling other Chinese, especially those considered one's social or cultural inferiors: rich merchants and the like. This was equally true for calligraphy and painting. Early writings on painting are full of references to forgeries,[4] and famous and respected artists are credited with making them—borrowing, perhaps, a painting they coveted, producing a convincing replica, and returning the replica to the unsuspecting owner. I say credited rather than accused, since the act seems to have brought them no moral opprobrium.

When we speak of "authenticity" we mean two separable but related things. An object can be authentic by being genuinely what it is presented as being—for instance, the work of a certain master or from a certain period; or else by being the product of authentic or genuine impulses: the maker is not trying to fool us, or make his creation seem what it is not. The latter sense takes us back to the 1960s, when some poems and pots and people were "authentic," some were not, and the idealistic young were very sure they could tell the one from the other.

Is there an equivalent to this compound meaning of "authentic" in China? Yes, if we attend only to the class of objects to which it is applicable, the ones that derived their value, in principle, from their being genuine products of the hands of particular people whose admirable character, so the theory went, would somehow impart a correspondingly admirable character to their artistic creations. The word *zhen*, for instance, with the basic meaning "real," can be used for "authentic" in the compound *zhenji* or "authentic traces" of some artist's hand—that is, a genuine work of painting or calligraphy. It can also be used in the compound *zhenren*, an "authentic person" or "realized person" in the Daoist sense.

The link between these, in art theory, is the idea of self-expression through the traces of one's hand, which were read as the imprints of one's mind, comparable to verbal expressions in poetry. Traces reliably from the hands of persons of a certain moral stature and spiritual attainment, then, were authentic in both senses.

A painting (much worn and retouched) in the Shanghai Museum represents an old, twisted tree, said to be from the hand of the great eleventh-century poet, statesman, and amateur artist Su Shi or Su Dongpo (1036–1101); another old tree and bamboo picture by a follower named Wang Tingyun, working about a century later, is in the Fujii Yurinkan in Kyoto.[5] Both are examples of literati or scholar-amateur painting, a movement that originated in Su Dongpo's time and was originally centered on him and his associates; their paintings and their theories were aimed at separating their works from the kind done by professional masters. Su's picture was read as a visible manifestation of his personal qualities and feelings; the trees and rocks in it were (in the words of his friend Mi Fu) "queerly tangled like sorrows coiled up in his breast." An early colophon to Wang Tingyun's painting likens viewing it to "seeing the man himself." For this kind of appreciation, attention to brushwork, the hand or touch of the artist, was paramount, far overriding any judgment of the work as representation, a category that was relegated to the lowest position on the scale of critical concerns. This emphasis on brushwork, along with a heavy reliance on documentary evidence—signatures, seals, inscriptions, records in catalogs— is the basis of traditional Chinese connoisseurship. My esteemed friend Wang Jiqian or C. C. Wang,[6] one of its two leading practitioners in our time, has for decades been urging on us an almost single-minded concentration on brushwork as the key to appreciating Chinese painting.

It is a tradition that merits our deepest respect. At the same time, I have come to believe, at this late stage in my career, that as a basis for deciding questions of authenticity it has serious limitations. I have even written (to the dismay of some former students, who rightly feel that it contradicts what I once taught them) that brushwork alone, apart from its representational function, is just about useless as a criterion for judging authenticity. To say this is not to depreciate C. C. Wang as a connoisseur, or traditional Chinese connoisseurship as a whole; he and his compatriot connoisseurs, I believe, are not really reading the brushstrokes purely as traces of the artist's hand, but are affected also, even when they deny it, by how the brushstrokes function descriptively within the whole pictorial structure. There is some gap, that is, between what is articulated and what is practiced.

The Chinese emphasis on the execution of the work, the "handwriting" of the artist, in judgments of authenticity in painting and calligraphy, has some validity when these belong to what Nelson Goodman calls "autographic" arts. An accurate copy of a literary text or a musical score cannot be called a forgery of that work, whereas even a good copy of a painting or work of calligraphy, done to deceive, must be, since even the slightest divergence between it and the original will be significant in betraying a different hand, a different period, a different intent.

An objection that is commonly, even endlessly, raised is, "If one cannot tell the difference between the original and the copy, why does it matter which is which?" But putting the question that way falsifies the situation one faces in real judgments of authenticity in art: if one cannot tell the difference, one goes back and studies the objects more, and tries to refine one's perceptions until one can. The objects will appear identical, that is, only until the differences between them, however subtle, are recognized. And typically, after some passage of time, they become so obvious that one cannot imagine how one ever missed them. That is also the answer to the collector's question, "Who cares whether it is a genuine

Wen Zhengming [or whatever] so long as I like it?" The time will very probably arrive, we reply, when your eyes will be opened to the real qualities of paintings genuinely by Wen Zhengming, and you will see how your picture falls short, after which you can never again, however hard you try, feel the same way toward it.

There are many cases, however, in which true and false are not so easily separated, and even major connoisseurs will fail to agree on whether or not a painting is from the hand of the master, purely on criteria of brushwork and other aspects of style. The two most famous connoisseurs in China, Xu Bangda and Xie Zhiliu, traveling with a group touring U.S. collections some years ago, reportedly disagreed constantly, one pronouncing a work genuine and the other fake; and numerous cases can be found in literary records of contradicting judgments by prominent connoisseurs.

We have begun in recent years to pay more attention to the social functions of Chinese paintings, in addition to their aesthetic qualities, and to read paintings for how they were designed to perform those functions. Attention to the question of how the pictorial structure works to deliver the intended meaning, on the assumption that the original artist cared about this more than a copyist or forger would, can often contribute importantly, I think, to a solution of authenticity problems. Comparison of an original painting by Wen Zhengming (1470–1559), his 1543 "Living Aloft,"[7] and a copy of it, illustrate this point. In looking at these aspects of the picture we shift attention from the idea of integrity in the artist to a kind of pictorial integrity in the work. That is, from the painting as the product of a particular master's hand we turn, if only for a time, to consider the painting as a picture, which can have its own integrity, as if apart from the identity and character of the artist. Western art historians have written about how in the past two centuries or so the experience of viewing European oil paintings was aestheticized and art historicized, from seeing them as pictures made under certain iconographic and other pictorial constraints to fulfill certain functions, to looking at them for their styles and aesthetic properties, and their authenticity as products of the hands of particular masters. The same recognition for Chinese paintings, of how the practice of connoisseurship has transformed the way they are read and evaluated, has been slower in coming. But I believe the concept or criterion of pictorial integrity to which it will lead can be useful, sometimes even decisive, in authenticity questions.

It frequently happens also that a copyist, attempting to replicate some painted form, will misunderstand and garble it; recognizing such pictorial misunderstandings, I have argued, should enable us to decide with some finality which is which. (This argument, I may say, has not been universally accepted.) The difference, which should be a clear one, is between an artist depicting some object in the world around him, and one who is attempting to copy a form from a painting, without necessarily having firsthand knowledge of the thing it was meant to portray, or even being quite clear about just what it was. I will show two examples.

A handscroll representing famous sites in the Wu or Suzhou region by the great Ming master Shen Zhou (1427–1509) exists in three versions: one on silk, now in the Allen Memorial Museum at Oberlin (fig. 1), and two on paper, one of them in the Nelson Gallery–Atkins Museum in Kansas City (fig. 2), the other in the National Palace Museum in Taipei (fig. 3).

Numerous telling comparisons of details could be made, but a single one will serve here to make the point, which I believe to be more or less inescapable: the passage depicting the ancestral shrine of Fan Zhongyan (989–1052) and the wall surrounding it. The Oberlin scroll (fig. 1) depicts faithfully a common feature of Chinese wall construction, to be seen in other paintings as well as in real, present-day examples: flat

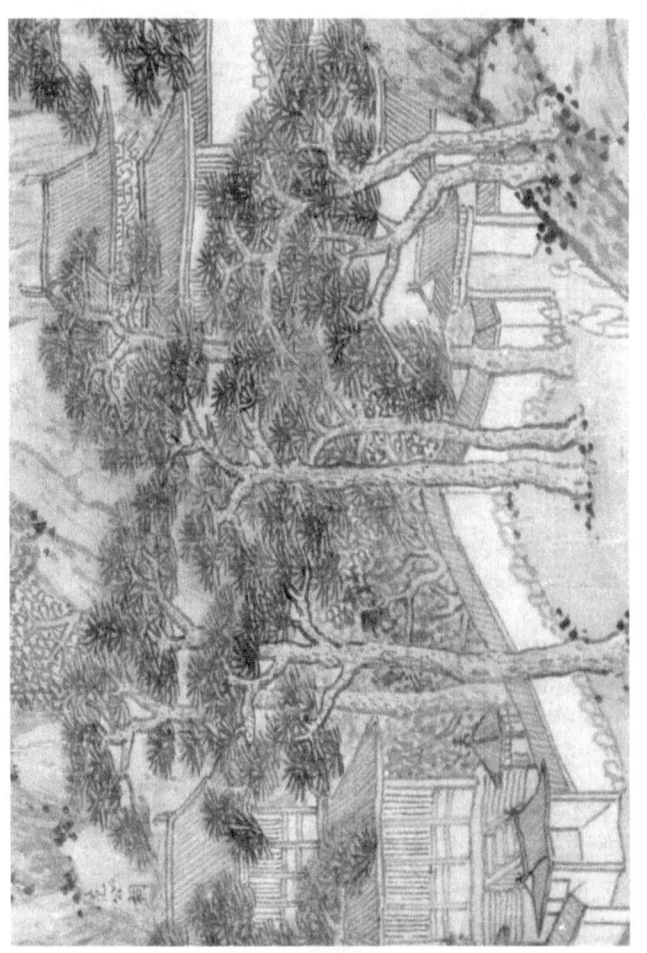

Figure 1. Shen Zhou, "The Shrine of Fan Zhongyan." Detail from handscroll, "Famous Sights of Wu," ink and light colors on silk, 37.3 × 936 cm. Allen Memorial Art Museum, Oberlin College, Ohio. Gift of Carol S. Brooks in honor of her father, George J. Schlenker, and R. T. Miller Jr. Fund, 1997.

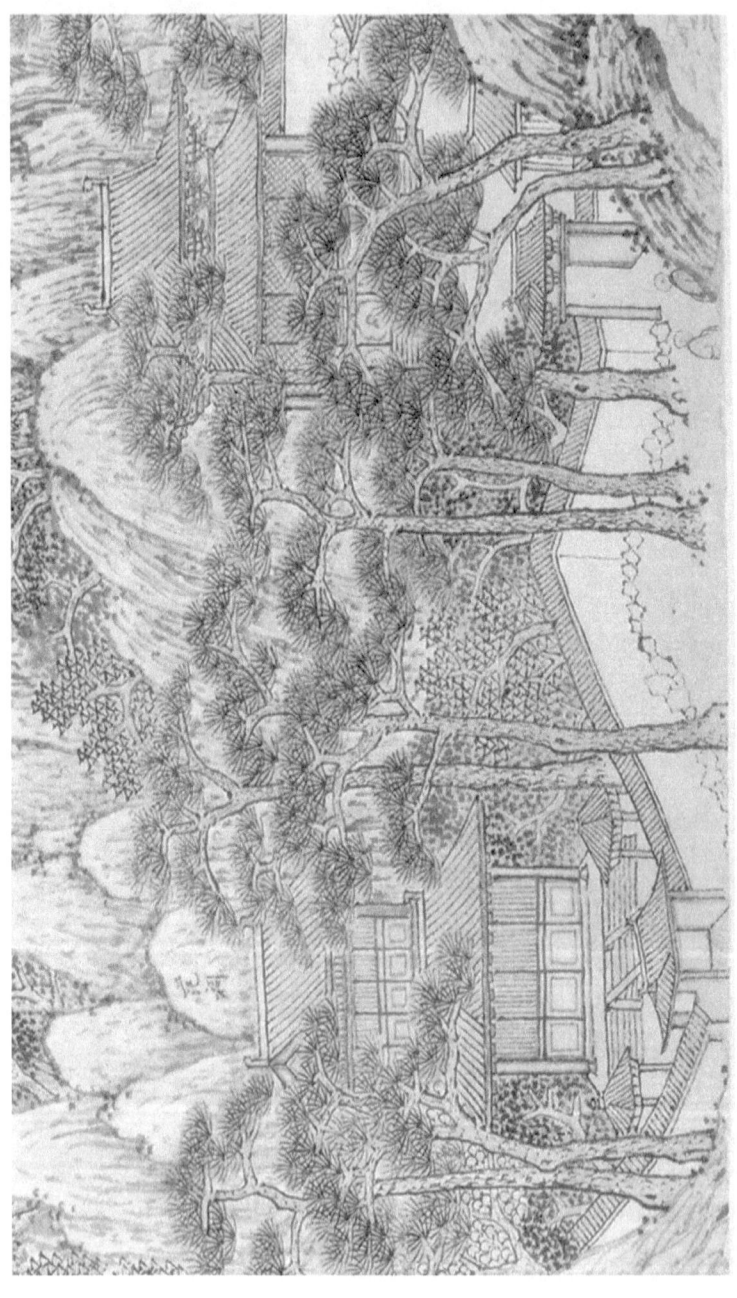

Figure 2. Shen Zhou, "The Shrine of Fan Zhongyan." Detail from handscroll, "Famous Sights of Wu," ink and colors on paper, 35.5 × 1799.5 cm. Nelson Gallery–Atkins Art Museum, Kansas City (70.25).

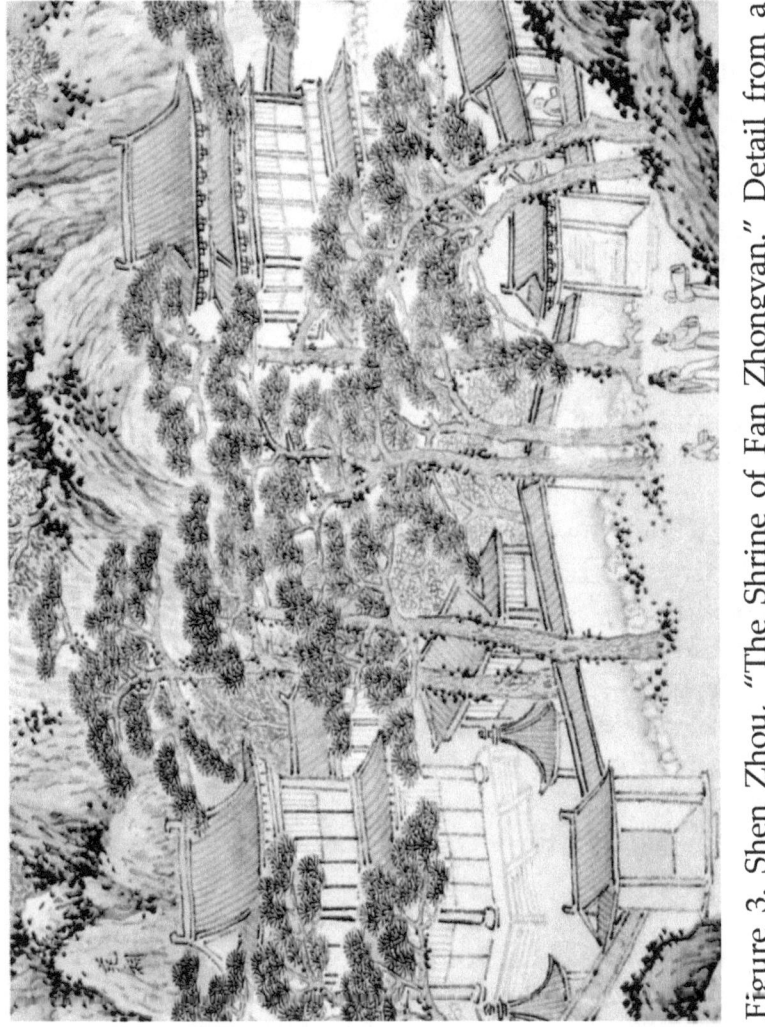

Figure 3. Shen Zhou, "The Shrine of Fan Zhongyan." Detail from a handscroll, "Famous Sights of Wu," ink and colors on paper, ht. 41.1 cm. National Palace Museum, Taipei.

stones set into the base to protect it from erosion and damage. In the Oberlin scroll, large stones alternate with smaller ones, and no stone, of course, overlaps where the wall changes direction. The copyist who did the Kansas City version (fig. 2) misunderstands this feature and draws large stones of irregular shape piled loosely against the base of the wall, not set into it (as their jagged lower contours make clear); one of them covers, impossibly, the join of two sections of the wall set at a right angle. The copyist of the National Palace Museum scroll (fig. 3), which must be one step further removed from the original, compounds the misunderstanding by adding shading to make the stones, now freely jumbled against the wall, stand out strongly from it. The artists of the two copies also add, absurdly, the bracketing proper for a heavy roof to the simple one over the gate. The copies must have been made by artists unfamiliar with what in Suzhou was a common sight; Shen Zhou could not have perpetrated such absurdities.

These pictorial blunders (and there are others in the scrolls, all favoring the Oberlin version) only confirm what I would conclude anyway from the style of the paintings by asking, In which one do the brushstrokes impart shape and volume to the terrain forms and in which do they flatten them? Although we should be able to agree on that as well, it appears that we cannot, and must use criteria that have a more objective, I would even say decisive, character.

The other case, on which I carried on a contentious correspondence with three colleagues that has been published in part,[8] deals with a well-known painting, "Examining Antiquities," supposed to be by the Ming master Du Jin (15th–16th century), in the collection of the National Palace Museum in Taipei (fig. 4). I will present my side of the argument in the briefest outline. It is a large horizontal painting, mounted probably originally as a screen like the ones represented in it.[9] A variant version of the left third of the composition, which seems to me more likely to be from Du Jin's hand, exists in a

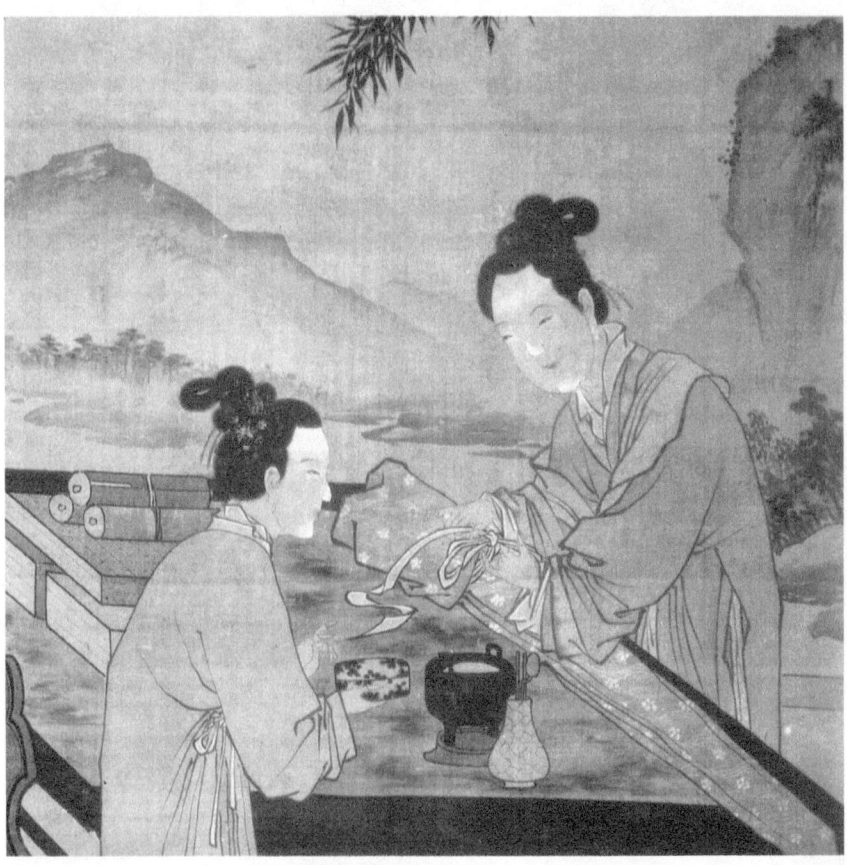

Figure 4. Du Jin, "Enjoying Antiquities," detail from a hanging scroll, ink and colors on silk, 126.1 × 187 cm. National Palace Museum, Taipei.

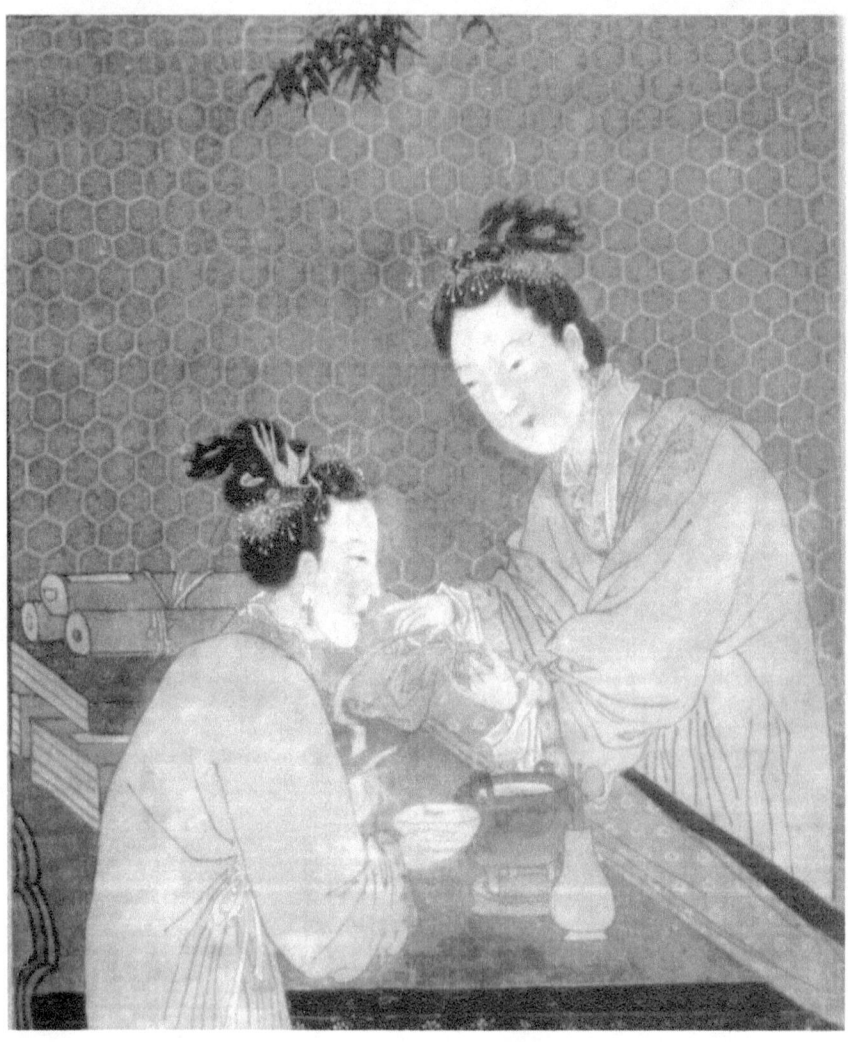

Figure 5. Du Jin, "Enjoying Antiquities," section of a hanging scroll, ink and colors on silk. Yale University Art Gallery.

Japanese collection and is discussed in the correspondence; another version of the right third is now in the Yale University Art Gallery (fig. 5). (Large horizontal pictures were often cut up in this way to make hanging scrolls that would fit into *tokonoma* alcoves and other places where space was constricted.) This one also seemed to me more acceptable as the work of Du Jin, or at least of a capable Ming master, than the same part of the Taipei painting. In this part of the composition two women are seen, each arranging objects on a table for the appreciation of the men, and removing the cover from a *qin* or zither, which one of the men will play.

Apart from quite a few details in which the Yale version (fig. 5) makes sense and the other (fig. 4) does not—the women's hair ornaments, the scroll ties, the rumpling of their robes—the spatial relationship between the two women is tight and effective in the Yale version, and quite lost in the other. But perhaps the most telling detail—so much so that after pointing it out I wrote that I would like to add *QED*, I have proved my case—is the bronze tripod. Its three legs, in the Yale version, are set properly into the circular recess in the shallow stand, which flares slightly at the base. The copyist responsible for the Taipei picture messes up this passage completely. Besides exaggerating the flaring of the stand into a grotesque form with a strange protrusion on the left side, he inserts two legs of the tripod at *diametrically opposite points* in the circular recess; realizes that if he were to paint in the third leg, it must hang out beyond the stand; and decides to leave it out, to avoid redoing the whole large and elaborate picture, hoping that his viewers would overlook his blunder. Indeed they have, through centuries of inattention to the pictorial aspects of paintings. I now refer to anomalies of this kind, when we encounter them in paintings, as "two-legged tripods," and make the contention, which seems to me self-evident and unassailable, that in cases such as this and the Shen Zhou scroll, the derivative works cannot be other than that—

cannot, that is, be reasonably understood as anything other than the outcome of garbled attempts to replicate preexisting pictorial configurations. No appeals to circumstances such as good artists having bad days, or to clumsy studio assistants (who would have quickly lost their jobs), or to the Chinese painter's scorn for petty matters of representation, can shake this. To say, as has been said, that I am advocating realism in Chinese painting, and that this is an inappropriate criterion, is to miss the point entirely and deliberately. Realism is not at issue; what *is* at issue is simply the need for the artist to draw forms that are representationally readable, as any good artist will do, whatever his style.

A different set of problems is presented by paintings wrongly attributed — works by lesser artists credited to greater ones, to increase their value, or works by painters whose skills permitted them to recreate, well enough to deceive their contemporaries, the styles of the old masters. One who could do this was the early Qing landscapist Wang Hui (1632–1717) — he is said to have been urged by dealers not to sign his works in old styles, so that they could be sold with spurious claims to antiquity. It seems likely that Wang Hui also made deliberate forgeries on occasion. The success he enjoyed in this may seem strange to us now, when his imitations leave us unconvinced. Until quite recently, a winter landscape by Wang Hui might have been seen hanging in the National Palace Museum in Taipei beside the great work of the 10th–11th century master Fan Kuan, one of the fairly few unquestioned masterworks of early landscape;[10] and Wang's work would have been identified in the wall label as by Fan Kuan's contemporary Xu Daoning (ca. 970–1052). In arguing why it cannot possibly be a work of early date or by Xu Daoning, we need to resort to criteria that are quite foreign to traditional Chinese connoisseurship: the idea of period style, or (as I would do) the impossibility of finding in early landscape any such violent distortions of natural form as are seen here. (Once one notices the human foot at the top, the picture can no longer be taken seriously.) One cannot arrive at a valid judgment in this case, I believe, by criteria of brushwork alone. But in resorting to other criteria, we open ourselves to charges of applying, in an Orientalist way, inappropriate western standards to Chinese painting.

It is not that the Fan Kuan painting has no distinctive brushwork, but that the hand of the artist is absorbed into the deeply naturalistic portrayal of geological forms and phenomena, and cannot be read as symptomatic of the artist's personality. The painting is genuine, then, not because it is "in the hand of Fan Kuan" but because it fulfills criteria we can derive from other reliable landscape paintings of early Song date, including the quality I am calling, while realizing that the term is imprecise and vulnerable, "pictorial integrity."

This lack of shared vocabulary and common conceptual tools for dealing with early painting makes it difficult for those of us trained in western art history to discuss questions of authenticity with Chinese colleagues, who are, some of them, extremely sharp-eyed—on the whole, probably better than we—for later Chinese painting, but less secure, I think, in the early periods. I have been challenged more than once in China, for instance, to explain why this work ascribed to Fan Kuan in the Tianjin Municipal Museum, much reproduced in Chinese books,[11] is not as believable for us as the painting in Taipei, and have not found it easy to do. (My argument, possible only in the presence of good reproductions or slides of the two paintings, depends on observing how elements of the artist's style that begin as descriptive of natural appearances end up as schematic and heavy-handed conventions in the works of followers.) The most famous connoisseur in China, Xu Bangda, was largely responsible for putting together the great Palace Museum collection in Beijing, so there can be no question about the high level of his judgments of authenticity in paintings. But when he writes about his methods, matters of style are scarcely brought into play. But he does it without articulating it; and that is probably true of a great deal of Chinese connoisseurship. But realizing this does not make our communication easier.

In a copy by Wang Hui of Fan Kuan's masterwork,[12] Wang does use brushwork and a system of forms that is more distinctively his own, and a judgment on the basis of brushwork could in principle be validly made. But we know that this copy was preferred by the eighteenth-century Qianlong emperor and his court connoisseurs to the original, as an early masterwork; and until fairly recently one could find it hanging in the Palace Museum as the work of Fan Kuan.

I should emphasize here that I am certainly not claiming infallibility—I could give another lecture on connoisseurial mistakes I have made, some of them quite embarrassing. I am only saying that if we can bring ourselves to look at the paintings as pictures, as they were originally intended, and look for what I now call pictorial integrity, we will often— not always, but often—find the solution to our problems at hand.

Finally, and briefly, the problem of the deliberate forger. For European painting, the most famous of recent times was Hans van Meegeren (1889–1947), the Dutch artist who in the 1930s forged Vermeer and other seventeenth-century Dutch painters, and whose success, for a limited period of time, has stimulated a whole reconsideration of the problem of forgeries.[13] For Chinese painting, it is without question Zhang Daqian (1899–1983). Zhang, whom I knew well, was much more likeable and stable than van Meegeren, who seems to have been embittered and neurotic. A major painter in his own right, Zhang Daqian was also a dealer—many genuine old paintings passed through his hands—and knowledgeable enough as a scholar to construct elaborate provenances for his forgeries, a function performed in the West usually by people other than the artist. As a forger Zhang was more brilliant and versatile by far than van Meegeren, since his fabrications covered most of the history of Chinese painting, at least from the eighth century to the eighteenth, and an astonishing number of artists — a circumstance that obviously calls into question any confidence in the "artist's hand" as an indicator of authorship. For certain painters, notably the great seventeenth- to eighteenth-century Individualist master Shitao, determining a reliable oeuvre is even today made difficult by the danger of including Zhang Daqian's forgeries in it.

Most interesting for the art historian, however, are Zhang Daqian's fakes of early paintings. Early in his career he visited the cave temples at Dunhuang and copied many of the Buddhist wall paintings; on this basis he went on to produce also quite a few forgeries of Dunhuang portable paintings on silk, of the kind that were found in some numbers in one of the caves. One of them was ably dealt with in the 1962 article by Wen Fong,[14] who recognized it as copied from one of the published wall paintings at Dunhuang. As Fong points out, the ability of the nameless Tang master to render three-dimensional form readably in volumetric line drawing (for instance, in the Bodhisattva's ear and hand) proves unrecapturable for the twentieth-century artist, however skilled he may be for his time. I could not easily tell you why, even if time permitted, except to say it is the same reason we cannot compose a completely convincing Shakespeare sonnet or Mozart quartet, or paint a Raphael or a Vermeer that will hold up for long. Wen Fong recounts how this painting was put through exhaustive technical analysis in Tokyo, and passed so swimmingly that "there were...plans afoot to publish the findings as a standard textbook analysis of a T'ang painting." Another of Zhang's Dunhuang forgeries was offered to the Freer Gallery of Art while I was curator there, in 1957 or 1958, and fared less well under examination: the yellow pigment proved to be a chemical compound not used until the 19th century, and our scroll mounter at the time, Takashi Sugiura, immediately pronounced the silk to be modern Japanese. Microscopic examination of the fibers of the silk, which had been artificially rent and discolored, showed them to be still strong, not deteriorated with age.[15] Technical examination of paintings can sometimes supply negative evidence; it can virtually never prove authenticity.

When Zhang was copying an earlier picture—and his sources were many and varied—his forgeries can sometimes be detected by identifying his model. He might begin with a woodblock print from an eighteenth-century Japanese book, and turn it into an eighth-century Chinese painting; or he might adopt the composition of a painting by the modern Japanese artist Hashimoto Kansetsu, done in 1929, and transform it into a long-lost work by the Tang (also eighth century) figure master Zhang Xuan. I have identified the sources of quite a few of Zhang's forgeries, and my colleague Fu Shen (Shen C. Y. Fu) identified others in the catalog for his 1991 Zhang Daqian exhibition, in which some of the forgeries were included as such.[16]

Hans van Meegeren raised an embarrassing problem for art historians in the European painting field; Zhang Daqian has done the same for us. Van Meegeren's "Disciples at Emmaus," the most successful of his Vermeer forgeries and the one on which he expended the most time and care, both in painting it and in aging it, not only convinced major specialists at the time, but still has its defenders, who insist that it should be exempted from the list of spurious works. And yet any good graduate student in that field could write a convincing essay now on why it cannot be a work of Vermeer or of the seventeenth century; and not simply by hindsight—it "looks" wrong, and is demonstrably wrong, in style. Among other criteria, our graduate student would use van Meegeren's later and more quickly painted forgeries, such as the "Christ Among the Doctors" or "The Last Supper," to identify the forger's style and hand and recognize them in the "Disciples at Emmaus."[17]

The same is true of Zhang Daqian's forgeries—collectively, they betray each other. Another painting, supposed to be by the Tang-period horse specialist Han Gan, was purchased for an unprecedentedly high price by the French government in the 1950s; this was before others of Zhang's forgeries in other public collections came to be identified and available for comparison.[18] An impressive list of eminent art historians and sinologues endorsed the purchase. While I was teaching at Berkeley, I regularly used the work as a test piece for students in my early Chinese painting class, and the sharp-eyed ones wrote about why it could not be a work of Tang date. The figures and horses, they observed, are completely flat and pressed together so that there is no convincing space around them; one figure is inserted where there is no place for him to occupy. The same fault exactly can be seen in van Meegeren's "The Last Supper." Neither Han Gan nor Vermeer could possibly have painted these pictures.

How to reconcile these judgments? I am certainly not claiming that my teaching methods turned my students into better connoisseurs than their well-established elders, any more than the hypothetical graduate student in European painting is better than the experts who authenticated the van Meegerens. I can only echo the common observation that forgeries have a limited life, and that impressive finish and an appearance of great age can divert even sophisticated viewers of a work of art into failing to subject it to a skeptical visual analysis, or to accept the outcome easily when it proves negative.

Those of you who keep up with events in the art world will be aware that I have avoided, as Jerome Silbergeld probably will avoid, touching on a work that has been a center of heavy controversy over the past two years or so, a work that I would regard as Zhang Daqian's "Disciples at Emmaus" in that it is his most carefully done, most successful forgery, so much so that many people who recognize the others still balk at this one. The painting, titled "The Riverbank," is now in The Metropolitan Museum of Art, New York, and bears a spurious signature of the tenth century master Dong Yuan. My arguments are put forth in "The Case against *Riverbank*: An Indictment in Fourteen Counts."[19] I suspect that the choice of "Connoisseurship of Chinese Painting" as the theme for this volume may attract readers well aware of the numerous reports of this controversy in the popular press, and the buzz about it in academic circles. Both Jerome Silbergeld and I felt, however, that we have talked and written and published enough about that painting and its problems already, and that a more general consideration of larger issues was in order. And yet, much of what I've written here is directly relevant to that work; especially in this last section, I have in effect been talking around it without mentioning it. There is quite enough to read on that subject for anyone who wants to pursue it.

Pictorial Integrity: The Readable Image as Indicator of Authenticity in Chinese Painting

Issues of authenticity continue to disturb Chinese painting studies, even while most in the field prefer, understandably, to turn their attention elsewhere. It seems worthwhile to set forth here, in general terms and for a wider readership, an argument that some of us have been making for a long time, but that still meets with surprisingly strong resistance. In its simplest form it goes like this: good Chinese paintings are among other things good pictures; a painting with serious representational mistakes, when ascribed to a respected master or an early date, should be held in suspicion of being a copy or forgery. This is because where the original artist was depicting objects (in whatever style), the copyist or forger was replicating or imitating preexisting artistic forms, and is likely, somewhere in the picture, to have misunderstood their representational intent and garbled them, rendering them unconvincing or even unreadable. We should be able to distinguish such garbling from expressive distortion, amateurish awkwardness, and other legitimate factors that work against realistic portrayal in genuine paintings. And we should recognize the irrelevance, in this context, of the old cliché about how Chinese artists "do not represent the outer appearances of things," and so forth. Purposeful departures from verisimilitude are not to be equated with pictorial blunders of the kind discussed here.

Most of what is quoted or summarized below has been printed already in some document, but several of these are not easily accessible to general readers. In citing others than myself I am not attempting to judge whether they are right or not in their conclusions, but only considering the kind of argument they make and the criteria they use.

In a trial conducted in New York in 1956 in which the dealer Walter Hochstadter sued the collector-dealer C. C. Wang, alleging that Wang had knowingly given him bad paintings in an exchange they had carried out, Sherman Lee testified on behalf of Hochstadter, relating in particular why he had rejected a certain work (a handscroll representing "Zhuangzi's Butterfly Dream" allegedly by the Yuan master Liu Guandao [active ca. 1275–1300]) when Wang had offered it to his museum for purchase. These are excerpts from Lee's testimony, taken from the transcript of the trial:[20]

> In judging a painting, I first study the painting itself, and if it seems to stand up internally, then I go to the external evidence, and if that will hold water, then in most cases I am reasonably satisfied about the authenticity of the painting. If there may be rather peculiar things in the colophons or seals and the painting is

good, that may have a slight effect on my judgment, but I have bought paintings which have definitely been fiddled with, in colophons or seals, but the paintings are in my opinion absolutely right. So I would say that the primary thing is the painting and the other material is secondary.

In this, for example [here he shows a slide], this vase here, the thing is flat. There is no weight, no solidity.... It is just a shape which is placed there flat on the surface.... (p. 235)

Now, there is one particular point in this painting where I think...we have what you might call a scientific proof of there being something wrong. [He points out a place where the drawing of the wooden bench is, he believes, wrongly continued over what he takes to be a false, deliberately made tear in the silk.] And the result is he [the forger] made a mistake. Now, somewhere along the line these people usually do make a mistake. And this is just the kind of thing that I try to find because...that is, I think, incontrovertible proof that this painting is a copy, or I would say, in my opinion, a forgery. (p. 239)

This kind of thing, once my suspicions were aroused... then you start looking, because sooner or later you find a place where they just make—sometimes a subtle mistake—or sometimes a very crude mistake, as you have here. (p. 244)

Later in the trial (p. 596), C. C. Wang responds to Lee, saying that he himself doesn't look at paintings that way, and that seals are more important to him. "He [Lee] used the Western way," he says, "and not the Oriental way.... It is not the way I learned in China, what was my own experience. It is entirely different...that is why he said some other paintings, he thinks...it is unbelievable." (I would read these partially and faultily transcribed words to mean: "Some other judgments Lee has made on this basis seem to me unsound, so I question the method.")

The way of reading and judging paintings described by Sherman Lee has been in use, then, for nearly half a century (and surely much longer, in unrecorded practice.) Why hasn't it been more generally adopted, when it is clearly so effective, sometimes even (as Lee claims, and I believe) decisive? An answer may be suggested by what Carlo Ginsberg writes about the "Morellian method" proposed in the 1870s by Giovanni Morelli, a way of analysis aimed not so much at determining authenticity as at identifying individual artists' hands in European, especially Italian, painting. We should examine, Morelli maintained (in Ginsberg's words), "the most trivial details that would have been influenced least by mannerisms of the artist's school: earlobes, fingernails, shapes of fingers and of toes." Although some of Morelli's new identifications of paintings were "sensational"—a picture that had been taken as a copy after Titian came to be recognized as "one of the very few authentic works by Giorgione"—Morelli's method, Ginsberg writes, was "heavily criticized, in part, perhaps, because of the almost arrogant certainty with which he applied it."[21] This raises a shocking possibility: can it be that Sherman Lee, with his "incontrovertible" and "scientific proof," and I myself with similarly positive claims, have been seen as—but no, perish the thought! Still, something other than academic disagreement must inspire the decades-long, heated opposition to this very reasonable procedure.

A two-day "Post-Mortem Symposium" to reconsider some of the paintings that had appeared in the Chinese Art Treasures exhibition from the National Palace Museum in Taiwan, organized by myself and held in the auditorium of Asia House Gallery in New York on October 4 and 5, 1962, was attended by virtually all the major scholars in the field, along with many who were then graduate students—it was the first in a succession of grand gatherings enjoyed by our highly specialized community. Later I sent out to all who had participated a summarized transcript of the discussions (checked and corrected by the speakers), a little-known but crucial document in the history of our field. Landscape paintings occupied most of our attention, but near the end we turned to the hanging scroll "A Literary Gathering" attributed to Emperor Huizong.[22]

The first to offer opinions on it were Sherman Lee and Laurence Sickman, both of whom began by calling it an academy work, probably of Huizong's time. Lee compared it (with a slide) to a copy in hand-scroll form by Qiu Ying of the Ming, and observed that in the version ascribed to Huizong, "the folds of the garments have weight" and that the details show "observation of actual objects, e.g. in the table setting," whereas those in the Qiu Ying picture are "symbols rather than actually real." Sickman commented on "the clean structure of the table in the hanging scroll [Literary Gathering] which is confused in the handscroll [by Qiu Ying.]" John Pope, a specialist in Chinese ceramics, then rose to claim that one of figures in the hanging scroll is holding "what can only be an early Ming blue-and-white dish," and the discussion turned to the identification of ceramics depicted in the painting—a telling criterion of age, obviously, since the painting cannot be older than the youngest identifiable and datable object in it. Later Alexander Soper, commenting on a different painting (attributed to Zhao Yan, "Eight Riders in Spring," *Chinese Art Treasures*, catalog no. 11) and arguing for a post-Song date, said this: "The 'Riders' balustrade can be fitted into an evolutionary sequence of architectural details as rendered by painters. Its dryness, flatness, and lack of reasonable articulation are typical late transformations of qualities that in Sung were still understood and appreciated."

These observations are directed, to be sure, toward somewhat different issues: a genuine painting versus a forgery, an original versus an honest copy, an early work versus a later one. But the criteria for making the distinctions are more or less the same, depending as they do on whether or not things in the painting are represented with real understanding based on observation, or are secondary forms imitated or copied from earlier pictures.

The method is less applicable to landscape paintings, for obvious reasons: the elements of landscape, less fixed in form than figures and artifacts, are less susceptible to "wrong" representation. Nevertheless, when we find, for instance, tree groups in which the individual trees cannot be disentangled, or spatial anomalies that appear inadvertent, not deliberate, or a water surface pattern that does not adapt to the flow of the water, or a river that turns into a path with people walking on it—all these and more were pointed out by Sherman Lee and myself as pictorial afflictions in the "Riverbank" landscape attributed to the tenth century master Dong Yuan (see above)—when the picture has *so much* wrong with it, we have reason to deny the work an early date or great-master authorship, since good early artists were too skilled and too respectful of nature to commit blunders of that kind.

That the "Admonitions to the Court Ladies" scroll attributed to Gu Kaizhi (ca. 345–406) exhibits visual anomalies indicative of a copy has been pointed out by a succession of writers during the century since its acquisition by the British Museum in 1903; Charles Mason, writing about the recent history of the scroll, states that those who believe it to be a copy typically cite "several passages in the scroll…where visual inconsistencies suggest the hand of someone imitating a design rather than painting a picture."[23] The most recent in this succession is Chen Pao-chen, whose sharp-eyed observations, delivered at a 2001 symposium on the "Admonitions" scroll, identify a number of copyist's errors in it, from the misunderstanding of multilayered garments to the misattachment of supports for the canopy of a palanquin.[24] And again, voices of angry opposition were heard from those who want to see the scroll as an original.

A similar examination with a similar outcome can be used, and has been, for the "Nymph of the Luo River" scroll also ascribed to Gu Kaizhi, even though the issue here is still another: a version in the Liaoning Museum believed to be an earlier and accurate copy of a lost original versus two less faithful and later copies, in the Palace Museum, Beijing and the Freer Gallery of Art. (I am told that the late Wai-kam Ho delivered a paper at a symposium at the Liaoning Museum in November, 2004, arguing for a pre-Song dating for their scroll.) Out of many comparisons of details that could illustrate the differences, I offer the boats from the Liaoning and Freer scrolls (figs. 6, 7). In the Liaoning picture, two flat bands of cloth hang over the canopy that covers the platform on top of the boat, their near ends blown slightly outward by wind, their far ends blown more strongly so as to almost touch the near side. In both the Beijing and Freer pictures, the near ends hang straight down; the far ends do the same, but are drawn as if they were hanging straight down *from the near side above*—negating, in effect, the depth of the canopy. That is, the feature of the wind-blown bands, readable in the Liaoning version, is misunderstood by the copyists. In the Liaoning and Beijing versions, thick wooden struts are laid at intervals on the outer deck, forming a kind of horizontal ladder against which the boatmen's feet push (a feature still to be seen on poled boats today). The painter of the Freer version, with no understanding of this construction, draws parallel lines readable only as flat boards set into the deck, useless to the boatmen. In these, too, there can be no question of which most faithfully reproduces the lost original.

My "two-legged tripod" argument (see above and figs. 4, 5) is another manifestation, admittedly, of Ginsberg's "almost arrogant certainty," with the predictable response: all three of my adversaries found ways (not the same ways, and in part

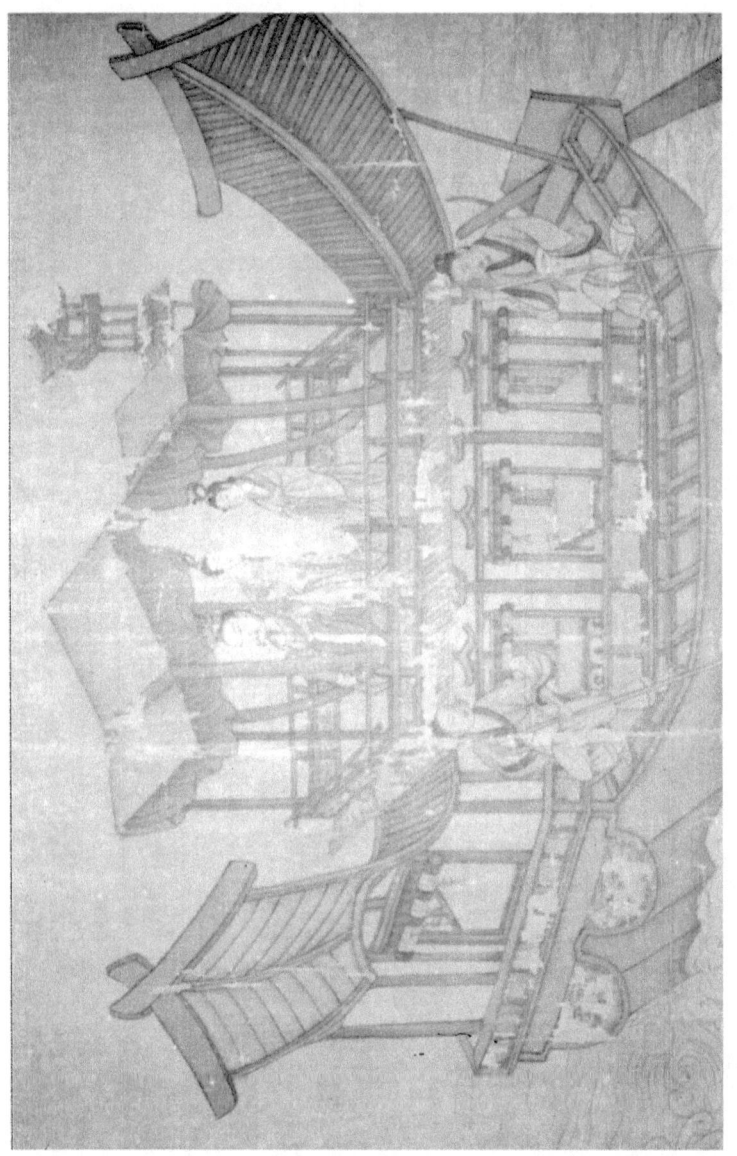

Figure 6. Attrib. to Gu Kaizhi. "Boat." Detail from "Nymph of the Luo River," handscroll, ink and colors on silk, 26 × 246 cm. Liaoning Provincial Museum.

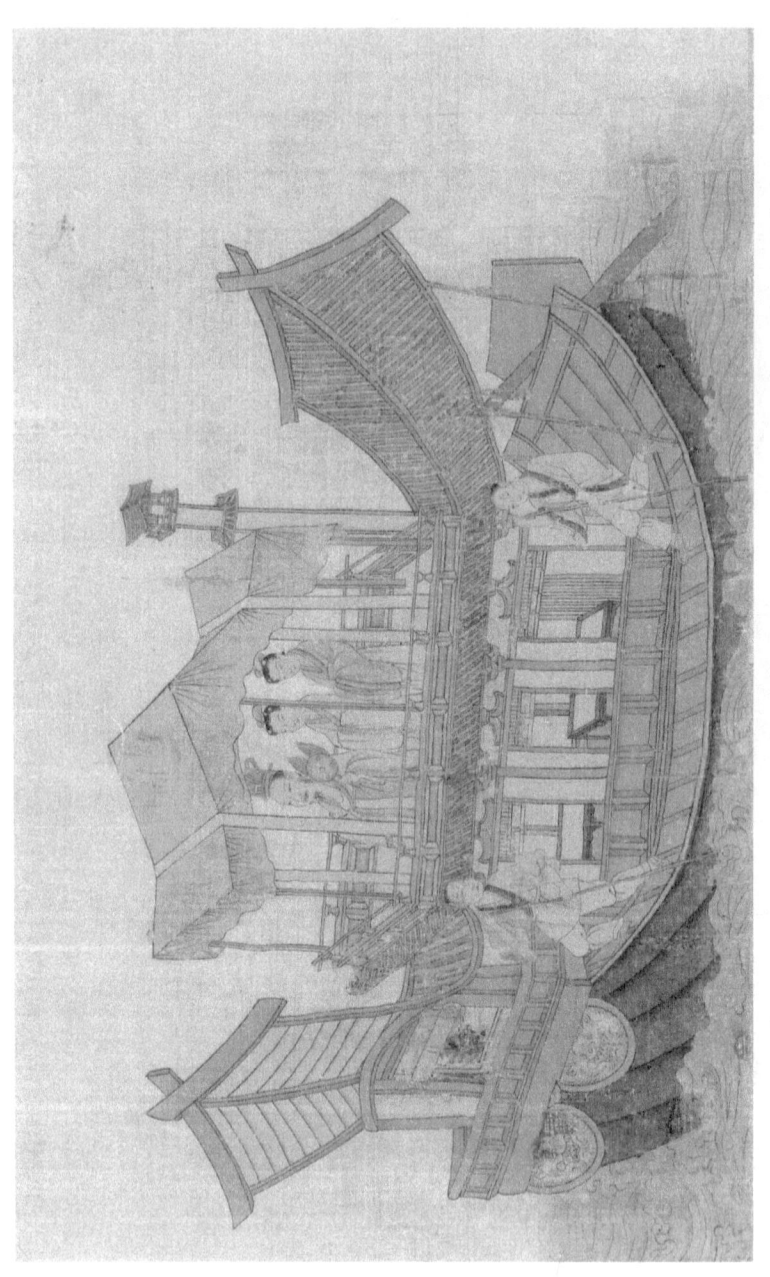

Figure 7. Attrib. to Gu Kaizhi, "Boat." Detail from "Nymph of the Luo River," handscroll, ink and colors on silk, ht. 9 1/2 in. Freer Gallery of Art, Washington, D.C.

mutually contradictory) to argue that the Palace Museum version is nonetheless, in some sense, a "real" Du Jin: the product of a studio assistant, a "cut-rate" version made within multiple production, and so forth.[25] We are still, that is, far short of agreement.

The buyer of such a painting in the artist's time would surely have complained about such representational flaws; connoisseurship based heavily on brushwork and professing to ignore readable imagery as a criterion of value belongs mostly to a later period and to the world of prestigious name-artist collecting. As all readers of Song-period writings on painting know, getting the image "right" was a major criterion at that time for identifying the best artists and pictures. In Japan, where imagery continued to be a major concern and brushwork in the Chinese sense was only imperfectly understood, *kanteika* or authenticators would often sketch copies of works they were called on to judge, in part to catch representational infelicities. And even within the orthodox tradition of connoisseurship in the later periods in China, no uniformity of practice can be assumed; there must always have been those who wanted, among other things, a good picture, even at the risk of being derided by their fellows for displaying such a philistine taste. I do not even believe, after spending many hours looking at paintings with the late C. C. Wang, paragon of traditional Chinese connoisseurship, that he truly was inattentive to the "scenery" (his dismissive term for representational content) in the paintings he judged.

And all of us, to the extent we are able, apply to the painting our understandings of individual style and period style, to see how the painting fits these, besides taking into account what Lee calls "collateral evidence"—seals, inscriptions, signatures, provenance, and so forth. The recognition of what I call "pictorial integrity," a quality I take to characterize good paintings of all periods and styles, does not replace these additional factors but augments them, permitting us to make judgments with more assurance, on more solid ground.

Attendees at the 1962 "Post-Mortem" symposium referred to above were dismayed to hear two leading authorities, Max Loehr and Alexander Soper, diverging by a millennium in their dating of the first painting considered, "Emperor Minghuang's Flight to Shu,"[26] Loehr making it eighth century and Soper, the eighteenth. At that time most of us were confident that this was only a symptom of the fledgling state of our field, and that we would reach a greater degree of consensus in years to come. But the "Riverbank" controversy of 1999, and the Gu Kaizhi symposium of 2001, have both revealed gaps as wide, or nearly so, in datings proposed by major scholars who took part. Either gap could, I think, be closed largely by a more widespread adoption of the method advocated here. One may hope that specialists of the next generation, looking beyond arrogance, will be willing to do that.

Notes

The first half of this essay was first presented at an American Academy of Arts and Sciences Western Center program, held at the Asian Art Museum, San Francisco, March 3, 2001. A shorter form was published in the academy's *Bulletin*, 55.1 (Fall 2001): 17–29, along with Jerome Silbergeld's commentary, titled "Three Paradigms for the Consideration of Authenticity in Chinese Art," at pp. 29–36. A revised version of Silbergeld's commentary appears as Chapter 3 of this volume. The second half of this essay is published here for the first time.

[1] Alexander Stille, "Faking It," *New Yorker*, June 15, 1998, 36–42.

[2] Nelson Goodman, "Art and Authenticity," in *The Forger's Art: Forgery and the Philosophy of Art*, ed. Denis Dutton (Berkeley: University of California Press, 1983), 93–114.

[3] See Susan Munro, "Cultural Property Law and the Hong Kong Trade in Chinese Antiquities," *Arts of Asia* (September–October 2000): 146–49; the relief was Lot 209 in Christie's New York "Fine Chinese Ceramics, Paintings and Works of Art," March 21, 2000. It was withdrawn from the sale.

[4] Conveniently collected in Wen C. Fong, "The Problem of Forgeries in Chinese Painting," *Artibus Asiae* 25, no. 2 (1962): 95–119.

[5] See James Cahill, *Three Alternative Histories of Chinese Painting* (Lawrence, Kans.: Spencer Museum of Art, 1988), 81 and 85.

[6] C. C. Wang died in 2003; see my obituary for him in *Archives of Asian Art* 54 (2004): 95–96.

[7] For this painting see James Cahill, *Parting at the Shore: Chinese Painting of the Early and Middle Ming Dynasty* (Tokyo, Weatherhill, 1978), color plate 13. The copy showed with my lecture was owned by a Hong Kong dealer.

[8] "The Tu Chin Correspondence, 1994–95," *Kaikodo Journal* 5 (Autumn 1997): 8–62.

[9] For the whole painting see my *Parting at the Shore* (see n. 7), fig. 73.

[10] Wang Hui ("Xu Daoning"), "Winter Landscape," and Fan Kuan, "Travelers Among Streams and Mountains." See *Three Hundred Masterpieces of Chinese Painting* (Taichung: National Palace Museum, 1959), 1:64, 75.

[11] The painting attributed to Fan Kuan in the Tianjin Municipal Museum is not reproduced in any easily accessible publication.

[12] *Three Hundred Masterpieces*, 1:65.

[13] See Hope B. Werness, "Hans van Meegeren *fecit*," in *The Forger's Art*, ed. Dutton (see note 2), 1–57. The paintings mentioned here are reproduced with this article.

[14] Both the original wall painting and Zhang's copy/forgery are reproduced and discussed in Wen Fong, "Problem of Forgeries" (see n. 4).

[15] This painting is reproduced as a color plate in Zhang Daqian's collection catalog, *Dafengtang Mingji* (Kyoto: Benrido, 1955), vol. 4.

[16] My identifications of the sources of Zhang's forgeries, delivered in an unpublished 1991 lecture, are incorporated in Shen C. Y. Fu, *Challenging the Past: The Paintings of Chang Dai-chien* (Washington, D.C., Arthur M. Sackler Gallery, 1991), 118, 200.

[17] John Kilbracken, *Van Meegeren, Master Forger* (New York: Scribner, 1968).

[18] Vadime Elisséeff, "Une peinture retrouveée," *Arts Asiatiques* 5, no. 3 (1958): 220–27. The list of authorities who supported the purchase appears at the end.

[19] For papers arguing both for and against its authenticity, given at a one-day symposium, see Judith C. Smith and Wen C. Fong, eds., *Issues of Authenticity in Chinese Painting* (New York: The Metropolitan Museum of Art, 1999). My article is on pp. 13–63. See also my brief follow-up, "The Present Status of 'Riverbank'," *Orientations* 32 (January 2001): 84.

[20] Walter Hochstadter v. Chi Chuan Wang. Supreme Court of the State of New York. October, 1956. Index No. 3205/1956. The final judgment (dismissing Hochstadter's complaint) was entered by Judge Louis J. Capozolli in Feb. 1957. His opinion was published in the *New York Law Journal*, February 5, 1957. Hochstadter then appealed March 6, 1957 (and lost).

[21] Carlo Ginsburg, *Clues, Myths, and the History of Method*, trans. John and Anne Tedeschi (Baltimore: Johns Hopkins University Press, 1984), 96–97.

[22] *Chinese Art Treasures: A Selected Group of Objects from the Chinese National Palace Museum and the Chinese National Central Museum, Taichung, Taiwan* (Washington, D.C.: The National Gallery of Art, 1961), no. 31.

[23] Charles Mason, "The *Admonition* Scroll in the Twentieth Century," in *Gu Kaizhi and the Admonitions Scroll*, ed. Shane McCausland (London: The British Museum Press, 2003), 293.

[24] Chen Pao-chen, "The *Admonitions* Scroll in the British Museum: New Light on the Text-Image Relationships, Painting Style, and Dating Problems," in *Gu Kaizhi*, ed. McCausland, 126–37.

[25] For all the counterarguments, see "Tu Chin Correspondence" (see n. 8).

[26] *Chinese Art Treasures* (see n. 22), catalog no. 1.

3

Three Paradigms for the Consideration of Authenticity in Chinese Art

Jerome Silbergeld

When Moses came face to face with God and received the tablets of the law, he then descended Sinai to watch his people dancing around a golden idol. Angered by their inability to see and realize what he himself had seen and realized, he smashed the sacred tablets (fig. 1). Later, when God offered the Israelites a second chance, he commanded Moses to prepare a new set of stone tablets, and we ought to wonder: under these changed circumstances, what else changed? For example, did God also change the text—dumbing it down perhaps, to meet lowered expectations? The answer may be surprising.

Remember, assuming the Bible's accuracy, that the Ten Commandments and the far more extensive Ordinances had already been written down by Moses and read to the Israelites well before this, to their public assent. God's writing this down *with his own finger* on the original tablets, *covering both sides* of two stone tablets that he himself had prepared, might have been redundant but it established his covenant with them. Despite the Lord's assertion to Moses that he would replace the broken tablets with "the words that were in the first" and that he would do this in his own hand, he must have changed

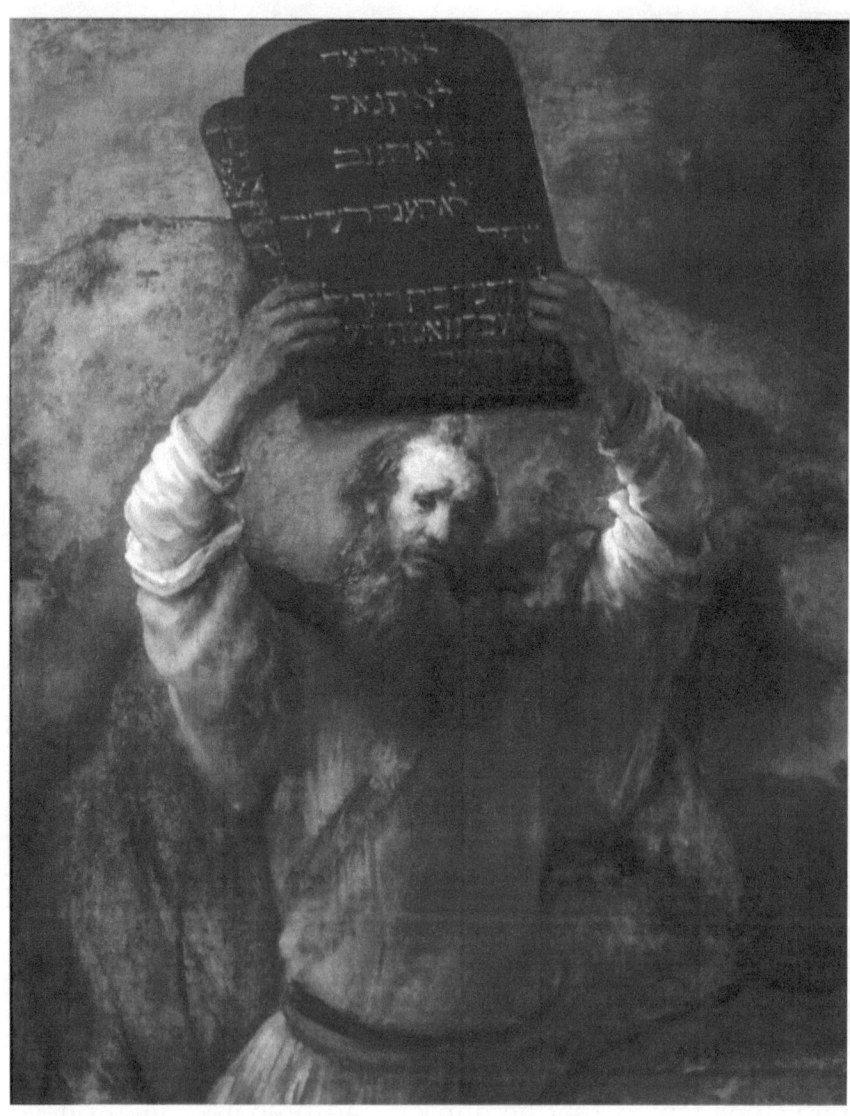

Figure 1. Rembrandt van Rijn, 1659, *Moses with the Tablets of the Law*. Oil on canvas, 168.5 × 136.5 cm. Gemäldegalerie, Berlin. (After Simon Schama, *Rembrandt's Eyes* [New York: Alfred A. Knopf, 1999], 622.)

his mind; for the tablets with which Moses descended on his last trip down the mountain were of workmanship inferior to the first, hewn by Moses himself, and written in Moses' hand, probably on one side only of the stones. In Talmudic interpretation, this reflected the lowered status of Israel after their disobedience. And the new tablets' content seems also to be different, perhaps much reduced from a lengthy original.

So even if Moses' replacement tablets still survived today, lodged somewhere in Jerusalem or in The Metropolitan Museum, would we be able to guess what God's original tablets looked like and what was written on them? Or if both sets miraculously survived intact, side by side—this might have to be in the Getty—would we correctly guess which one was which? And what would be our guide? Would it be style? Text? Materials?

Such questions might seem of greater interest to religious scholars than Chinese art historians, but they are very much like the ones we are here considering: dual questions, of authenticity and authentication. These are very old problems. The difficulties of judging distant events, of discerning original identity, of relying on problematic texts; the complex nature of copywork; separating the role of a dominant patron (in this case, God himself) from that of an obedient workman; the preconceived expectations brought to the viewing of canonized works; the impingement of uncertain contexts and indeterminate events on object production—these are our prime factors.

With Israel and China, we have two cultures distinguished by a profound respect for writing, based on an early association of the word with sacred and authoritarian communication. In China, the elevated status of painting evolved very gradually, through strategic comparisons of painting with writing (artists, for example, borrowed the word *xie*—originally, "to write"; later, "to paint"); and these two arts alone, calligraphy and painting, among all other media were considered to reveal a distinctive "hand," associated with individual personality, defined in terms of originality, and regarded as "high art" (in modern Chinese, *meishu* as opposed to *gongyi*, or craft). I wonder how the Chinese, who have almost as many words and shades of meaning for copywork as the Eskimos reputedly have for snow, might have regarded Moses' handiwork: as *mo*, an exact copy; or *lin*, a freehand copy or close approximation; as *fang*, inspired creativity, freely done in the manner of someone else; as *zao*, an outright original; or as a *daibi*, literally a "substitute brush," following the dictates of, and standing in for, a fellow artist.

I concur wholly with James Cahill's assertions in the previous chapter about the Chinese long-standing alertness to questions of authenticity; about differentiations made according to different media; and their placing a moral onus less on the clever forger than on the uneducated sucker who can't tell the difference. The Chinese have long differentiated the varied contexts in which copywork was generated and distinguished between innocent copywork and outright forgery. To quote Wen C. Fong:

> There are copies, imitations, or downright fakes that were made at dates considerably later than that in which the intended artist had lived. There are "studio" products, contemporary imitations, or minor works of the period which had been erroneously attributed—either by mistake, by wishful thinking or as a result of some dealer's dishonest manipulation—to great masters. There are relatively unimportant works of a later period with forged inscriptions or colophons added to make them appear much earlier. Finally, there are partial forgeries, like altered or over-restored pictures, and—a unique Chinese invention—stripped or peeled paintings.[1]

I agree quite readily with the bulk of Cahill's comments in the previous chapter, but I would like to shift our attention from authenticity to the scholarly act of authenticating. And rather than emphasizing what disagreements exist between us, which I'll save for later, let me first locate his approach in relation to the rest of the field of Chinese art-historical practice, to place him in a larger landscape.

As my title suggests, I would like to succinctly outline three approaches to what we call the "authentication" of Chinese art; and, given the limitations of space, I confine my remarks to the art of painting. I also cannot resist saying at the outset that the term *authenticating* always makes me cringe, for a number of reasons. First, although the process of identification questions the pretenses that a work brings to the viewer, confirming or denying its claims to date and authorship, such "authentication" is applied as often as not to innocent works that have claimed for themselves neither date nor authorship. Second, the authentic date and authorship of a work is an immutable fact in its own right, and all that our "authenticating" consists of is an attempt to get our perceptions to coincide with the truth; so we're really authenticating not works but our opinions, while the truth remains both unchanging and yet all but indeterminate. Third, given the uncertainties and shortcomings inherent to the practice, which I will be discussing, there's the sheer intellectual hubris of the term's self-confident air, but I won't go further into that.

So let me address authentication itself, those who do it and how, by delineating three paradigms of how this has been approached by modern historians of Chinese art. The first group of connoisseurs—another vain and misleading term, etymologically meaning those who know and judge, rather than those who study and struggle, who doubt and regularly change their minds, which is what a good connoisseur must do—this first group I would label as *intuitive* and say that they are best characterized by what they are not: they are by intention and disposition not very systematic. The elements of routine are there but not thoroughly applied. The intuitors typically know how to practice the arts of calligraphy and painting, and they are very likely to be native Chinese. They are the traditionalists in their approach. They know their materials (such as the typical silk weaves used at various times, even the smell of certain silks, and changes in paper making), as well as the various materials and techniques used for making a work look older than it really is; they intimately know the history of calligraphy and of the seals impressed on works of art; they are knowledgeable about the inscriptions later added to works and about the numerous informational catalogs composed and handed down through the centuries; and of course, they are widely experienced in the viewing of paintings in private and public collections. All this is highly informative and *could be* made more systematic, but there is in my opinion a long-standing faith in the subjective, highly personal judgment that derives from the traditional Chinese understanding of the gentleman, the scholar-statesman as defined in Confucian and neo-Confucian terms, a judgment that stands in the way of too much rigor. As Confucius himself puts it in his *Analects*, "The gentleman is not an implement." One doesn't find clear and concise statements describing this paradigm because that in itself would contradict the values. Instead, one reads statements like this old one, from the fourteenth century:

> The power [of money] makes a collector; the power of a good eye makes a connoisseur…. [Gentlemen] show each other objects and compare their relative merits, without any wish to boast of their unusual qualities or wrangle over their rarity. Shallow people…[as] soon as they see something good in another man's possession…will disparage it and pick away at its faults, in order to be able to buy it for themselves…. [But true]

connoisseurs and high-minded gentlemen...will never let themselves speak too bluntly.[2]

Such "true" connoisseurs, in their writing as in their thinking, indulge heavily in such aesthetic and vaguely spiritual terms as *shenhui*, "spiritual communion," or *qiyun*, "life-breath," to distinguish good works from bad (the tautology: if it's good, it has *qiyun*, whatever that means), and they spend their time looking for *zhenji*, "authentic traces." The bulk of western literature before 1960 was blanketed in such mystifying terms. Usually, brushwork is the intuitionist's ultimate criterion, exemplified in modern times by Wang Jiqian, whom Cahill has referred to repeatedly in his paper. Cahill's statement that "brushwork alone, apart from its representation function, is just about useless as a criterion for judging authenticity" is sheer heresy—if taken at face value—way out there! And while I'm usually delighted by such provocative remarks, I'm not sure how to comment on it in two hours or less, except to say that it's best taken other than literally, for (I think) it means actually more than it says and suggests a broader critique of this whole intuitive approach to judgment. Cahill has also written sardonically about how the greatest of these contemporary practitioners traveled the United States together in the early 1990s to compile a massive compendium separating the authentic works from the mere pretenders, but managed to disagree among themselves far more often than they agreed. That's group number one.

Cahill belongs to practitioners of a second paradigm, not rejecting these tools but adding to them and attempting to establish some more systematic basis for judgment. I refer to this loosely as the "scientific" paradigm. Fong specifically labels as scientific his efforts to define "period styles" on the basis of ever-more naturalistic ground planes (fig. 2), developed with increasing naturalism from the Six dynasties through the middle Yuan, fourth century to fourteenth. The

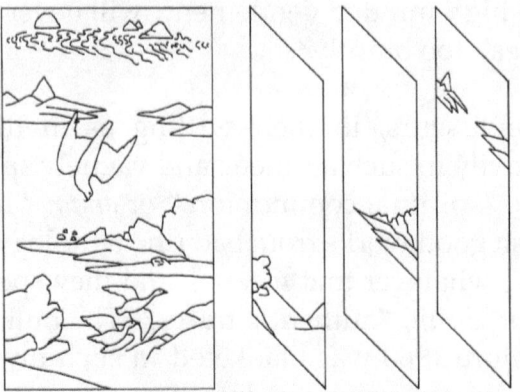

Figs. 13a, b. Diagrams of *Hawk and Ducks*, fig. 18, showing additive mountain motifs receding in three separate stages

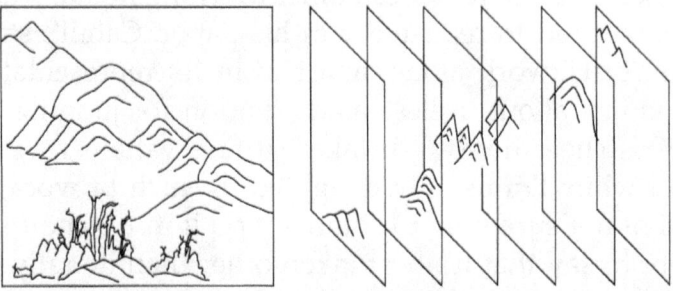

Figs. 14a, b. Diagrams of Li-sheng, *Dream Journey through the Hsiao and Hsiang Rivers*, fig. 53, showing overlapping mountain motifs receding in a continuous sequence

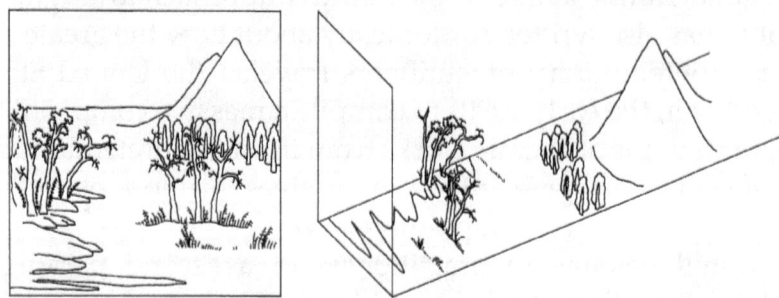

Figs. 15a, b. Diagrams of Chao Meng-fu, *Autumn Colors on the Ch'iao and Hua Mountains*, fig. 66, showing landscape elements arranged along a continuously receding ground plane

Figure 2. Wen Fong, Diagrams showing landscape elements arranged in separate stages, a continuous sequence, and along a continuously receding ground plane. (After Wen Fong, *Images of the Mind* [Princeton: The Art Museum, Princeton University, 1984], 21)

term *period style* itself, of course, refers to the predictable characteristics that any work of a given time will exhibit, or which if lacking will reveal the work as an imposter. Period style, in my opinion, is a problematic formulation that can be very useful when used flexibly, allowing for anomalies, but which proves counterproductive when applied too rigorously. And since connoisseurship is concerned with screening out anomalies, period style works well in describing a history of works already agreed upon but serves as a connoisseurial filter only in the most obvious cases.

I don't know if Cahill welcomes the term *scientific* applied to his own work or not, but like Fong he takes formal structure as his leading guide. He has been increasingly emphatic in articulating the approach used here, exemplified by Du Jin's two-legged *ding* (chap. 2, fig. 4) and Wen Zhengming's stone that wouldn't turn the corner. Fong has written that "when a copyist or a forger imitates or appropriates an ancient style... he inevitably creates form relationships and visual structures more characteristic of his own time." Cahill agrees with this but goes beyond it in asserting that:

> the "good"...painting will always be the one in which the brushstrokes, lines, and so on best perform their descriptive function. That has proven true for me so consistently that I'm ready to make a rule of it. The point is that the original artist is principally concerned with *depicting something*...while the copyist isn't.[3]

To evaluate this, you must note that Chinese painting history can be divided roughly into two broad stylistic phases. Earlier, as seen in works from the second century BC through the fourteenth AD, naturalism was generally pursued and eventually grasped. To introduce a painting that Cahill has conscientiously avoided in the first part of his essay and which I promise not to judge here, The Metropolitan Museum's

Riverbank, which bears the signature of a tenth-century artist but Cahill believes is twentieth century, there are a number of spatial contradictions that he finds unacceptable by the stylistic standards of that period (fig. 3). You can see a good example of what he means if you follow a single contour line that descends from the base of a plateau just to the right of a pool in the midst of the waterfall (fig. 4). The contour line drops right to the base of that pool, but a steeper line of descent from the same point on that plateau lands far front of the waterfall itself, having somehow traversed several other vertical lines in the process, and ultimately results in an ambiguous reading of spatial structure. The space above is impossibly compressed compared to the extension of space below. But look at an undisputed late tenth-century illustrated Buddhist sutra, *Bizangquan*, and you find a similar kind of spatial contradiction in the pair of trees by a pavilion, both trees set behind the architecture but the more distant tree projecting in front of the pavilion eaves (fig. 5). And in an archaeologically excavated painting from the same quarter century, the central mountain is far too large for the space its base must fit into; above, it looks like a massive, distant peak, but below, the nearest reach of its base lies closer to us than the main gateway (fig. 6). Even though I could cite various other examples to question the status of visual naturalism in art at that time, these two could just be anomalies, but so too could the landscape in question. The whole process of trying to fit each and every work into a rigid framework of period style enters the troubled territory of norms and anomalies. I trust that most of you know something of Thomas Kuhn's writing on scientific norms, anomalies, and methodological revolution, as well as the concerns of his critics, all of which ought to be instructive and cautionary to art historians as well.

As for later Chinese painting, for a variety of subtle and important reasons most scholar-painters abandoned the

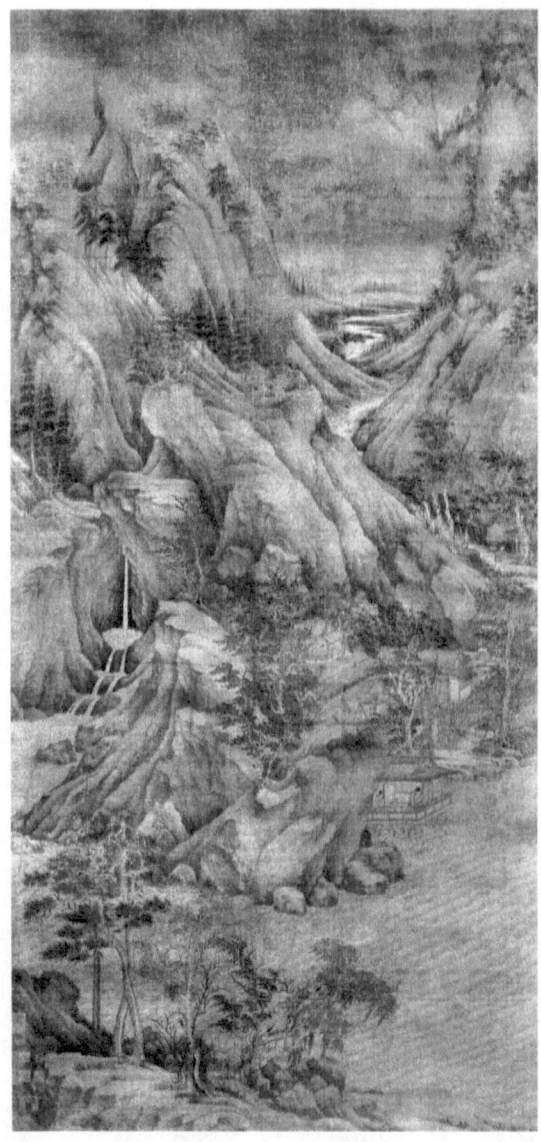

Figure 3. Attributed to Dong Yuan, 10th century, *Riverbank*. Hanging scroll, ink and color on silk, 221 × 109 cm. The Metropolitan Museum of Art (after Maxwell Hearn and Wen Fong, *Along the Riverbank: Chinese Paintings from the C. C. Wang Family Collection* [New York: The Metropolitan Museum of Art, 1999], 2).

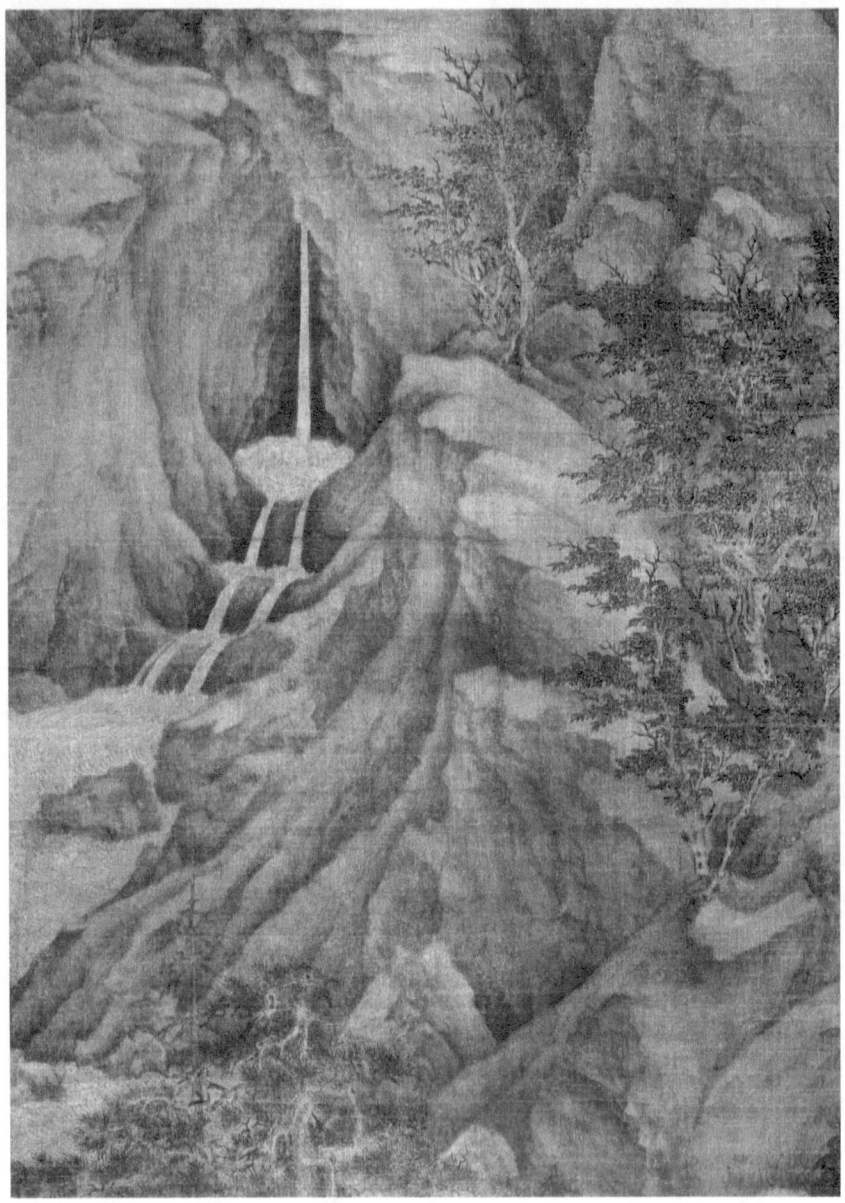

Figure 4. *Riverbank,* detail of waterfall (after Hearn and Fong, *Along the Riverbank,* 10).

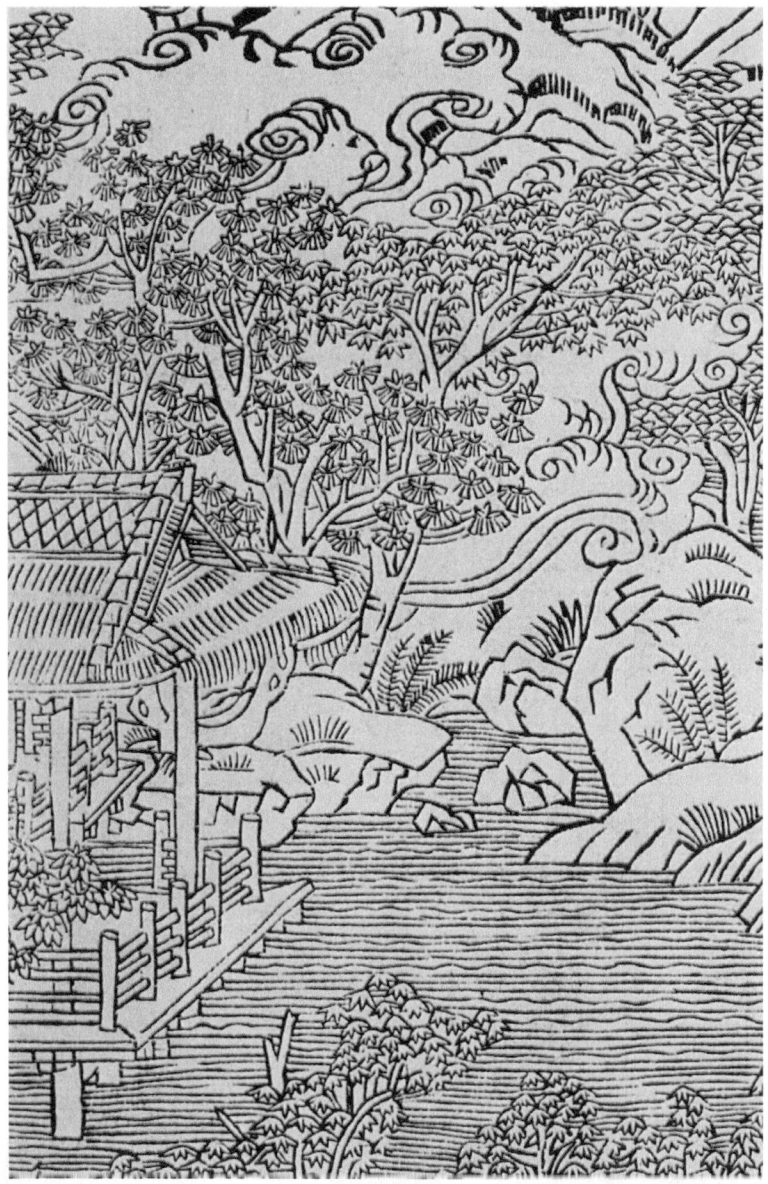

Figure 5. Unknown artist, 10th century, *Bizangquan*. Woodcut, detail. Arthur M. Sackler Museum, Harvard University, Cambridge, Massachusetts (after Max Loehr, *Chinese Landscape Woodcuts* [Cambridge, Mass.: Harvard University Press, 1968]).

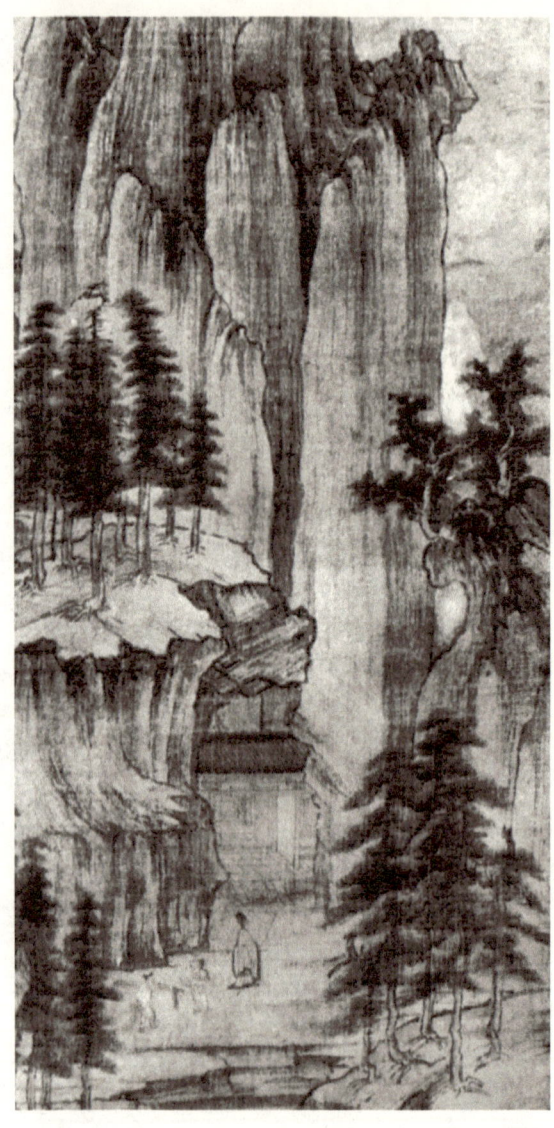

Figure 6. Unknown artist, 10th century, *Landscape* excavated from a tomb at *Yemaotai*. Hanging scroll, ink and color on silk, 106.5 × 65 cm. Liaoning Provincial Museum (after Judith Smith and Wen Fong, eds., *Issues of Authenticity in Chinese Painting* [New York: Department of Asian Art, The Metropolitan Museum of Art, 1999], 118).

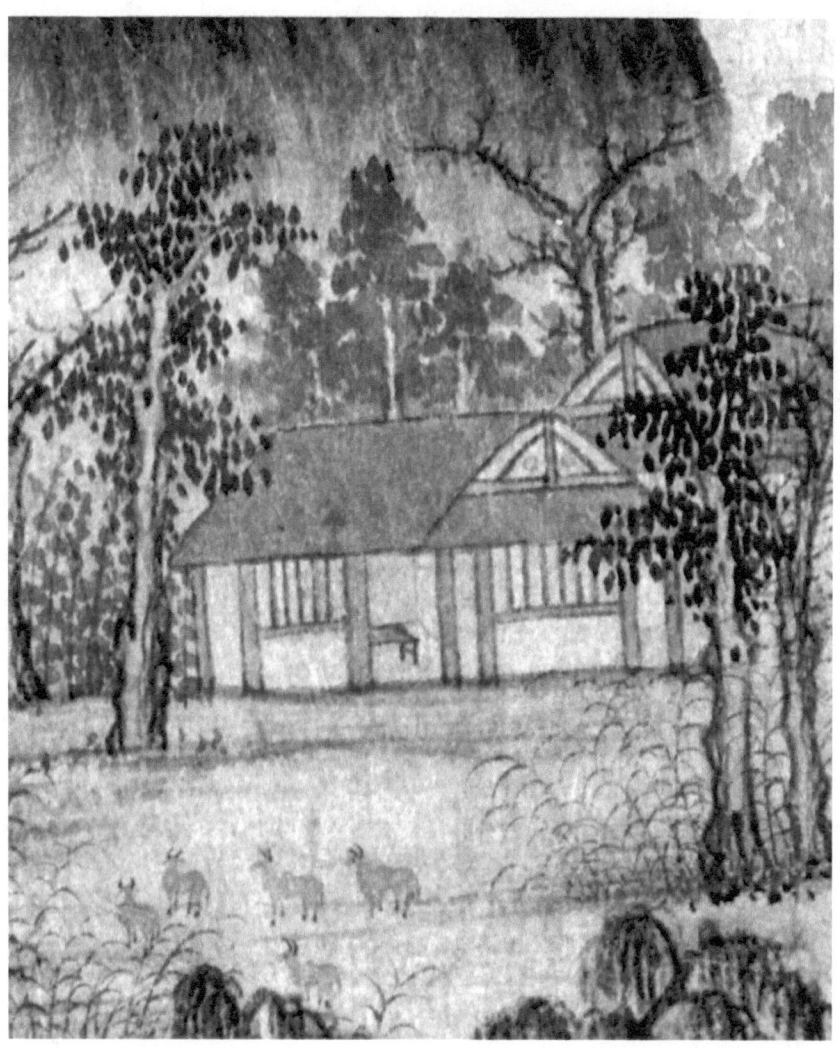

Figure 7. Zhao Mengfu, 1296, *Autumn Colors on the Qiao and Huu Mounluins*. Handscroll, ink and color on paper, detail. National Palace Museum, Taipei, Taiwan (after Yang Xin et al., *Three Thousand Years of Chinese Painting* [New Haven: Yale University Press, 1997], 146).

naturalistic standard, and they were as likely to look back to early, "primitive" paintings as their model as they were to look at nature itself. Recently, this period is compared to postmodernism and described as "posthistorical"; and while that's something of an overstatement, "period style" provides little adequate guidance. A pioneer in this phase was Zhao Mengfu. Look at a detail of a painting from 1296, where the eave line of his farm houses behave at the corner very much like the errant example shown by Cahill (fig. 7). This isn't sloppy, I would contend, but a conscious and careful assertion of non-naturalistic values, art freed from objective constraints, the artist no longer (in Confucius's terms) "a utensil." And if Cahill's examples weren't the products of careful non-naturalism but only unintended mistakes, well, I can only say that I've personally watched fine contemporary artists make such technical mistakes, unconcerned, right down to misdating their painting by ten years and not hesitant to let these works go forth in public. It seems to me that even the careful copyist, not having to generate his own composition and free to concentrate on details, is as likely as the original artist to avoid mistakes and to clean up an original mistake when he finds one. Cahill mentions two versions of the famous Fan Kuan landscape, of which we all agree about which is original and which is copied, but look carefully and you'll see that it is in the original that space is artificially compressed and flattened, while in the copy, even if aesthetically inferior, the forms are more naturalistically three-dimensional, and there is ample space in which a figure might much more readily walk about. Perhaps the Qianlong emperor preferred the fake because he held and applied the same standards as Cahill.

We live in a world where science calls the shots. Scientists design the nuclear weapons, they control genetic engineering; they alone can stare into deep space and explain our astronomic origins, or peer into smallness to explain what things are made of. But let me express that differently. Many humanists and most of the general public *think* that scientists call the shots. We humanists may feel that we have only mystery on our side, the mystery of human creativity, while scientists have clarity, truth, and understanding. We may suffer from what Edward Rothstein has called "science envy." And yet, since the 1920s the greatest of mysteries have been the property not of humanists but of scientists. As a colleague of mine, a geophysicist, said to me recently in discussing the concept of "entanglement" (which I don't understand) and the incompatibility of relativity with quantum mechanics: what actually goes on in an atom can be compared to putting a playing card on end, very unstable, and letting it fall—which it will—to one side or the other. We can observe which way it falls; but in the case of an atom, only our observation—our intrusive observation—makes things seem to resolve one way or the other. In reality, if the card were like the spin of an electron, or like its position in relation to a known momentum and we didn't intrude in order to measure it, then the card would actually fall *both ways at once,* and we don't really understand what that means. People, both inside and outside the art world, when the question of authenticity is involved, want the professionals, the connoisseurs, to just get on with it. If you can't come up with a consensus, then scrape off a little material, put it under a spectrograph of some sort, and come up with a date. People like Cahill and myself, humanists trying to understand complex historical puzzles, agree that the historical data has to be correct before it becomes usable— you can't use a painting historically if you don't know when it was made. And we would like to think that if only we could be more rational, more scientific, in considering all the factors that the history of a work would come clear on its own. But we rarely stop to think that maybe, just maybe, the more we knew, the less we understand. Einstein and Planck and Heisenberg and their heirs have taught us that in the world of nature there are some things, some very fundamental things, that stretch human conception to its limits, or lie beyond. And that, it seems to me, may be as true in art history as it is in science.

Just as a photon may behave like a wave or a particle, depending on how one intervenes to observe it, so too the same work of art can appear entirely different in two different observations (fig. 8). Looking at the water in *Riverbank*, the distinguished museum curator Sherman Lee publicly stated, "The Chinese word for a landscape is *shanshui*, or mountain-water picture. Water content is paramount, and it is a lively thing, curving patterns observed at close range and at a distance. When patterned, it is a pattern that convinces and shows the mastery of the brush.... The wash-board effect in the *Riverbank* [is] tiresome to look at and just as certainly must have been tiring to paint.... Nowhere does it dance and flatten in response to the variations in the surface tension. It is not the *shui* observed in early works. Only a modern [artist] could fail to see the varying tensions when observing water in nature." At the same public forum, looking at the same detail of the same work, Richard Barnhart stated, "Nowhere else in Chinese painting has the subject of water been treated with such an observant interest in how it falls, how it splashes on the rocks, and how it flows on toward the sea, nor depicted it with such beauty. For its water alone, it is one of the finest early Chinese landscape paintings in existence." What do such wildly differing perceptions of the same image say about the possibility of constructing that objective framework for authentication known as period style?

The Metropolitan Museum did subject *Riverbank* to extensive scientific scrutiny, doing thread counts of the silk, digital enhancement, and so forth and so on—but Professor Cahill and similar thinkers about this work remain entirely unconvinced by these results. So what to do? My third group of art historians is entirely skeptical about the connoisseurial mission, put off by the shortcomings of the process, and interested

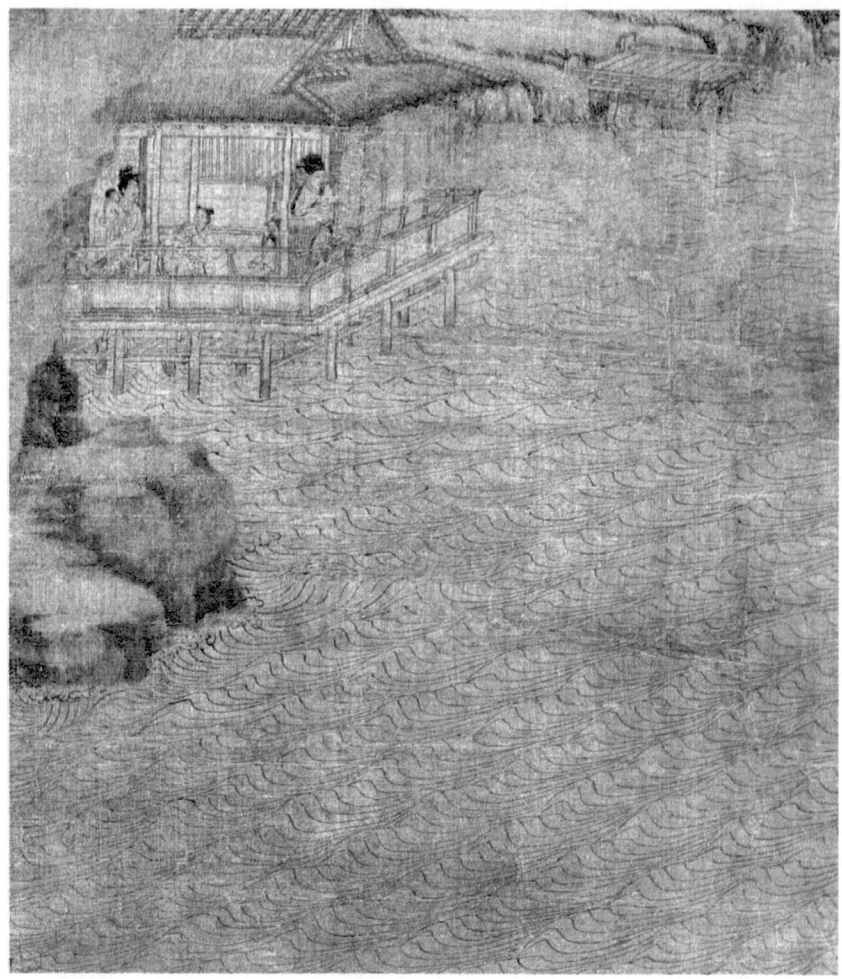

Figure 8. *Riverbank,* detail of water (after Hearn and Fong, *Along the Riverbank,* 9).

in contextual interpretation practically to the exclusion of all else. Their paradigm parts ways with the logical positivism of the former two groups. They are, in a word or two, relativists, deconstructionists, less concerned with "scientific" analysis than with the Foucaultian "gaze" — changing ways in which such works have been produced and perceived down through the ages. Cahill "despairs" (his word) at their abandonment of completing a chronological foundation for Chinese painting history before attempting to build their interpretive structure. (If the generation of Cahill and Fong is like Moses coming down the mountain side bearing a covenant with history, then here are the worshippers of the golden calf!)

Let me illustrate with a single brief example how this group treats questions of authenticity. I was previously a discussant for a paper by Maggie Bickford, who looked at a number of works attributed to China's greatest painting emperor, Huizong, who ruled in the early twelfth century. Huizong worked so closely with his royal atelier that even in his own time it was considered highly problematic trying to distinguish his work from theirs. Bickford describes a massive atelier project whose intent was to replicate in painting a series of heaven-sent auspicious omens, retaining in the paintings their original magical efficacy, which she tells us required that individual artistic agency and authorial identity be entirely suppressed. In such a case, she tells us, trying to distinguish the role of the emperor from that of his artisans is to miss "the most appropriate questions." In her fine tuning of the word "by," she sounds a bit like Clinton facing the prosecutor:

If here the word *by* means "painted by Huizong" (his fingers grasping the brush that touches the silk), I think that we will not be able to deal definitively with these possibilities. If we mean *by* in the sense of "with the authority or sanction of Huizong" or of "in the manner of Huizong," we open up other avenues of access to this valuable visual evidence and, consequently, to understanding the art of Huizong, as properly construed.[4]

If not the end of history, then at least this represents the end of connoisseurship as we know it, the art object supplanted by its own function.

Returning now to where I began, I assume that no one here would imagine it possible in the present to accurately reconstruct the tablets brought down the slopes of Sinai. How much more possible do we think it would be to reconstruct the entire artistic structure of China a thousand years ago, based on a handful of undisputed works scattered among the competing claims of hundreds or thousands of copied, and forged, and unsigned or undated paintings, subjected to a variety of modern interpretive visions every bit as disparate as those of Jews and Christians and Muslims, orthodox and reformed, believers and atheists? It just might take a miracle.

Notes

This essay was first presented at an American Academy of Arts and Sciences Western Center program, held at the Asian Art Museum, San Francisco, March 3, 2001. A shorter form was published under the same title in the academy's *Bulletin*, 55 no. 1 (Fall 2001): 29–36.

[1] Wen C. Fong, "The Problem of Forgeries in Chinese Painting," *Artibus Asiae* 25, no. 2 (1962): 95–119, at 101–2.

[2] Tang Hou, *Hua lun*, quoted in ibid., 99.

[3] James Cahill, in Richard Barnhart, James Cahill, Maxwell Hearn, Stephen Little, and Charles Mason, "The Tu Chin Correspondence, 1994–95," *Kaikodo Journal* 5 (Autumn 1997): 8.

[4] Ironically, Bickford then proceeds to provide some of the finest connoisseurial analysis seen in our generation. This was first published as Maggie Bickford, "Emperor Huizong and the Aesthetic of Agency," *Archives of Asian Art* 53 (2002–3): 71–104, see at 74–75; a more extended version has recently been published as Maggie Bickford, "Huizong's Paintings: Art and the Art of Emperorship," in *Emperor Huizong and Late Northern Song China*, ed. Patricia Buckley Ebrey and Maggie Bickford (Cambridge, Mass.: Harvard University Asia Center, 2006), 453–513.

4

What Is an Original?

Richard E. Spear

The focus of this paper is a number of seventeenth-century artists represented in the 2002 Australian exhibition "The Italians," though the issues it raises concern the entire social history of art. That is because its topic, attitudes toward originals and copies, reflects much wider cultural and economic values. To give one example from our own society, where the cult of the original has become all-pervasive: why should we care, as the ad-men think we do, if a good rip-off isn't an original Mephisto (fig. 1)? Is it because the shoes might not be as well made? Because they are not as beautiful? Or because they lack what Walter Benjamin famously called the "aura" of an original, even though in this example there are thousands of mechanically made originals? Or is it because ethically it doesn't seem quite right for someone to copy, particularly without permission?

These, in fact, are the key questions when it comes to paintings, too. Since I have side-stepped from the seventeenth century into the world of shoes, I might note that once upon a time the most illustrious of Americans, like their continental counterparts and many Australians, wanted copies.[1] For example, prior to going to Europe, Thomas Jefferson drew up a list, based on reproductions, of which famous paintings he should have copied for hanging at his great Virginia estate

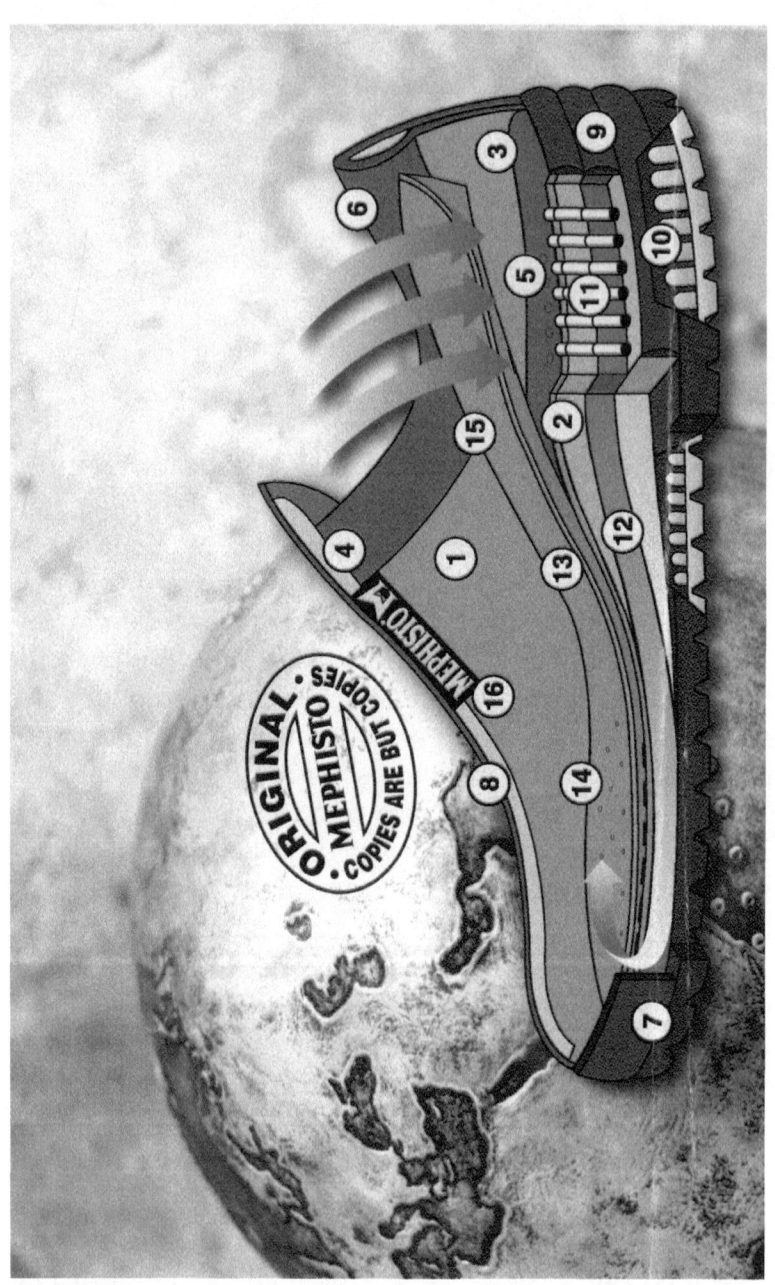

Figure 1. Advertisement from Mephisto shoes brochure.

called Monticello. How utterly different that seems from our notion of fine art and discriminating taste. Can one imagine Brian Kennedy, as director of the National Gallery of Australia, commissioning a copy of Caravaggio's *The Cardsharps* (Fort Worth, Kimbell Art Museum) for his museum? If not, why not? What has changed since 1832, when Samuel Cabot proudly commissioned a copy of Caravaggio's *The Cardsharps*, which later was given to the Fogg Art Museum at Harvard, where happily it remains, despite the current fashion of deaccessioning any work whose originality is in question—a practice I predict will be regretted when the wheel of taste and historical understanding turns and copies are appreciated once again.

In the first half of this paper I will survey a variety of problems that copies and variants pose. In the second part I will discuss a number of complex issues they raise, always within their seventeenth-century context. When I use the word *originality*, I must distinguish between two different meanings of the term regarding pictures. So far I have been using it to differentiate an autograph work from a copy, an imitation, a reproduction. That is, original/originality in the sense of what we mean when we ask, "Is this an original picture?" But originality can also pertain to the uniqueness of design and style in the creative sense, that is, to that which makes something appear to be new or original. Thus one can say, paradoxically, that an original picture need not display much originality; and that a picture is a copy, yet after a work with much originality.

What did the Bolognese artist, Domenichino, have in mind when he painted *The Last Communion of St. Jerome*, an altarpiece he signed and dated in Rome in 1614 (fig. 2)? Surely an earlier altarpiece by his teacher, Agostino Carracci, representing the same, rare subject (fig. 3). But what did Domenichino's rival, Giovanni Lanfranco, have in his mind about eight years later when he was competing with Domenichino to get the commission to decorate the church of S. Andrea della Valle in Rome, and sent his student, François Perrier, back to Bologna to make an etching of Agostino's picture? He then passed the etching around Rome to reveal that Domenichino's design had been taken from the earlier work, in order to damage Domenichino's reputation.

Before saying more about this famous incident,[2] I should mention that previously I thought it was the first charge of plagiarism in the history of Western visual arts, but recently I recognized a precedent in the life of the Florentine artist Ludovico Cardi, called Cigoli, written around 1628 by his nephew; the incident emerges again in Baldinucci's biography of Cigoli.[3] They relate that Cigoli was in Rome in 1604 working on an altarpiece for St. Peter's depicting *St. Peter Healing the Cripple at the Golden Gate*. He had completed only the sketching-out of the composition on the slate support *in situ* when he returned to Florence to work for the Grand Duke. But by the time he resumed painting the altarpiece in mid-1606, he had revised its design. His motivation to do so reportedly was the consequence of artistic envy. Some Roman artists resented Cigoli's favored position with the Medici and therefore, during his absence in Florence, managed to get inside his enclosure in St. Peter's to assess the work in progress. They engraved what they saw and passed it around Rome in order to show that Cigoli was plagiarizing "una stampa forastiera," a foreign print.

Although Cigoli's altarpiece is destroyed, other engravings document its design, which in fact has no known connection with any foreign, or Italian, print. All we can conclude is that here is a parallel with the more famous Domenichino-Lanfranco story, including that a print was made to expose the alleged plagiary, and that envy motivated the action. Inasmuch as Cigoli's nephew was writing his uncle's life around 1628, just a few years after Lanfranco had Perrier make his etching, one wonders if he might have appropriated the story

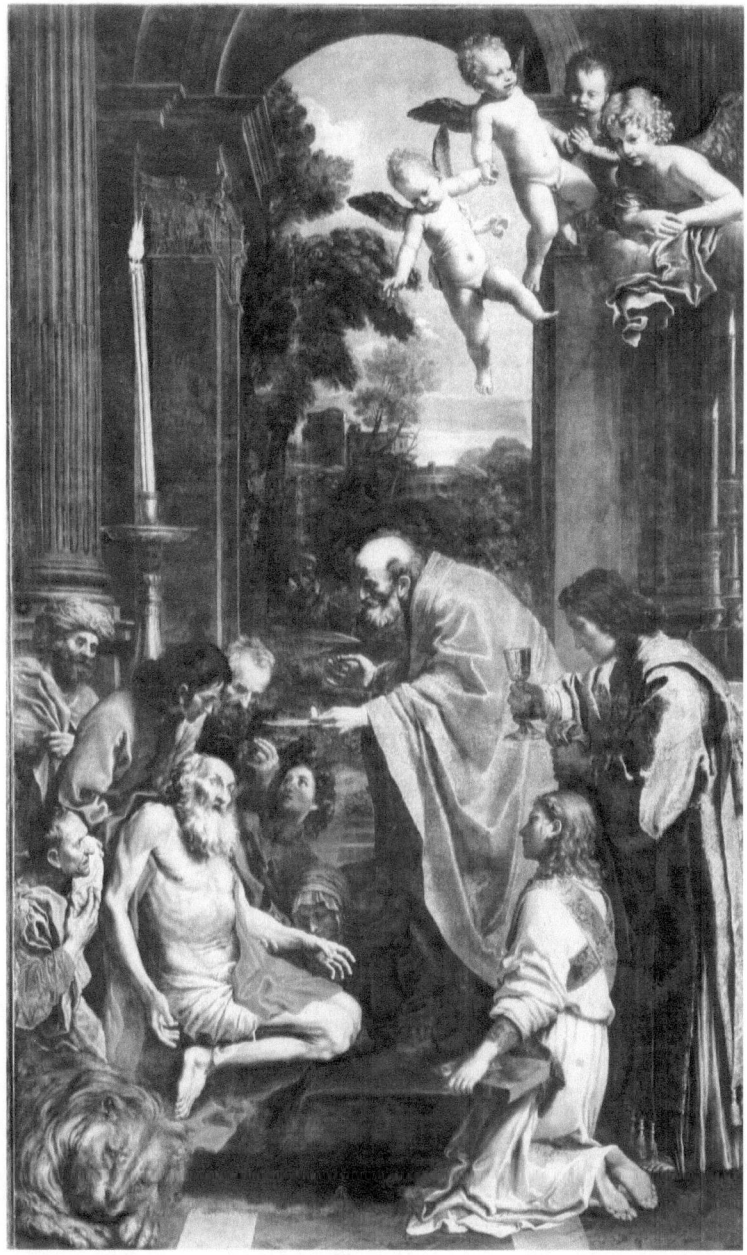

Figure 2. Domenichino, *Last Communion of St. Jerome*, 1614. Oil on canvas, 419 × 256 cm. Rome, Pinacoteca Vaticana.

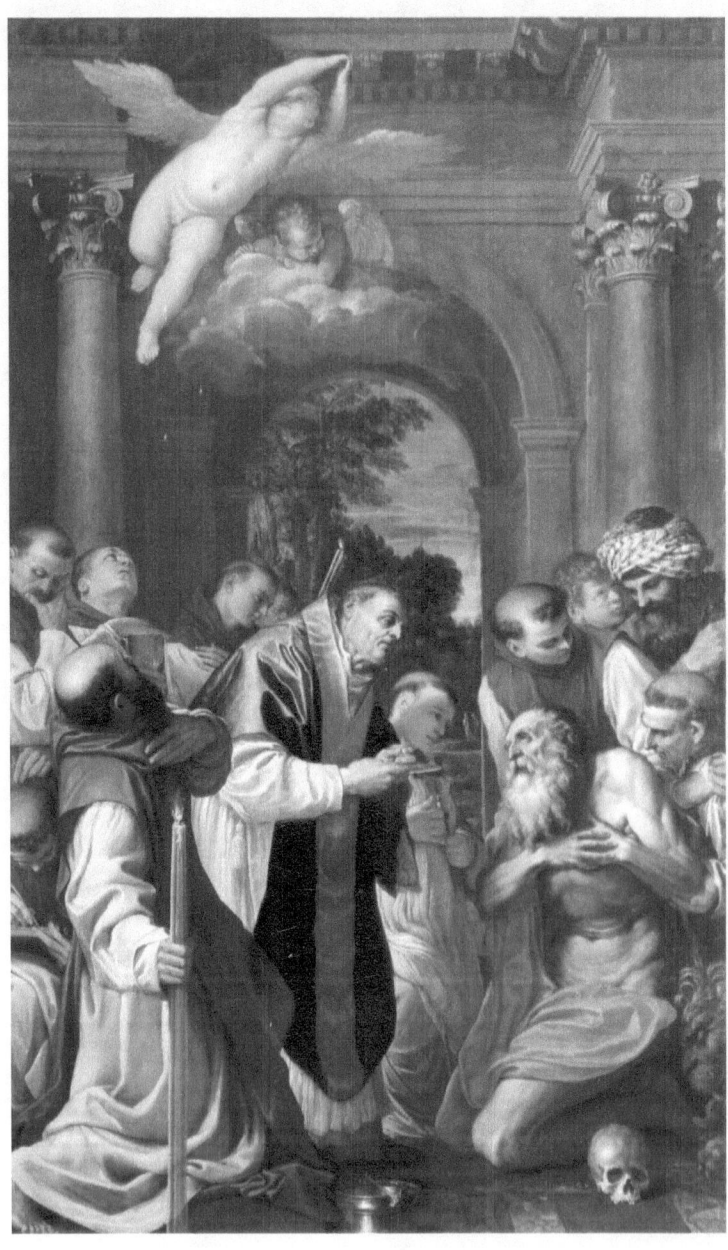

Figure 3. Agostino Carracci, *Last Communion of St. Jerome*, 1590s. Oil on canvas, 376 × 224 cm. Bologna, Pinacoteca Nazionale.

for his own purpose, and that the Domenichino-Lanfranco affair was the first instance of a charge of visual plagiary after all.

Be that as it may, artists and writers took sides on the more famous issue, though it is telling that no one denied the compositional connection between the altarpieces because such borrowing was commonplace at the time. Some painters, including the great French artist Nicolas Poussin, strongly defended Domenichino, finding in the relationship praiseworthy emulation. Poussin—to whose ideas on copying I will return—would have found that Domenichino heeded Petrarch's advice when the Renaissance poet said, "A proper imitator should take care that what he writes resemble the original without reproducing it. The resemblance should not be that of a portrait to the sitter—in that case the closer the likeness is the better—but it should be the resemblance of a son to this father."[4]

Lanfranco probably thought that his accusation had merit because Agostino's picture was back in Bologna and that Domenichino was hiding his source, which was against the tacit rules of Imitation, wherein one openly acknowledges one's models. I will not discuss this complicated case further because I am focusing on the other meaning of originality, that is, originals, variants, and copies. Nonetheless, it is essential to bear in mind that neither Domenichino nor Lanfranco nor their audiences would have thought of the relationship between those compositions or similar borrowings in terms of copies, but rather as Imitation, a method of creative emulation with roots deep in ancient rhetoric and literary theory. Imitation in this meaning represents the embracing of revered works as worthy models: it is the conscious open reliance on, and reverence for, past achievements.

Copies, on the other hand, we tend to think of as second-rate works of art and, by definition, as not-authentic, as Jonathan Richardson succinctly put it in 1719: "The Ideas of Better, and Worse are generally attached to the Terms Original, and

Coppy."[5] But some artists complicated these assumptions by repeating themselves, by copying their own original designs. Yet typically they made some kind of adjustments, which after all is only natural artistic practice — to fiddle with this or that detail when given a chance to repeat and rethink a solution. For instance, Orazio Gentileschi revised many aspects of his *Finding of Moses* (ca. 1630–31, private collection; fig. 4) when he replicated its design a couple of years later in the version in the Prado Museum (fig. 5). Not only did he reconsider the dramatic role of the maidens behind the infant Moses, but he adjusted, and improved I think, the color scheme by adding a marvelous blue dress on the right.[6] Conversely, when the workshop copyist of the beautiful Orazio of *Judith with Her Maidservant and the Head of Holofernes* in Hartford made the version in the Vatican Pinacoteca, not only was he unable to replicate its magical lighting and textures, but he altered nothing in the design.

From my experience with these and many other examples, including non-autograph versions of Caravaggio's *Una Musica* and *Doubting Thomas* in bank vaults in Chiasso, Switzerland and Trieste, respectively, I resist the fashionable rush to maintain that Caravaggio painted identical replicas.[7] His *St. Francis in Meditation* from Carpineto Romano in "The Italians" (no. 50) (fig. 6)[8] is a perfect case in point, since scholars argue over whether it, or the replica in the Capuchin church in Rome (fig. 7) is the original; or if both are copies of a lost original; or, a minority opinion, if both are autograph. The Capuchin version had more support as being the original until x-rays swung the balance to the canvas from Carpineto Romano. My aim is not to resolve this connoisseurial problem but to observe that the pictures are virtually identical in design and therefore, in my judgment, that only one, if either, is likely to be autograph.

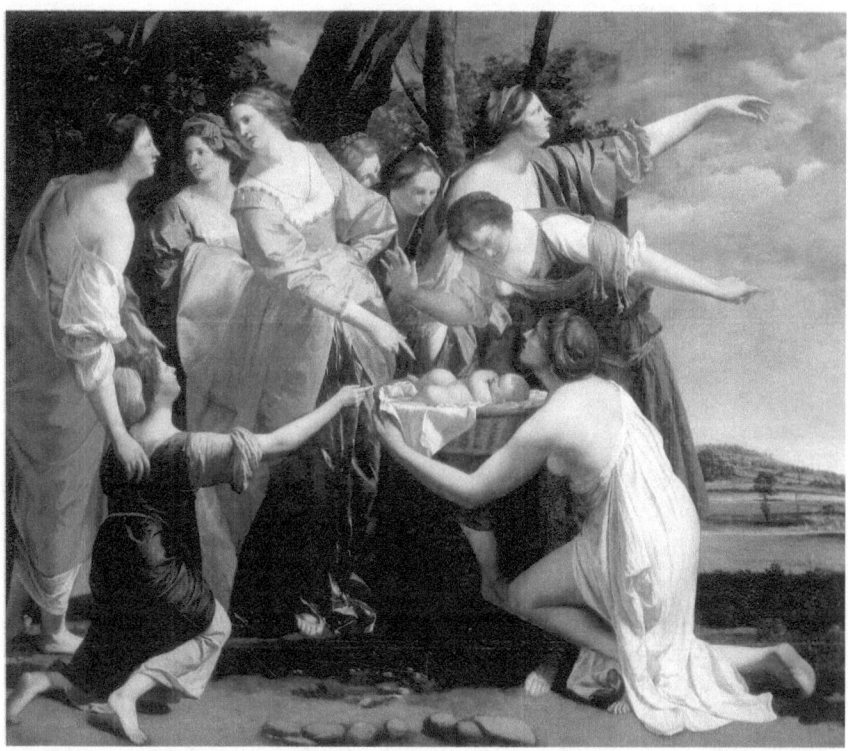

Figure 4. Orazio Gentileschi, *The Finding of Moses*, ca. 1630–31. Oil on canvas, 257 × 301 cm. Private collection.

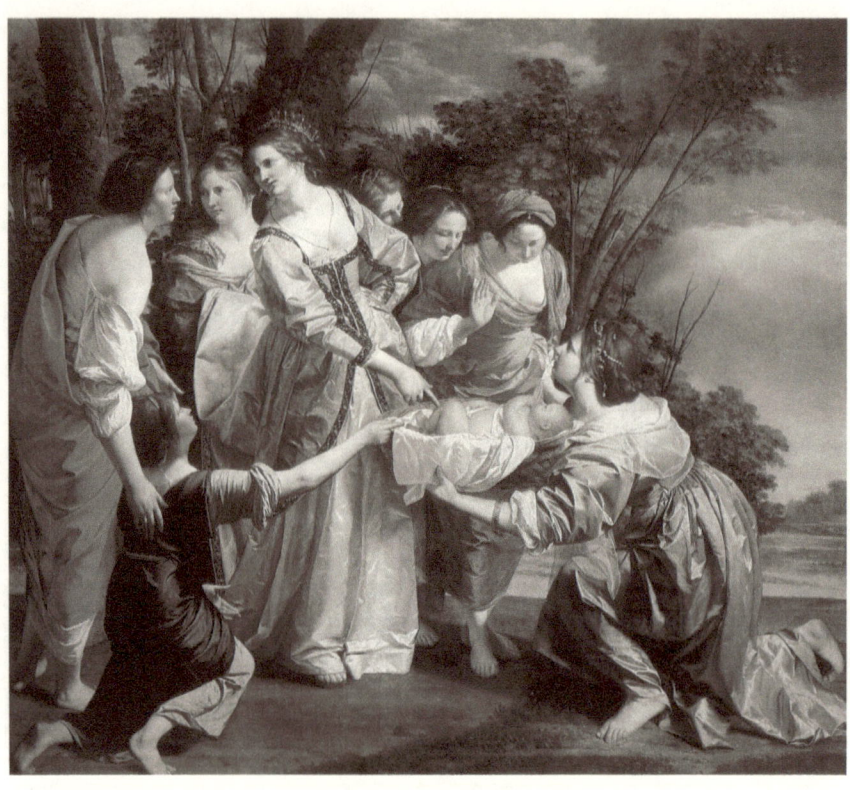

Figure 5. Orazio Gentileschi, *The Finding of Moses*, 1633. Oil on canvas, 242 × 281 cm. Madrid, Museo del Prado.

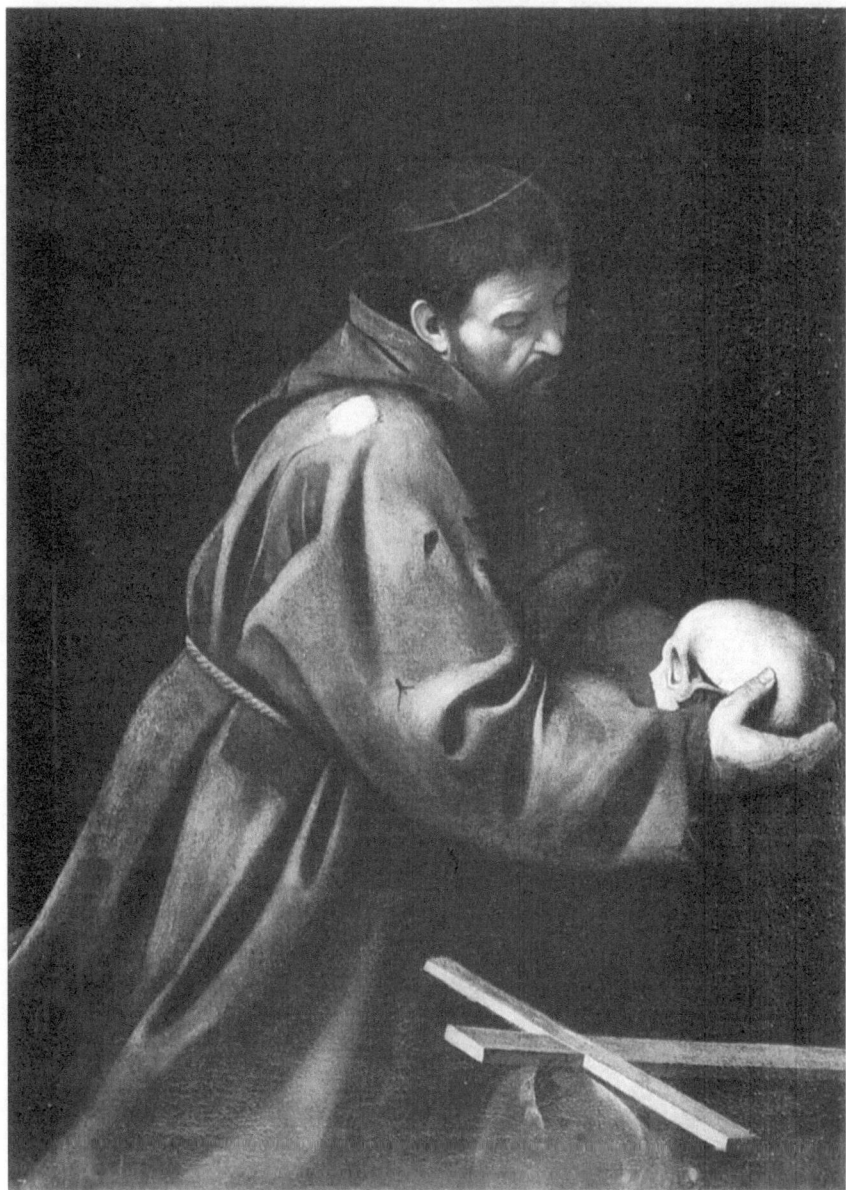

Figure 6. Caravaggio (?), *St. Francis in Meditation*, ca. 1603. Oil on canvas, 128 × 94 cm. Carpinetto Romano, S. Pietro. (Archivo Fotografico Soprintendenza Speciale per il Polo Museale di Roma.)

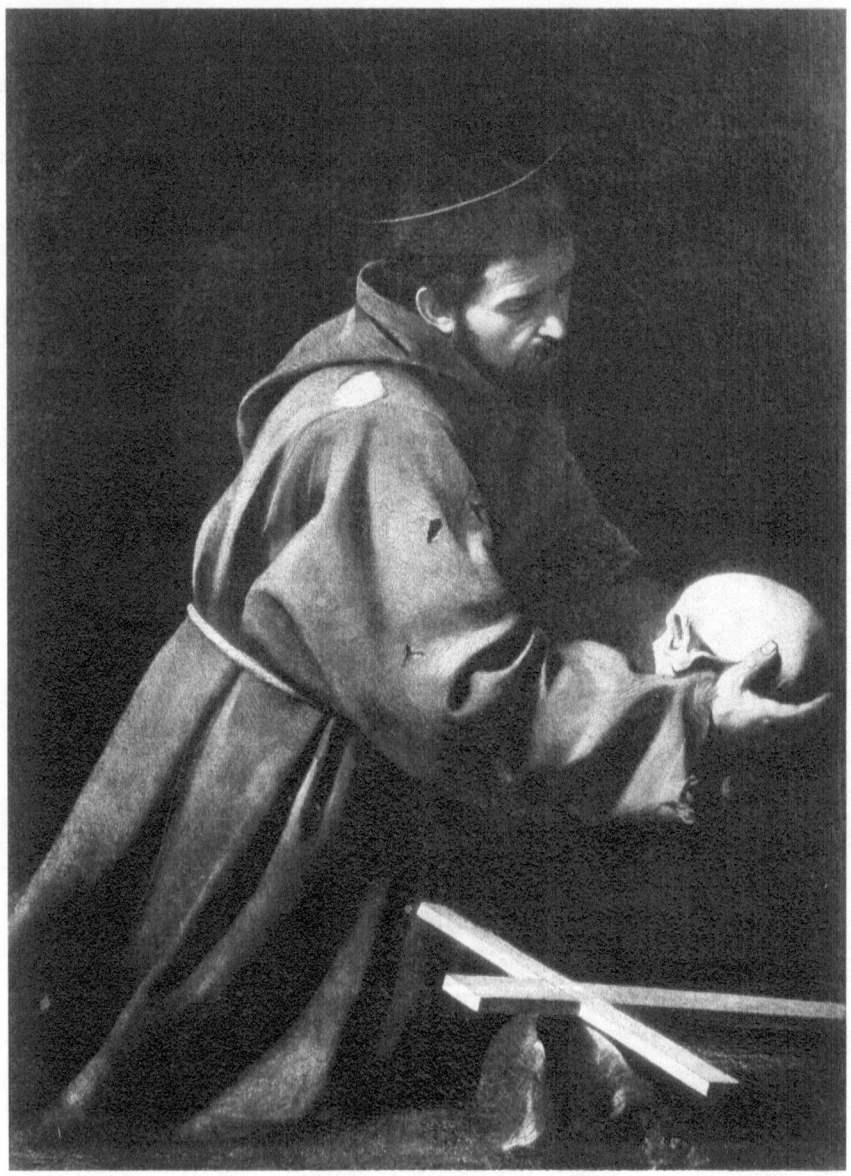

Figure 7. Caravaggio (copy after?), *St. Francis in Meditation.* Oil on canvas, 128.5 × 97.5 cm. Rome, S. Maria della Concezione. (Archivo Fotografico Soprintendenza Speciale per il Polo Museale di Roma.)

Another instructive case is a *Pietà* by Orazio Borgianni, one of Caravaggio's earliest followers. He probably invented the composition for a now heavily overpainted fresco in the sacristy of S. Salvatore in Lauro, Rome. Then he used it for the oil painting in the Galleria Spada ("The Italians," no. 54). Next he explored the dramatic effect of adding a third mourner. Finally, with another change in medium, he etched the composition with three mourners. Every one of the other canvases that repeats Borgianni's design is a non-autograph copy. Thus all four originals vary from one another, whether in composition or medium.

One more example of this pattern might be cited from "The Italians." Lanfranco essentially copied his huge canvas of *The Multiplication of the Loaves* painted for S. Paolo fuori le Mura, Rome (now Dublin, National Gallery of Ireland; fig. 8), which measures over 2 × 4 m, in a much smaller version: 1.43 × 2.18 m ("The Italians," no. 41) (fig. 9). Not only was there a radical change in size in the autograph replica, but Lanfranco also adjusted many of the colors and deleted a figure seated in front of Jesus.

This broad but not invariable pattern—that in one way or another most artists reworked compositions when repeating them—is one reason why, when in 1981 the Cleveland Museum of Art acquired the then little-known version of Poussin's *Holy Family of the Steps* (fig. 10) and it seemed so right stylistically as Poussin's own work, yet it replicated bit by bit the very famous picture in the National Gallery of Art in Washington (fig. 11), I was immediately suspicious of the latter version. I was suspicious, too, on the grounds of what Poussin himself wrote about copying, which is one of the most important statements on the subject by any seventeenth-century artist. Poussin's great Parisian patron, Paul Fréart de Chantelou, had asked the painter for copies of the *Seven Sacraments* that he had done for Cassiano dal Pozzo. Chantelou was fully content to have Poussin arrange for copies to be made by another

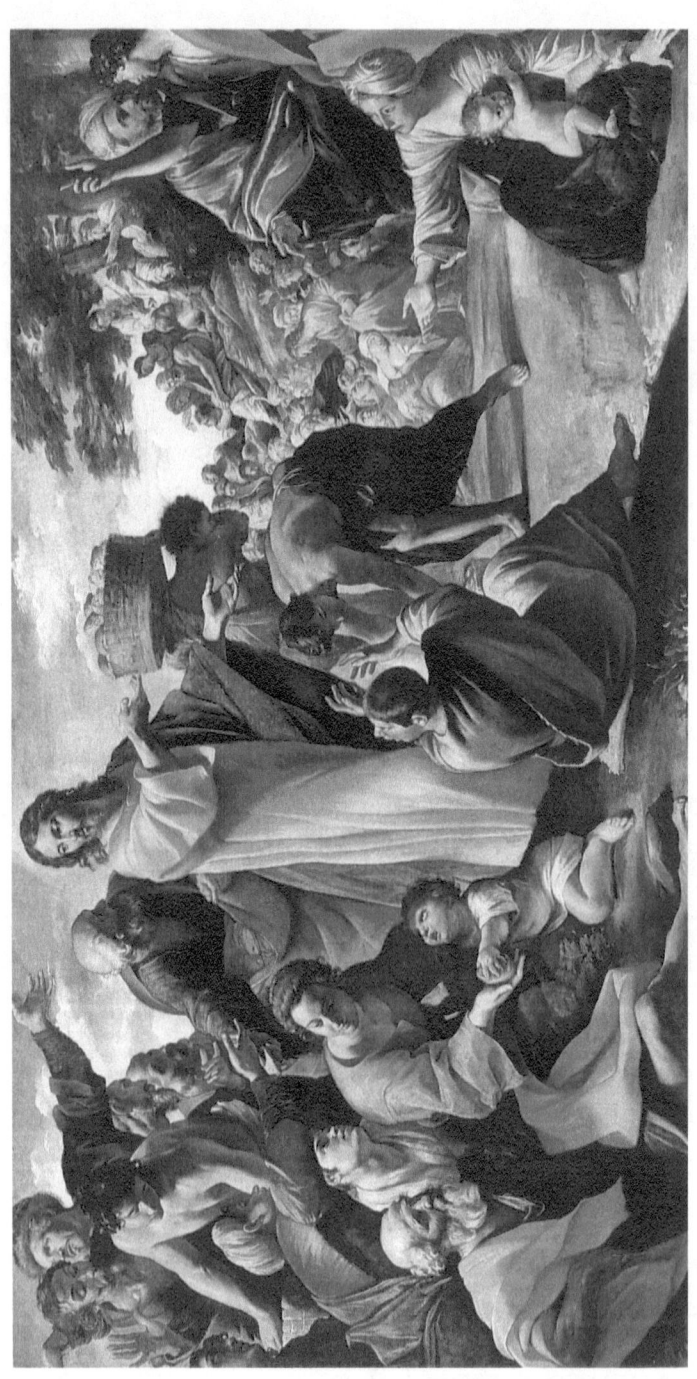

Figure 8. Giovanni Lanfranco, *The Multiplication of the Loaves*, 1624–25. Oil on canvas, 229 × 426 cm. Dublin, The National Gallery of Ireland.

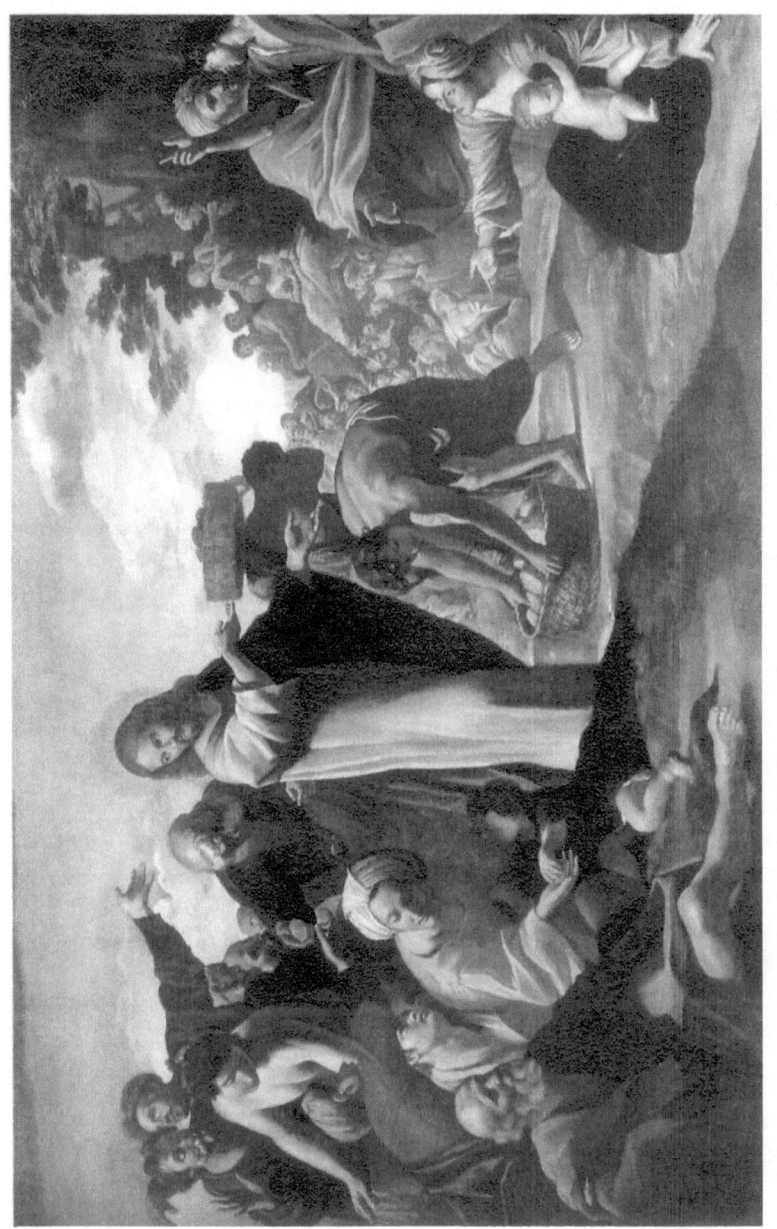

Figure 9. Giovanni Lanfranco, *The Multiplication of the Loaves*, 1631(?). Oil on canvas, 143.5 × 218.5 cm. New York, private collection.

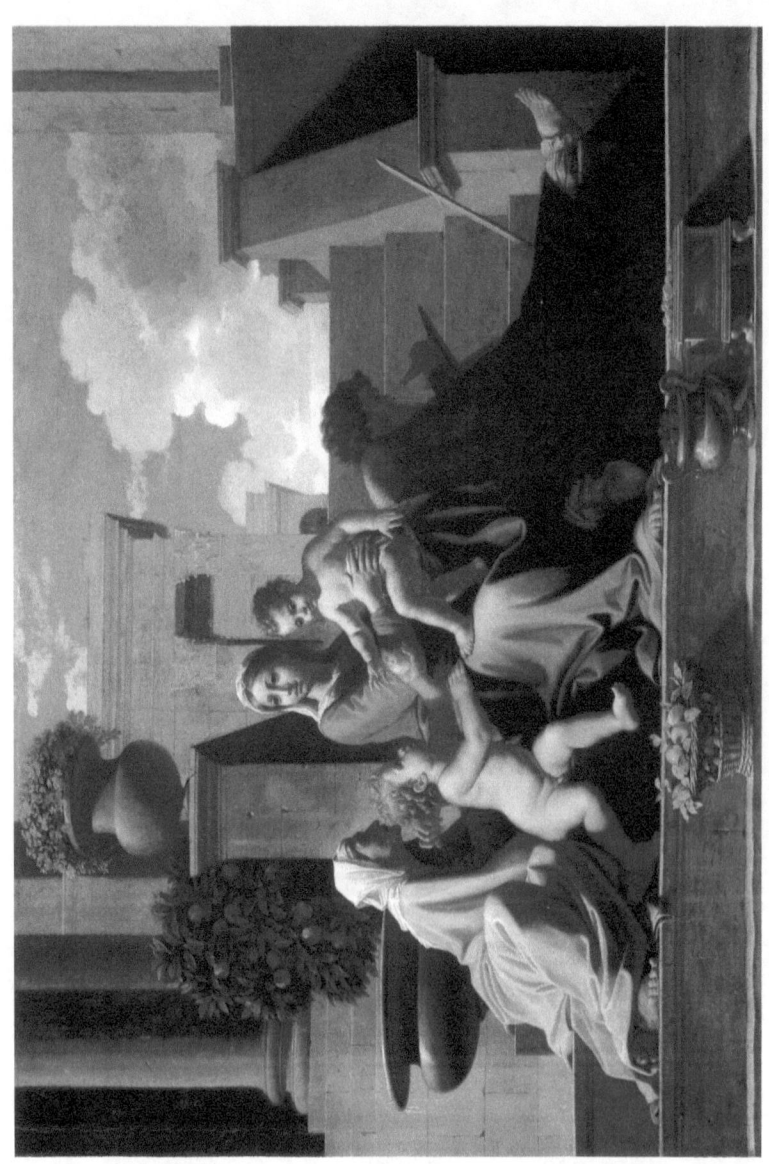

Figure 10. Nicolas Poussin, *The Holy Family of the Steps*, 1648. Oil on canvas, 73.4 × 111.7 cm. Cleveland, Ohio, The Cleveland Museum of Art, Leonard C. Hanna, Jr., Fund, 1981.18.

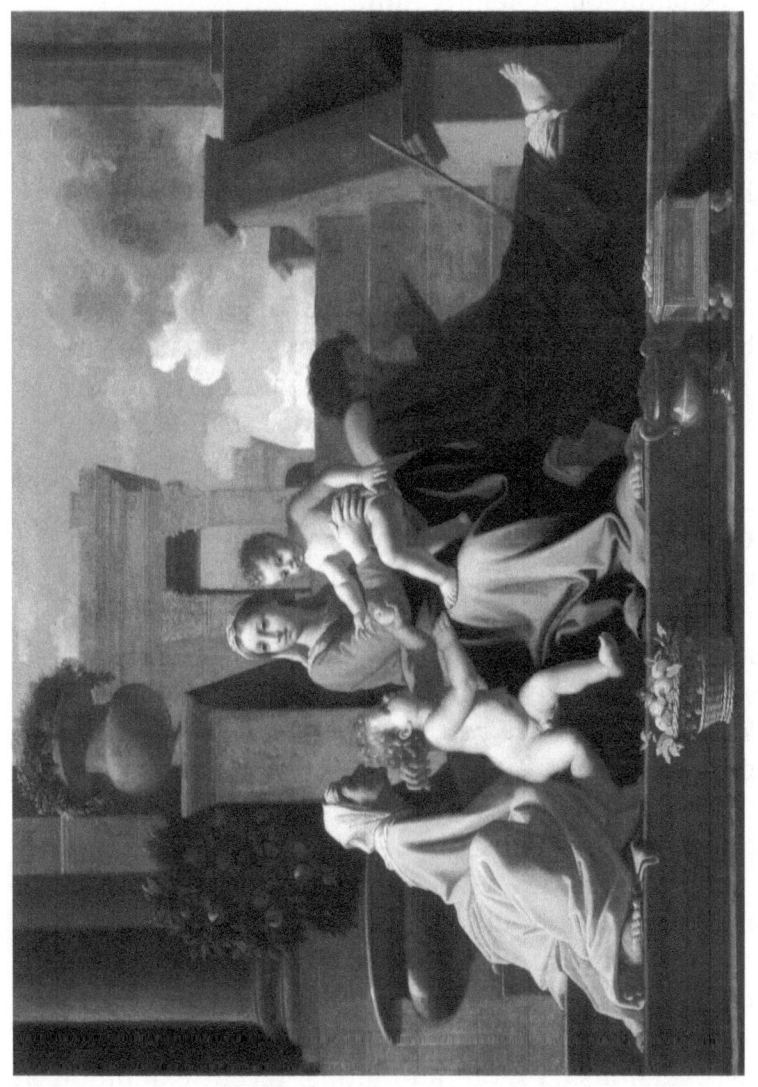

Figure 11. Nicolas Poussin (copy after), *The Holy Family of the Steps*. Oil on canvas, 68.7 × 97.8 cm. Washington, D.C., National Gallery of Art.

artist, a point worth stressing because it shows that a very discriminating collector who owned many originals by Poussin was eager to acquire copies as well. But in 1644 Poussin answered Chantelou by telling him:

> I've thought a thousand times about the too little love, care, and clarity that our professional copyists bring to what they imitate and of the price they ask for their daubs. And I have marveled altogether how so many people enjoy them. It is true that, seeing beautiful things and not being able to own them, one is obliged to content oneself with copies, even badly made, which, in truth, could diminish the name of many good painters, if it weren't that their originals are viewed by many who know well the extreme difference that exists between them and the copies. But those who don't see other things than the bad imitation easily believe that the original is not great.... Reflecting myself on all of these things, I thought I did well for my honor and your pleasure to let you know that.... I would wish myself to be the copyist...either of all seven or a portion; or rather make them a new arrangement [*une autre disposition*]. I assure you, Monsieur, that they will be better than copies.[9]

True to his word, Poussin provided Chantelou not only with seven canvases from his own hand, but with entirely new compositions, undoubtedly finding the prospect of self-repeating both unworthy and boring. In 1994 Cleveland lent their *Holy Family of the Steps* to the National Gallery of Art, where a day-long symposium was devoted to the problem of the two versions. A more ambitious, recent exhibition in Cleveland repeated the exercise.[10] Seeing the two canvases side-by-side clinched the matter: Washington's painting is a good early copy, surely not by Poussin, who almost certainly would have changed some aspect of the design had he been the copyist himself. I say "clinched the matter" on the basis of connoisseurship, a method I will discuss shortly.

It would be misleading, however, to claim that Poussin's view as expressed to Chantelou about copying his *Sacraments* was the norm, even though I believe that it was far more common than often is recognized. Some seventeenth-century artists did repeat themselves almost exactly, especially those who worked on a small scale and those who were portraitists. Moreover, attitudes varied not only from artist to artist, but also from region to region.

In Rome and Bologna, precise self-copying seems to have been relatively uncommon. Andrea Sacchi (e.g., "The Italians," no. 62) and his student Pier Francesco Mola are two exceptions. A particularly interesting story is recounted by Sacchi's early biographer, Passeri, who tells that, when Pope Alexander VII wanted something from Sacchi's hand, the painter presented him with reduced copies of two of his most famous compositions. Initially pleased, the pope became angry when he was told by his more discerning friends that they were just "lousy copies [*copiaccie*] not from [Sacchi's] hand but by his students." While Passeri maintains that in fact they were originals, he nonetheless felt that Sacchi deserved blame for his laziness in not inventing something new for such a distinguished client.[11]

Evidently following in his teacher's footsteps, Mola, too, marketed many copies of his designs. Passeri explains that, especially embittered over a failed commission at Valmontone, Mola allowed others to paint copies of his work, which he'd give a few brushstrokes (*poche pennellate*) and then sell as originals, creating confusion over what is "la leggitima verità del suo pennello" (the real truth of his brush).[12]

In Venice self-copying seems to have been much more frequent—I do not know why. But its tradition might shed light on why in Spain El Greco, who had studied in Venice, organized a studio that turned out countless replicas, although it also could have been due to the artist's background in Crete making icons, which by even longer tradition were based on pre-existing patterns. A perfect example is El Greco's *St. Martin and the Beggar*. A signed original from the late 1590s and a smaller workshop version perhaps by El Greco's son Jorge Manuel are in the National Gallery of Art, Washington. Four other small versions are known, which progressively move away from the autograph prototype. Jonathan Brown has proposed that one of the four is from El Greco's studio, sometime around 1600–1614; a second from El Greco's studio, 1610–14; the third by his son Jorge Manuel, around 1615–20; and that the last, also by Jorge Manuel and the latest and most independent of the group, was painted in the 1620s.[13]

Among the artists included in "The Italians," Bernardo Strozzi well represents the Venetian practice of self-copying. His beautiful *St. Catherine* in the Wadsworth Atheneum, Hartford, to cite just one example, is known in a large number of variants and copies.[14] A version of particularly high quality that is very similar in design to the Hartford picture is held by Strozzi specialists to be a second original, but even then Strozzi rethought its colors. His *Parable of the Wedding Guest* ("The Italians," no. 30) (fig. 12) raises different yet related issues, because it is a preparatory study for a large, destroyed ceiling painting; there is another, closely related preparatory oil study in the Uffizi (fig. 13). Again the two studies differ in palette and in this case in design, so here is a classic example of autograph replicas that record an artist's compositional experimentation.

It was long assumed that another seventeenth-century artist active in Venice, the German Johann Liss, made many autograph replicas.[15] But on the occasion of the exhibition of his work in Augsburg and Cleveland in 1975–76, it became clear to me that something was untenable about that view. Of 46 presumed originals, no fewer than 24 were alleged to be

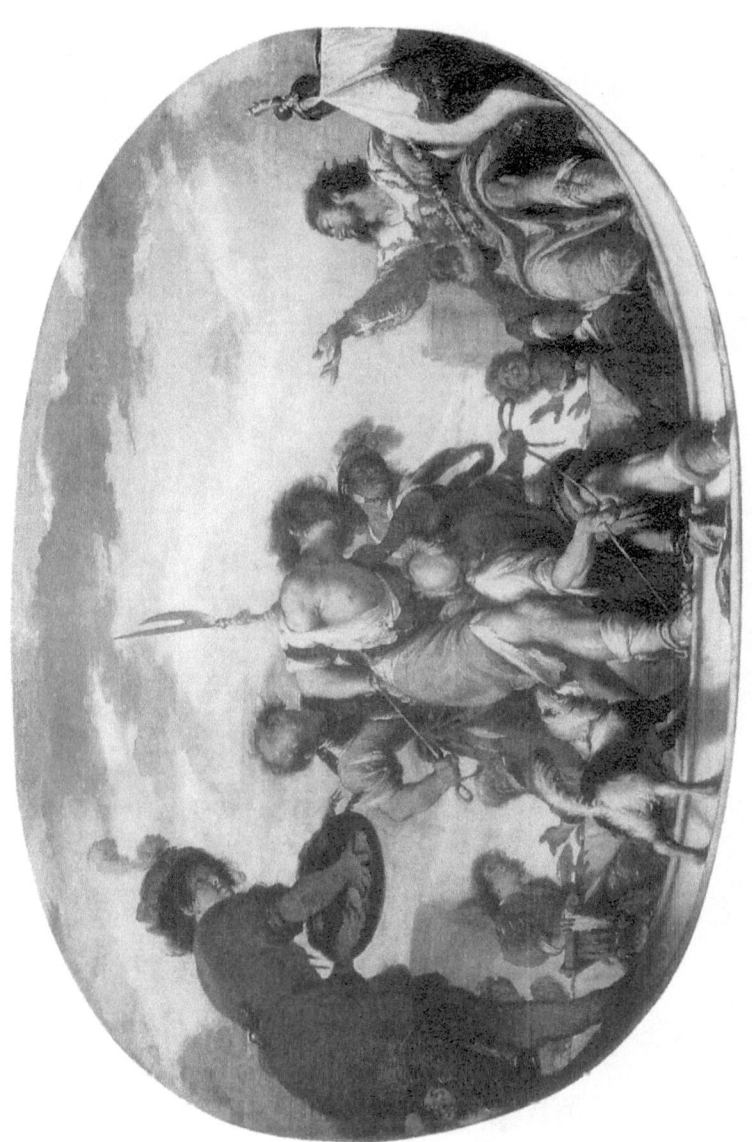

Figure 12. Bernardo Strozzi, *Parable of the Wedding Guest*, 1636. Oil on canvas, 136 × 191 cm. Genoa, Museo dell' Accademia Ligustica di Belle Arti.

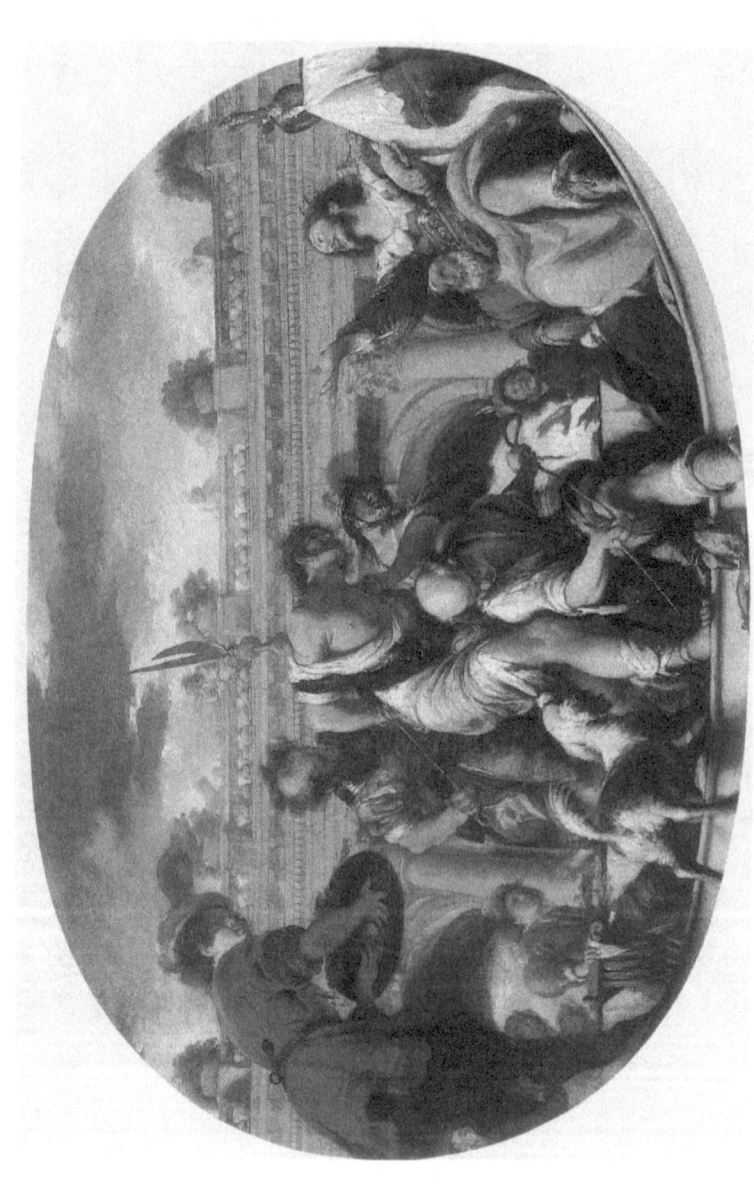

Figure 13. Bernardo Strozzi, *Parable of the Wedding Guest*, 1636. Oil on canvas, 127 × 190 cm. Florence, Galleria degli Uffizi. (Gabinetto Fotografico della Soprintendenza Speciale per il Polo Museale Fiorentino.)

autograph replicas. Not only was there no documentary evidence supporting the existence of so many self-copies, but the quality and stylistic variety of the pictures on view strongly argued against that notion. This is not the occasion to repeat my analyses of his *Peasant Brawl* in Nuremburg and its copy in Innsbruck; the original *Banquet of Soldiers and Courtesans* in Nuremburg and its copy in Kassel; or Liss's *Satyr and Peasants* in Washington and its copy in Berlin. Suffice to say that, in my judgment, a third of all of the pictures in the Liss exhibition were later copies, and that I have little doubt that close examination of many other artists' oeuvres would yield similar if not quite as dramatic results.

By the standards of the time, however, an "original" work did not have to be "autograph," meaning truly by the master's hand, for some artists sold paintings as originals when they themselves had scarcely touched them. Titian was so accused, as would be Mola. Guido Reni's early biographer, Malvasia, tells how Reni's teacher, Denis Calvaert, had his promising pupil do most of the work on small copper panels that Calvaert then marketed as his own.

In the Baroque period, the problem of what "original" and "fully autograph" or "partially autograph" could mean is perfectly epitomized in Rubens' work. In a famous series of letters to the collector-politician Dudley Carleton, who had written to Rubens complaining that some of the pictures Rubens had sent him were by his pupils, the great master replied that they "are not simple copies but are so well retouched by my hand [*si ben ritocce de mia mano*] that it would be difficult to tell them from originals [*difficilmente si distinguerrebbono dalli originali*]—signifying that he had given them his approval before they left the studio and were just as good—but that if Carleton had told him that he wanted entirely autograph originals, he happily would have sent them instead.[16] So, for Rubens, as for Mola, Guido Reni, and many other painters included in "The Italians," an original was not necessarily autograph, but a work that the master sanctioned as being up to par, regardless of his personal involvement in its execution.

By those terms, two similar paintings in Madrid and Washington of *The Meeting of Abraham and Melchizedek* are both Rubens originals, even though the former is not from the master's hand. Like the one in Washington, which probably is autograph, the painting in Madrid is an oil study for a tapestry in the *Triumph of the Eucharist* series. There is a full-scale version of the composition as well (Sarasota, Ringling Museum of Art), prepared for the weavers to follow. It, too, is an original Rubens, even if not painted by the master. Studio demands simply necessitated a lot of collaboration.[17]

Three broad questions arise from these representative cases of "originality problems." Was the seventeenth-century viewer aware of the distinctions between autograph originals, studio originals, and copies, and if so, what attitudes toward them prevailed? Second, given that so many copies existed, how were they made? Finally, why were so many copies wanted?

Here I can provide only outline answers to these questions, since each is very complex and points to still other issues. Moreover, there was no uniform opinion toward originals and copies in the seventeenth century, so no categorical answer can be given. In order to avoid as much as possible the superimposition of modern values onto those of the seventeenth century, I will rely on evidence from artists, collectors, and writers of the period.

As for the first question, whether or not there was an awareness of distinctions between originals, studio variants, and copies, the unqualified answer is, yes. I will limit my evidence chiefly to two Italian authors of the time, Giulio Mancini, a doctor from Siena who wrote an unusually perceptive treatise on art while practicing medicine in Rome during the first quarter of the seventeenth century, and Filippo

Baldinucci. It is important to know whether a painting is a copy or an original, Mancini said, "because sometimes the originals are so well imitated that it is difficult to tell. Besides, those who want to sell copies for originals darken them with smoke from wet straw, so as to give them a certain coating similar to that which time produces. Moreover," he goes on to say, "in order to make the deception more effective, they take old panels and paint over them. Even with all this, those who are experienced unmask all these forms of deception."

Mancini's remarks are particularly interesting because they document an early awareness of fraudulent copies and how some clever ones were made; and also because Mancini was convinced that the connoisseur could detect the copy or fake, and that it mattered. Mancini actually coaches us on how to distinguish a copy from an original, in one of the formative texts in the history of connoisseurship (that is, the practice of visual comparison that, based on long, close familiarity with art, and utilizing one's memory, aims to attribute works by school, artist, and date, and to evaluate their quality).[18]

Guido Reni's full-length *Penitent Magdalene* from the Palazzo Barberini in "The Italians" (no. 44) (fig. 14), whose autograph status has never been doubted, puts Mancini's guidelines to the test when two closely related pictures are taken into account (figs. 15, 16). Can Mancini's advice help determine the comparative quality of these pictures? "The first thing to consider," the doctor writes, "is whether the painting in question has the degree of perfection that is characteristic of the artist under whose name the work is offered and sold." That is, one needs to be familiar with Reni's art before making a judgment, for otherwise one can be led astray by bringing to the problem irrelevant criteria or simply inadequate expertise.

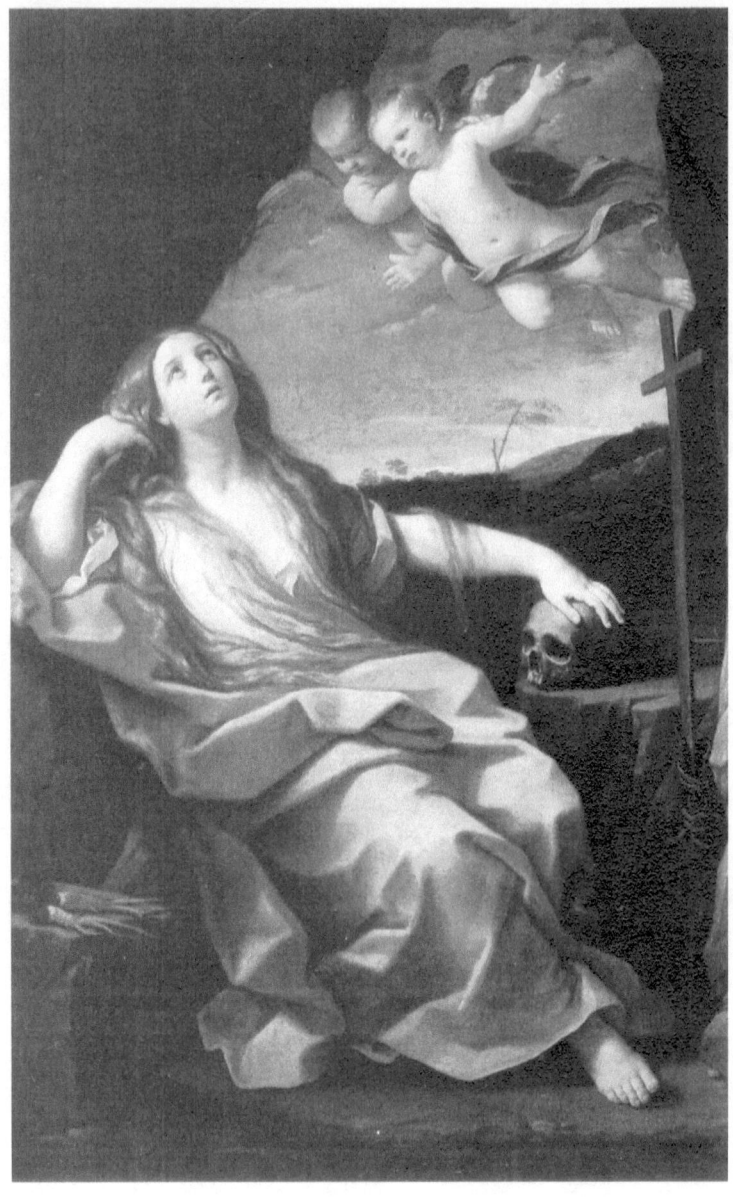

Figure 14. Guido Reni, *Penitent Magdalene*, ca. 1630–32. Oil on canvas, 231 × 152 cm. Rome, Galleria Nazionale d'Arte Antica, Palazzo Barberini. (Archivo Fotografico Soprintendenza Speciale per il Polo Museale di Roma.)

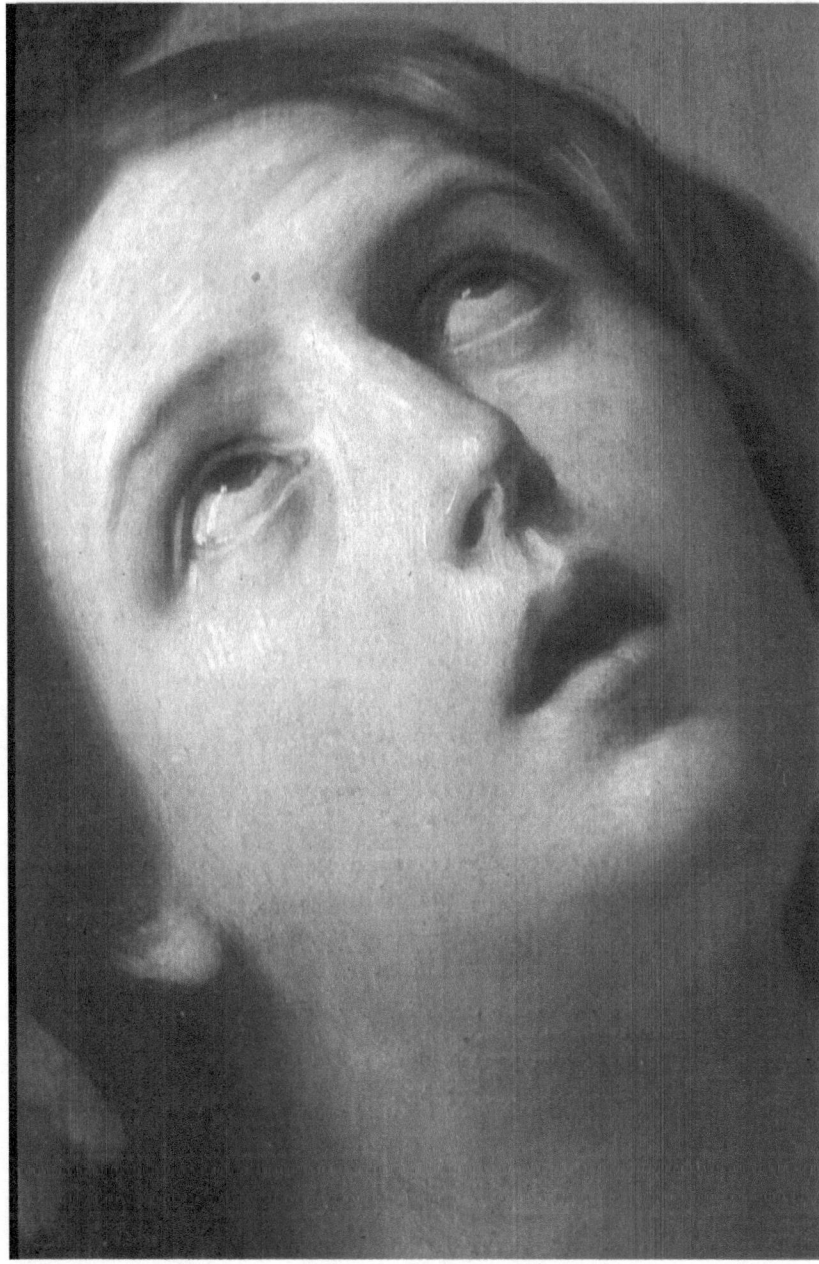

Figure 15. Guido Reni, *Penitent Magdalene* (detail), ca. 1627. Oil on canvas, 175 × 135 cm. Private collection.

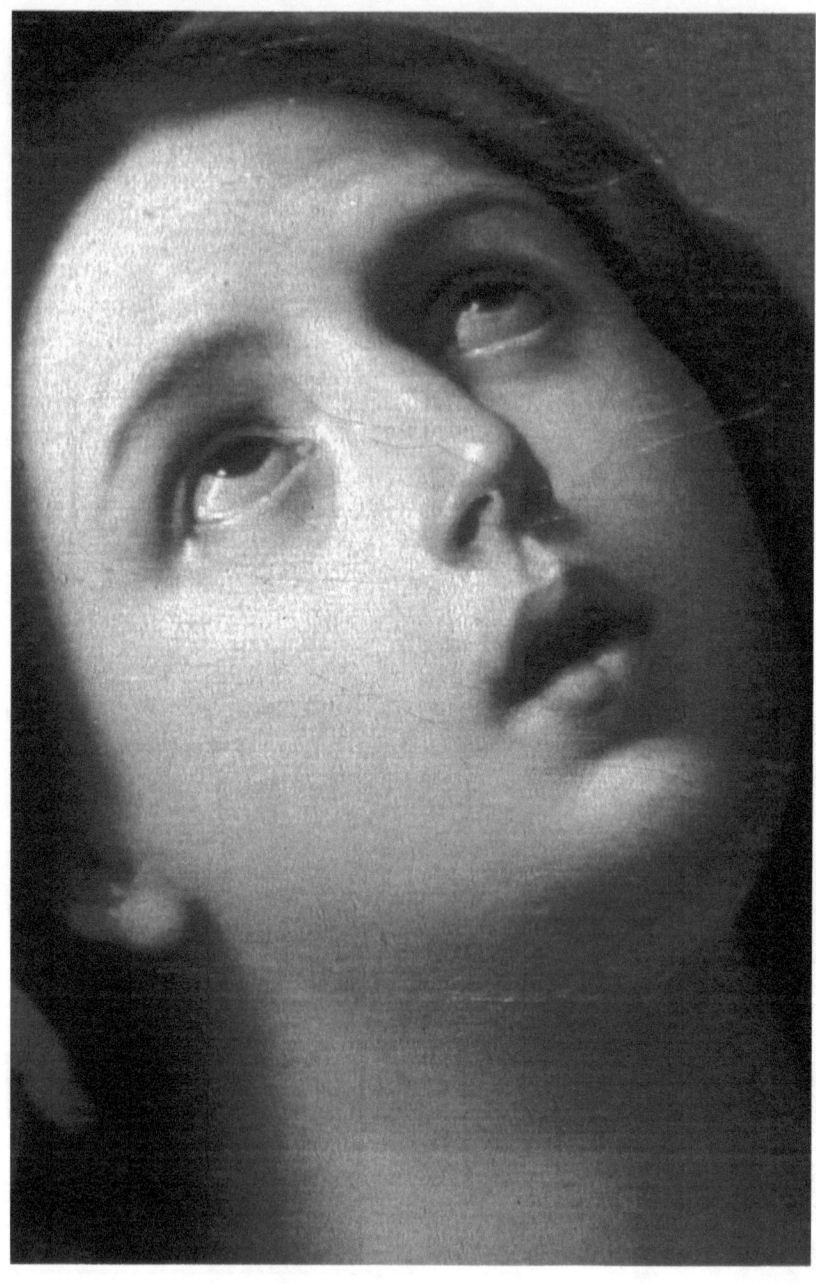

Figure 16. Guido Reni (copy after), *Penitent Magdalene* (detail). Oil on canvas, 156 × 131 cm. Private collection.

Mancini continues:

one should consider whether the painting reveals the assurance of the master himself, above all in those parts that are executed with a degree of boldness that cannot be well imitated. This is especially true of the hair, the beard, and the eyes. When [copyists] have to imitate the ringlets of hair, they do so with a certain awkwardness that is apparent in the copy.... You can see the same thing in those touches and dabs of highlights, scattered here and there. The master places them instantly and decisively, with brushwork that cannot be imitated, which depends more on the imagination and the fantasy of the master than on the actual appearance of the object.[19]

Which of the two Magdalenes (figs. 15, 16) should be assigned to Reni? Which head seems to reveal a better understanding of the suppleness of skin and nuances of light, which Reni mastered so thoroughly? Which has a more complex, subtle grasp of variegated coloring in the face? Which more successfully conveys the kind of pathos that Reni communicated so effectively, in this example that of a tormented, repentant saint turned toward heaven, yearning for a sign of divine forgiveness?

There is little question, once Reni's authentic, documented paintings are studied, particularly the Palazzo Barberini *Magdalene* (fig. 14). The version of this composition in a private collection (fig. 15) is by the master, whereas the head illustrated in figure 16 is by a copyist who was not even an assistant in Reni's studio, since it is far from Reni's personal manner. It has a slick, superficial aspect, and I mean superficial both literally and metaphorically, because everything appears to be right there on the surface, as is typical of so many copies, which often are made that way. That is, instead of being built up as originals are, they frequently rely on shortcuts that replicate only the final, surface layer of their models and hence end up looking like decals. Frequently, as in the painting illustrated in figure 16, the copy seems harder and less unified. It should be noted that the autograph *Magdalene* illustrated in the detail in figure 15 preceded the full-length version in "The Italians" (fig. 14) and depicts only a three-quarter length figure; so while the heads of the Magdalene in the two originals are nearly identical, the designs of the paintings are not.

A group of recently discovered letters by Mancini proves that the author had intimate knowledge of copies.[20] As early as 1606, the year Caravaggio left Rome for good, Mancini was involved in having copies made of Caravaggio's paintings, including *Una Musica*, *The Cardsharps*, and the *Fortune Teller*. Copies of paintings weren't cheap. Mancini wrote to his brother that those he commissioned cost him fifteen *scudi* apiece, more than Caravaggio was paid for some of his youthful originals twenty years earlier, though prices for his work soon skyrocketed. In 1613, three years after Caravaggio died, his *Fortune Teller*, probably the version in the Louvre, sold for 300 *scudi*, about forty times its original price, so by those standards a copy was a bargain.[21]

Most interestingly, Mancini's letters document that some owners actually opposed the copying of their pictures because they wanted to protect their uniqueness. Mancini characterizes the consequences of copying with the vivid verb *sverginare*, to deprive of virginity or to deflower. Referring to copies after Caravaggio, he also says that some were painted by the master's *scholaro* or pupil, but who Mancini meant is unknown.

If owners could object to copying, could artists, once their works left their hands? This question points to a key term I have avoided so far, copyright, because copyright did not exist as a legal concept for paintings in seventeenth-century

Italy. Anyone who had access to a painting could copy it, regardless of whether it was the original or a copy. But there is an important exception, with a telling explanation. Printers and printmakers could get what were called privileges, issued by the Church or State. For instance, in 1642 Louis XIII granted the printmaker Abraham Bosse "permission to engrave and print, sell and have sold and invoice suitable buyers everywhere in our realm all drawings of his invention or copied from others for the period of twenty years after pulling the first impression; anyone who copies his prints without his or his heirs' permission will pay a fine of 3000 *livres* and have all their impressions confiscated."[22]

The reason Bosse and others enjoyed legal protection was economic in origin. The capital investment that printing required was what merited protection, not the originality of an artist or designer. Another motivation behind the system of privileges, especially in Rome and France, was political, that is, the desire to control the content of what was being disseminated. Bosse's privilege extended to prints after other artists, whose permission to have their works copied was not required. Only in the eighteenth century would this situation change with Parliament's passing of the Hogarth Act in 1735, but it, like the French Copyright Act of 1793, is a much later story.[23]

Bosse, like Mancini, argued in his own treatise on originals and copies that, with experience and careful looking, one can discern copies because they always are inferior in rendering volume and look flat and labored. Another seventeenth-century author who wrote on the subject, Filippo Baldinucci, was not just an important biographer of artists but also a curator for the Medici. Baldinucci published advice reminiscent of Mancini and Bosse on how to tell copies from originals.[24] He recognized that "from copy to copy there is quite a difference," because masters, for instance, might touch up their pupils' copies—as Rubens, Reni, and Mola were wont to do—thereby confusing the visual evidence. Bosse, in fact, had warned that those were the hardest kind of copies to recognize.

"The Italians" bears this out. The seventeenth-century biographer Bellori tells that Annibale Carracci had his studio assistant, Lucio Massari, who was expert at copying his master's work, excerpt a figure from Annibale's altarpiece of *The Madonna with St. Luke* for the beautiful *St. Margaret* in the exhibition ("The Italians," no. 38), and that then Annibale touched it up. To this day experts disagree on how much of the painting is by Massari, how much by Annibale, perfectly proving Baldinucci's and Bosse's point.

Baldinucci goes on to caution that there are copies of the old masters by highly talented artists, for example, that Annibale and Agostino Carracci copied Titian, Correggio and Parmigianino. Probably the most notorious case of this is described by Vasari, who tells that Andrea del Sarto's copy (Naples, Museo di Capodimonte) of Raphael's *Portrait of Pope Leo X with Cardinals Giulio de' Medici and Luigi de' Rossi* (Florence, Galleria Palatina) fooled even Giulio Romano, who himself had helped Raphael paint the original. Vasari adds that Ottaviano de' Medici, "for all his understanding in matters of art, could not tell the one from the other, nor distinguish the real and true picture from the copy; especially as Andrea had counterfeited even the spots of dirt, exactly as they were in the original." When finally Giulio Romano was convinced that what he insisted was Raphael's original was del Sarto's copy, he said, according to Vasari, "I value it no less than if it were by the hand of Raffaello—nay, even more, for it is something out of the course of nature that a man of excellence should imitate the manner of another so well, and should make a copy so like."[25]

One looks for the artist's own hand in the original, Baldinucci advises, not only in what he terms the *franchezza*, the assurance, of contours, but "in the laying in of the colors and tints...and in many certain strokes, which we would say are negligible, almost put down by chance...." Here Baldinucci anticipates by more than two centuries Giovanni Morelli's methodical connoisseurship, which also stresses the importance of studying certain kinds of seemingly negligible details.

It is clear, then, that during the seventeenth century some lovers of art thought a lot about originals, retouchings, and copies at a time when the market was flooded with replicas and the two kinds of originality I defined moved closer together. They did so partly through the rising appreciation of the novelty and spontaneity of artistic design and execution, which was linked to the concurrent growth in the appreciation of drawings. That is, behind the judgment of the worth of originals versus copies, and behind the appreciation of originality as newness, often went a taste for the artist's unfettered hand at work, which is just what Mancini, Bosse, and Baldinucci were looking for.[26] Connoisseurship as we know and practice it grew out of these issues, since it depends directly not just on the recognition of individual styles, but on a concept of value residing in distinguishable artistic personalities.

How were all of these copies made?[27] One of the simplest methods was to reuse a cartoon, that is, a full-scale working drawing or a smaller study that could be enlarged. For example, a small pastel drawing from Reni's studio (Bologna, Pinacoteca Nazionale) must have been copied and varied in paintings over and over again, whether by the master or his pupils, with or without permission, with or without Reni's retouchings.[28] John Shearman has postulated that Andrea del Sarto personally made only the preparatory drawings for some of his paintings that were produced in his studio, in which case no autograph original ever existed. A possible example of this procedure is his *Virgin and Child* in Ottawa (fig. 17), about which Shearman wrote, "the *pentimenti*...indicate that this is

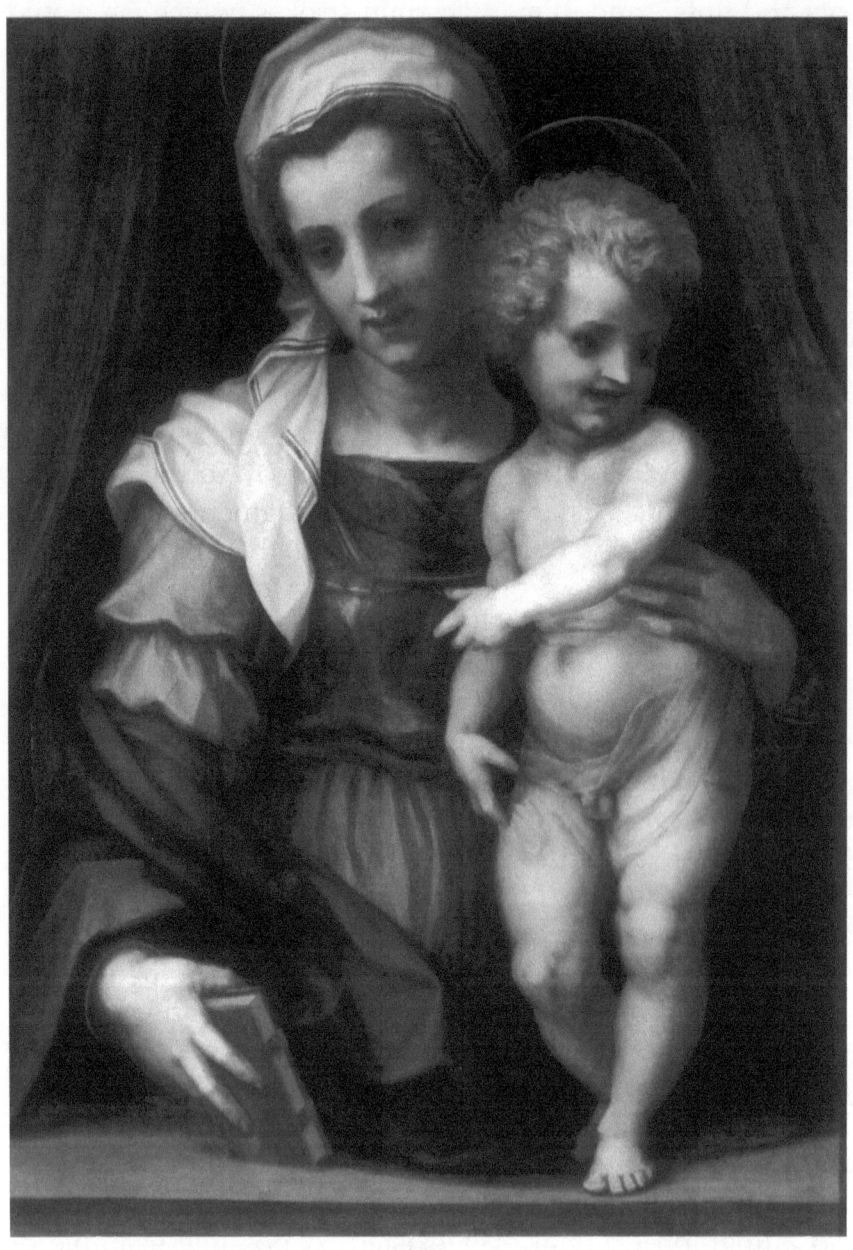

Figure 17. Andrea del Sarto, *Virgin and Child*, ca. 1515–20. Oil on panel, 85.6 × 62.5 cm. Ottawa, National Gallery of Canada.

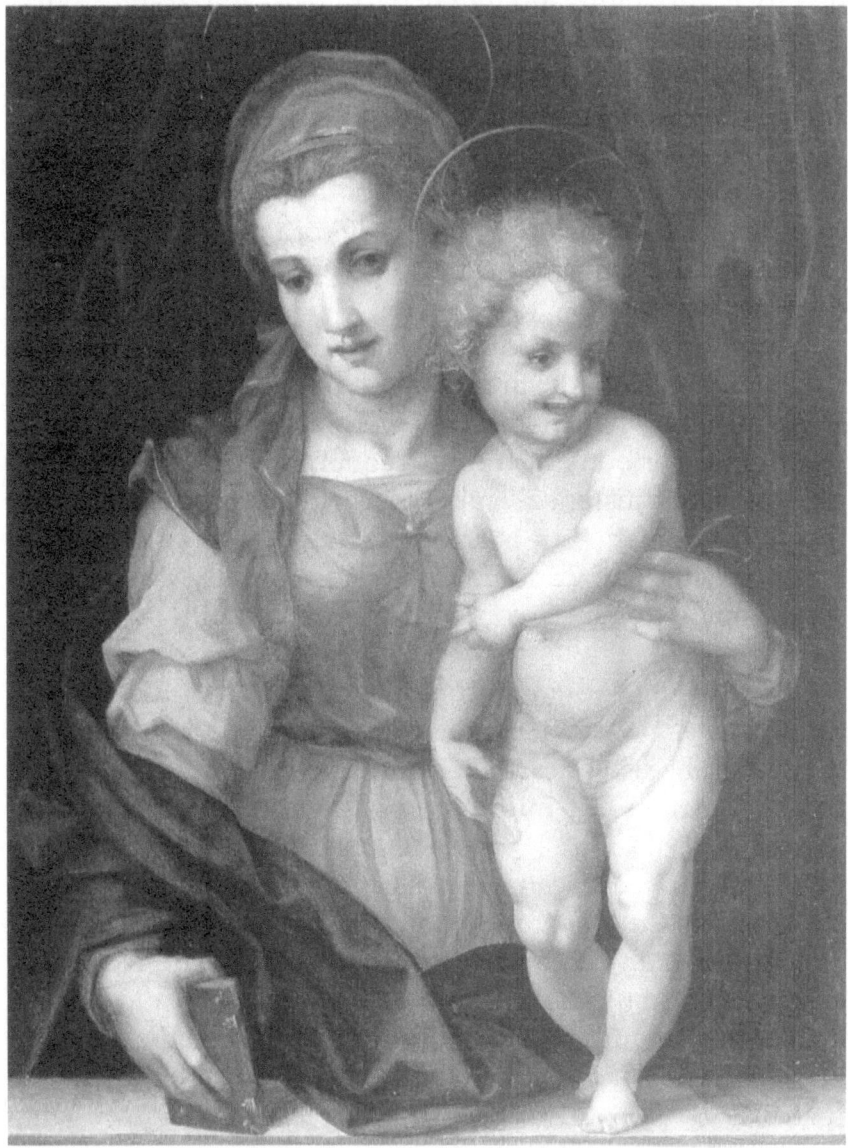

Figure 18. Andrea del Sarto, *Virgin and Child*, ca. 1515–20. Oil on panel, 89 × 66.6 cm. London, The Matthiesen Gallery.

the primary version, and that there is no lost original. The quality is very high, and it may be, in part, autograph...but... the execution was largely left to assistants." Shearman later changed his mind and believed that the Ottawa panel is entirely autograph. A recently discovered version of that panel is in "The Italians" (no. 5) (fig. 18). Subtle differences between them and *pentimenti* suggest that both are probably derived from the same lost cartoon and that both may be autograph. Moreover, the same lost cartoon seems to have been reused for other variants.[29]

Another way to produce replicas with cartoons was further removed from the artist's hand: paintings could be made from cartoons that themselves were copies, whether copies of original cartoons or, more frequently, copies of finished paintings. For instance, a pricked cartoon in the Uffizi is not by Giulio Romano but is a copy after his *Madonna of the Cat* (Naples, Museo di Capodimonte). It apparently was made to serve copyists, whose works therefore are copies of copies of an original.[30]

An exacting copying technique, tracing from the original, unfortunately was widespread during the seventeenth century. Like the use of cartoons and drawings, it was centuries old at the time but much more dangerous. Barocci's great *Entombment of Christ* (Perugia, Cathedral), for instance, was nearly destroyed because it was copied so often by tracing. Referred to as *lucidare* in Italian, the process is described in two seventeenth-century treatises, one by Richard Symonds, an Englishman who traveled to Italy around 1650 and learned a great deal about artistic practices in Rome from Domenichino's student, Canini; and the other by a Venetian artist and forger, G. B. Volpato. Volpato says that tracing makes copying much less tedious; that it allows students to reproduce their teachers' works with accuracy; and that then they can be retouched and passed off as originals.[31]

The dull copy of Orazio Gentileschi's *Judith with Her Maid-servant and the Head of Holofernes* (Rome, Pinacoteca Vaticana) already referred to was made with a tracing. So was Orazio's *Danaë* in the Cleveland Museum of Art, but in that case Orazio himself probably replicated his prime original and in doing so characteristically made some changes, notably in the color of the coverlet on the bed.[32]

To make a tracing, as explained by Volpato, paper was oiled to render it transparent, rather like modern glassine; then it was pressed onto the surface of the original picture so that the contours of the design could be seen through the paper. Next, the design was outlined with chalk or pen or, worse, with a stylus, some sharp tip such as the end of a small brush. As if this were not dangerous enough, some originals needed strengthening because important passages were not legible through the oiled paper. One method was to put chalk onto selected dark parts of the original canvas, hoping it would show through, and even by applying to the original surface a lake paint so that obscure areas could be read and traced more readily and accurately. Raphael's *Sibyls* in the Chigi Chapel in S. Maria della Pace in Rome suffered from copying with greasy and oily liquids. Volpato condemned the "sacrilegious blockheads" who oiled Titian's highly admired *Martyrdom of St. Peter Martyr* in Venice, which later was destroyed in a fire and ironically is known today only by way of many copies. Elsewhere Volpato writes that "such [tracers] ought to have their hands cut off as punishment for the crime of spoiling such rare gems."

A method moderately safer than tracing was to use a *velo*, a transparent veil or piece of black gauze, which unfortunately also was laid right onto the surface of the original, whose outlines then were drawn onto the gauze with gesso and subsequently transferred to the newly prepared canvas.

Symonds writes that the preferable method is neither tracing nor using a *velo*, but instead a *graticola*, meaning a netlike device whose chalked threads were pressed onto a new canvas, not the original, making a white pattern of squares. Then the same net was set up in front of the original painting, which was viewed through it and, by way of this squaring method, the composition was divided up into sections for copying without ever touching the original surface.[33] The squaring grid had a long history because it served for study of perspective and proportion, and hence was familiar as a learning tool to many artists, though some theoreticians criticized its mechanical nature, believing that it would lead to a lazy hand and deficient eye.

Neither Volpato nor Symonds bothered to discuss the absolutely safest way of copying, simply by eye, as some students and professional copyists still do in museums today, though shortcuts were desired when the demand for variants and copies was far greater.

The third and final question I posed is, why were so many copies made in the first place? Not just young but older, established artists copied works of earlier masters in order to learn their secrets. The great copies that the mature Rubens made after Titian come to mind. Artists also copied to prove their talent, that is, to demonstrate that they were equal to the revered masters and, as beginners, to attract attention. For instance, Passeri reports that Pietro da Cortona's important patron, Marcello Sacchetti, first recognized Cortona's talent when he spotted the young painter's copy of Raphael's *Galatea* (Rome, Villa Farnesina).[34] Pascoli, another of the early biographers of Italian painters, similarly wrote that Gian Andrea Carlone found patronage by way of a copy after Veronese.[35]

A remarkable discussion of originals and copies was published in 1625 by Cardinal Federico Borromeo, who introduced another justification for copying. Borromeo chastised snobbish collectors who, in his words, being arrogant and thinking themselves to be discerning critics, as soon as they see a painting that copies some masterpiece, they immediately scorn and reject it. "I then say to these people that all human things perish; therefore it is desirable for the good of humanity that, just as copies of ancient books came down to us, so would those of the most famous ancient [artists]. How precious would the copy of any painting by Apelles or Zeuxis be today! How useful to the progress of art! And at the same time, how much pleasure we would draw from it!"[36]

Borromeo is proven right by the copies after Titian's destroyed *Martyrdom of St. Peter Martyr*; the engraving by Marcantonio Raimondi after a section of Michelangelo's lost cartoon for the *Battle of Cascina*; and Rubens' drawing after Leonardo's lost cartoon for the *Battle of Anghiari*, among many others. Such copies have become precious and admired records of otherwise lost masterpieces, even if few copies were made for that documentary purpose.

More prevalent was the lucrative copy, which El Greco, Calvaert, Reni, Lanfranco, Mola, del Sarto, and others turned out. When the Bolognese painter Francesco Albani's older brother died and left him with staggering debts, Albani worked doggedly for the rest of his life to pay them off by selling replica after replica. Some scholars seek theoretical explanations for such artistic practice, but mundane circumstances, such as Albani's debts or Reni's well-documented huge loses from habitual gambling, were important motivating factors, too.[37]

Another type of copy was made to replicate subject matter, whether secular or religious. Portraits of famous individuals especially were copied, and not always by second-rate painters. For example, Tintoretto, Bassano, Palma, and Veronese were all sought out to copy Scipione Pulzone's portrait of Bianca Cappello, the wife of Francesco I de' Medici.[38] Sometimes artists themselves produced the replicas of their famous sitters, with scant if any modification, as Baciccio was wont to do ("The Italians," no. 64). Clearly, portraits of popes and cardinals, like those of secular heads of state, had broad political use, as modern totalitarian leaders particularly appreciate.

With regard to copies of religious images, undoubtedly the largest category of all, a fascinating exchange of opinions occurred at the opening of the eighteenth century in Rome.[39] The French-born sculptor Pierre II Le Gros wanted to move his marble statue of St. Stanislas Kostka (fig. 19) from its initial location in the room where Kostka died to a more prominent position in the adjacent church, Bernini's S. Andrea al Quirinale. He proposed replacing the original with a stucco copy that he would make personally. The Jesuits in charge refused, saying that it would strip the room of the piety the statue instills; that the original work of art would not be as effective because it could not be seen as close-up in the church; that a plaster replica simply would get damaged it time; and, to quote the documents, "few people will come to see the copy and it will inspire little piety if the original is exposed to the public in the church."

Le Gros replied, claiming that a plaster would not be damaged because, in his words, it is adored, not caressed, and that "it is not the material that stimulates piety but rather what is represented by it, whether it is marble or plaster or metal." The sculptor continued to press his case with arguments at the heart of the early copying of religious imagery:

> The statement that if the statue were duplicated it would no longer be venerated is also without foundation [he argued] nor can anybody see why this should be so. If one induces piety, more of it will be induced by two, placed, however, in different locations. No one will ever say that the duplication of the images of the Crucifixion, of the Virgin, or of the saints in many, many churches diminished piety. Instead the veneration given to God and the saints increases through the multiplicity of their images...in venerating [images]

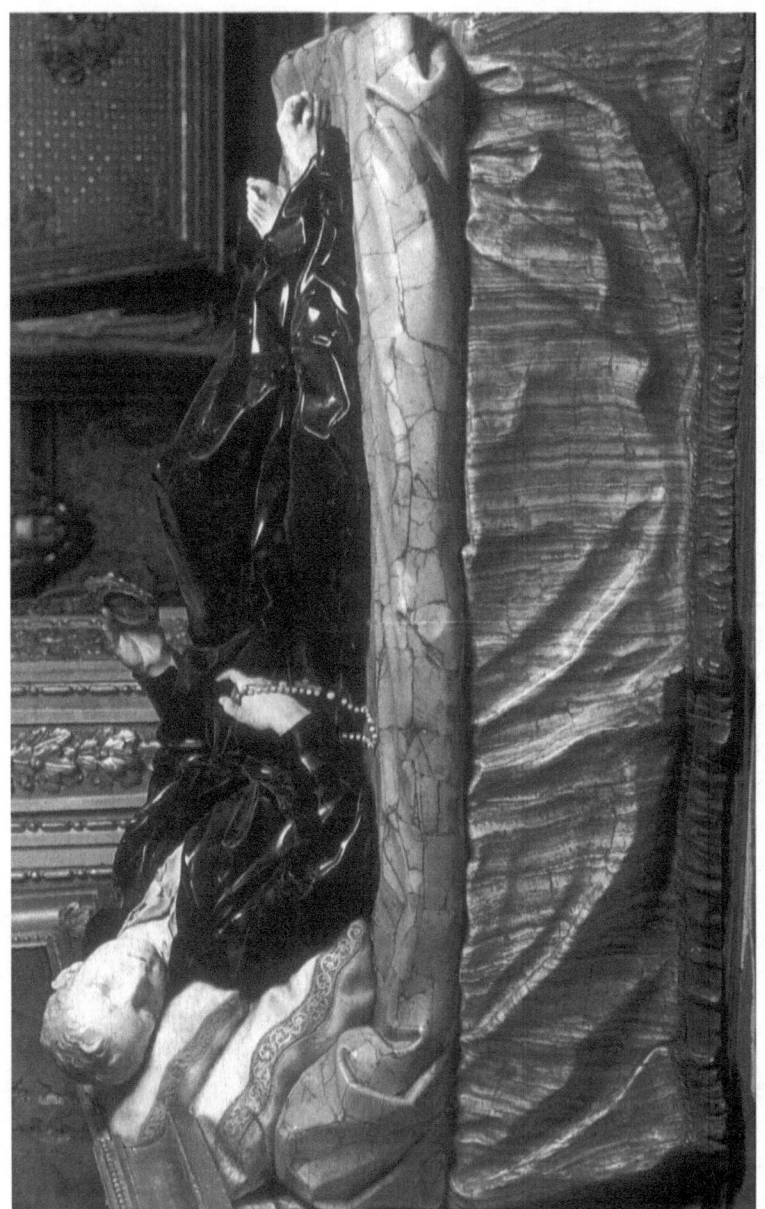

Figure 19. Pierre II Le Gros, *St. Stanislas Kostka*, 1703. Marble. Rome, S. Andrea al Quirinale, Chamber of St. Stanislas Kostka.

one does not think about whether they are originals or copies after an artist.

Le Gros finally covered himself on all fronts by assuring the Jesuits that, "by having the same artist make the copy...it will be possible to say that both are originals and both will be capable of exciting the same devotion in he who adores them."

Nonetheless Le Gros, like his patrons, apparently could not escape from thinking that for many of the viewers it did matter if a work was an original or a copy, and—for Le Gros anyway—if a copy was an autograph copy. It mattered because, ever since the generation of Leonardo, Raphael, and Michelangelo, the artist increasingly had a respected place in society as a thinker, not just as a maker. His inventions, his designs, took on new significance as the manifestation of his superior mental, not just manual, talent.

Thus we have one last reason that copies were made—the fame, the name, of the artist. Our post-Romantic cult of individuality, by exulting originality at the expense of copies and banishing them to basements, distorts history. Early in the eighteenth century Jonathan Richardson still believed that "A Coppy of a very Good Picture is preferrable to an Indifferent Original; for There the Invention is seen almost Intire, and a great deal of the Expression, Disposition, and many times good Hints of the Colouring, Drawing, and other Qualities. An Indifferent Original has nothing that is Excellent...."[40] Most painters and collectors of the Renaissance and Baroque would have agreed with Richardson, preferring a fine copy to a mediocre original. Despite our age of simulacra, virtual originals, and what Baudrillard calls the hyperreal, or maybe because of it, today's museum directors, curators, and collectors disagree by worshipping the authentic. Personally I think Richardson had the better case. In any event, he certainly had history on his side.

Afterword

The guidelines Giulio Mancini provided around 1620 for telling an original from a copy are not unlike what historians of Chinese painting identify with the traditionalist's, or Chinese, approach to authenticity, namely assessment of brushwork. "One should consider whether the painting reveals the assurance of the master himself...the master places them instantly and decisively, with brushwork that cannot be imitated, which depends more on the imagination...than the actual appearance of the object." The last words indicate that in Mancini's judgment—as in Jerome Silbergeld's—spontaneous creativity is a more important criterion for spotting authenticity than structural accuracy, James Cahill's position. As the authentic Buddhist sutra, *Bizangquan*, has "spatial contradictions" (Silbergeld), so do many indisputably authentic paintings by the arch-naturalist Caravaggio have "representational mistakes." To adopt mimetic accuracy—"getting it right"—as the key test for Caravaggio would mean rejecting many of his masterpieces.

Baldinucci, too, probably would have endorsed Silbergeld's views, since he stressed that one should look for the artist's own hand in the original, not only in what he terms the *franchezza*, the assurance, of contours, but "in the laying in of the colors and tints...and in many certain strokes, which we would say are negligible, almost put down by chance...." But the difficult question, of whether behind those positions were Western eyes looking at Western painting or some timeless, universal way of judging artistic authenticity, would require another volume of essays.

Notes

This paper was originally presented at a symposium held August 9–11, 2002 at the University of Melbourne, in conjunction with "The Italians," the

2002 exhibition in Canberra and Melbourne (the National Gallery of Australia, Canberra, 28 March–16 June 2002 and the Melbourne Museum 7 July–5 October 2002, with an accompanying catalog, Gilberto Algranti, ed., *Titian to Tiepolo: Three Centuries of Italian Art*, exh. cat. [Milan: Skira, 2002]). It was previously published in David R. Marshall, ed., *"The Italians" in Australia: Studies in Renaissance and Baroque Art* (Melbourne: University of Melbourne, 2004). I am very grateful to Jaynie Anderson and her colleagues, especially David Marshall, for their invitation to participate in the Melbourne symposium and their many courtesies during my stay in Australia. I am grateful to David Marshall for granting permission to republish my essay. A brief version was presented at the 2003 Summer Institute of Connoisseurship of Chinese Calligraphy and Painting at the University of Maryland. In order to preserve the nature of this paper, conceived as an introductory address for a broad public, I have limited references to essential literature, which should be consulted for additional bibliography.

[1] On one aspect of collecting of copies in Australia, see Alison Inglis, "'A Mania for Copies': Replicas, Reproductions and Copies in Colonial Victoria," in *The First Collections: The Public Library and the National Gallery of Victoria in the 1850s and 1860s*, exh. cat., University Gallery, University of Melbourne Museum of Art, 14 May–15 July 1992 (Parkville, Vic.: The Museum, 1992), 31–37.

[2] Richard E. Spear, *Domenichino* (New Haven and London: Yale University Press, 1982), 1:34–36.

[3] Idem, *From Caravaggio to Artemisia: Essays on Painting in Seventeenth-Century Italy and France* (London: Pindar Press, 2002), 394–95, with further references.

[4] From Petrarch's letter to Boccaccio, quoted and discussed in Thomas M. Greene, *The Light in Troy: Imitation and Discovery in Renaissance Poetry* (New Haven and London: Yale University Press, 1982), 95, the essential study of literary imitation.

[5] Jonathan Richardson, *Two Discourses* (1719), ed. London, 1725, reprinted in Aesthetics: Sources in the Eighteenth Century, ed. John Valdimir Price, vol. 4 (Bristol: Thoemmes Press, 1998), 176.

[6] For excellent color reproductions of both versions, see *Orazio Gentileschi at the Court of Charles I*, exh. cat., ed. Gabriele Finaldi (London: National Gallery, 1999), 40–41.

[7] After close study of the picture in Trieste in 1999, I reported to the owners that, despite a favorable expertise written by Maurizio Marini in 1996, the picture is a non-autograph copy of the Potsdam original. For its subsequent inspection by a team of Italian experts in 2002 (who reached the same conclusion I did) following its sensational "discovery" the previous year, see the articles in *Il piccolo di Trieste*, 29 November and 14 December 2001, and 16 May 2002.

[8] All subsequent parenthetical references to catalogue numbers are to the catalogue that accompanied the exhibition "The Italians" held at the National Gallery of Australia, Canberra, 28 March–16 June 2002 and the Melbourne Museum 7 July–5 October 2002: Gilberto Algranti, ed., *Titian to Tiepolo: Three Centuries of Italian Art*, exh. cat. (Milan: Skira, 2002).

[9] Ch. Jouanny, *Correspondance de Nicolas Poussin*, Société de l'histoire de l'art français, Archives, 5 (Paris: J. Schemit, 1911; repr. 1968), 242–45, no. 100 (12 January 1644). I have previously discussed Poussin's views in The *"Divine" Guido: Religion, Sex, Money and Art in the World of Guido Reni* (New Haven and London: Yale University Press, 1997), 266.

[10] See the issue of *Cleveland Studies in the History of Art* 4 (1999), devoted to the exhibition "A Painting in Focus: Nicolas Poussin's *Holy Family on the Steps*."

[11] Giovanni Battista Passeri, *Die Künstlerbiographien von Giovanni Battista Passeri nach den handschriften des autors herausgegeben und mit anmerkungen versehen*, ed. Jacob Hess (Leipzig and Vienna: H. Keller, 1934; repr. 1995), 301–2.

[12] Ibid., 373.

[13] For discussion and illustrations of all these versions, see Jonathan Brown and Richard G. Mann, *Spanish Paintings of the Fifteenth through Nineteenth Centuries*, The Collections of the National Gallery of Art Systematic Catalogue (Washington, D.C.: National Gallery of Art, 1990), 47–51, 78–83.

[14] Louisa Mortari, *Bernardo Strozzi* (Rome: De Luca, 1995), 108–9, cat. nos. 115–22 (nos. 115 and 118 for the Hartford painting and its high-quality replica).

[15] There is detailed discussion and illustrations of these pictures in Richard E. Spear, "Johann Liss Reconsidered," *The Art Bulletin* 58 (1976): 582–93, reprinted in Spear, *From Caravaggio to Artemisia* (see n. 3), 289–318.

[16] This much-cited letter of 12 May 1618 is discussed by Jeffrey M. Muller, "Measures of Authenticity: The Detection of Copies in the Early Literature on Connoisseurship," in *Retaining the Original: Multiple Originals, Copies, and Reproductions*, Studies in the History of Art 20 (Washington, D.C.: National Gallery of Art, 1989), 143 and 148, n. 24, for the Italian text. For further examples of what was considered to be an "original" picture, see Spear, *"Divine" Guido* (see n. 9), chapters 13 and 14 (a variant of the latter chapter, "Di sua mano," has been recently published in *The Ancient Art of Emulation: Studies in Artistic Originality and Tradition from the Present to Classical Antiquity*, Memoirs of the American Academy in Rome, supplementary vol. 1, ed. Elaine Gazda [Ann Arbor: University of Michigan Press, 2002], 79–98).

[17] For discussion of all three paintings and a fourth oil sketch for the tapestry (Cambridge, Fitzwilliam Museum), see Julius S. Held, *The Oil Sketches of Peter Paul Rubens: A Critical Catalogue* (Princeton: Princeton University Press, 1980), 1:143–45, cat. nos. 90–92.

[18] The literature on connoisseurship is large. The best introduction to its history is Carol Gibson-Wood, *Studies in the Theory of Connoisseurship from Vasari to Morelli* (New York and London: Garland), 1988. Also see the discussion of connoisseurship regarding copies in Antoine Schnapper, *Collections et collectionneurs dans la France du XVIIe siècle*, vol. 2, *Curieux du Grand Siècle* (Paris: Flammarion, 1994), 55–69, including remarks on Chantelou's request for copies from Poussin (p. 68).

[19] Giulio Mancini, *Considerazioni sulla pittura*, ed. Adriana Marucchi and Luigi Salerno (Rome: Accademia nazionale dei Lincei, 1956–57), 1:134–35, trans. Robert Enggass and Jonathan Brown, *Italy and Spain 1600–1750: Sources and Documents* (Englewood Cliffs, N.J.: Prentice Hall, 1970), 34–35. Mancini's concern with detecting forgeries and copies was anticipated by Enea Vico's study of fraudulent ancient coins, on which see Muller, "Measures of Authenticity" (see n. 16), 141–42, and was followed by various seventeenth-century authors, such as Abraham Bosse and Roger de Piles.

[20] Michele Maccherini, "Caravaggio nel carteggio familiare di Giulio Mancini," *Prospettiva* 86 (1997): 71–92.

[21] Mancini's remarks on the prices of originals and copies are discussed in a broader context of seicento artists' earnings (including Caravaggio's) in Richard E. Spear, "Scrambling for *Scudi*: Notes on Painters' Earnings in Early Baroque Rome," *The Art Bulletin* 85 (2003): 310–20.

[22] I paraphrase the text of the privilege, which is published in Bosse's own treatise, *Sentimens sur la distinction des diverses manières de peinture, dessein & graveure, & des originaux d'avec leurs copies* (Paris, 1649), 114. On privileges in post-Tridentine Rome, see Francesca Consagra, "The De Rossi Family Print Publishing Shop: A Study in the History of the Print Industry in Seventeenth-Century Rome," (Ph.D. diss., The Johns Hopkins University, 1992), 383–88; Eckhard Leuschner, "The Papal Printing Privilege," *Print Quarterly* 15 (1998): 359–70; and Michael Bury, *The Print in Italy 1550–1620*, exh. cat. (London: The British Museum, 2001), 128–31.

[23] For a recent study of the later developments, see Anne L. Schroder, "Reversals of Power: Artistic Property, Counterfeiture, and the 1793 French Copyright Act," *Visual Resources* 16 (2000): 143–54 (special issue on plagiarism in art and art history).

[24] *Lettera di Filippo Baldinucci fiorentino nella quale risponde ad alcuni quesiti in materie di pittura all'Illustrissimo...Vincenzio Capponi* (Rome, 1681). See Spear, *"Divine" Guido* (see n. 9), 272–74, for further discussion of Baldinucci's text.

[25] Giorgio Vasari, *Lives of the Painters, Sculptors and Architects*, trans. Gaston du C. de Vere, ed. David Ekserdjian (New York: Alfred A. Knopf, 1996), 1:844–45.

[26] For a penetrating study of painterly brushwork, see Philip Sohm, *Pittoresco* (Cambridge: Cambridge University Press, 1991).

[27] The best overview of early copying methods is Mary Beal, "A Study of Richard Symonds: His Italian Notebooks and Their Relevance to Seventeenth Century Painting Techniques" (Ph.D. diss., Courtauld Institute of Art, 1978), 198–202.

[28] The pastel and some of its many spin-offs are discussed and illustrated in Spear, *"Divine" Guido* (see n. 9), 236–38.

[29] For detailed analysis of the *pentimenti* and the relationships between the panels in Ottawa and that exhibited in "The Italians," with illustrations of the other variants and references to previous literature, see *A Del Sarto Rediscovered*, ed. Beverly Louise Brown (London: Matthiesen, 2001).

[30] Carmen C. Bambach, *Drawing and Painting in the Italian Renaissance Workshop: Theory and Practice 1300–1600* (New York: Cambridge University Press, 1999), 112–13, fig. 105 for the cartoon.

[31] A bilingual publication of Volpato's treatise is in Mary P. Merrifield, *Medieval and Renaissance Treatises on the Arts of Painting* (1849; repr. Mineola, N.Y.: Dover Publications, 1999), 721–55.

[32] Keith Christiansen, "The Art of Orazio Gentileschi," in *Orazio and Artemisia Gentileschi*, exh. cat., ed. Keith Christiansen and Judith W. Mann (New York and New Haven: Yale University Press, 2001), especially the section "Replication," pp. 21–27.

[33] Beal, "Richard Symonds" (see n. 27), 201–2.

[34] Passeri, *Künstlerbiographien* (see n. 11), 374–75.

[35] Lione Pascoli, *Vite de' pittori, scultori, ed architetti moderni* (Rome: 1730–36; repr. Amsterdam: Boekhandel & Antiquariaat, 1965), 2:189–90.

[36] Spear, *"Divine" Guido* (see n. 9), 267 with further references to literature on Borromeo's treatise.

[37] Ibid., 216–19 (Albani) et passim (Reni).

[38] See the letter dated 20 April 1586 in Paolo Barocchi and Giovanna Gaeta Bertelà, *Collezionismo mediceo: Cosimo I, Francesco I e il Cardinale Ferdinando: Documento 1540–1587* (Modena: Franco Cosimo Panini, 1993), 283–84.

[39] Brown and Enggass, *Italy and Spain* (see n. 19), 59–68, and, for a view of the documents that partly differs from mine, Evonne Levy, "Reproduction in the 'Cultic Era' of Art: Pierre Legros's Statue of Stanislas Kostka," *Representations* 58 (1997): 88–114.

[40] Richardson, *Two Discourses* (see n. 5), 179.

5

Connoisseurship: Conceptual and Epistemological Fundamentals

John H. Brown

The following essay attempts to lay out the basic epistemology of connoisseurship. It approaches the subject from a general philosophical perspective. While striving to be relevant to the practice of art history, illustrating the theoretical points with examples drawn from the literature of that discipline, it makes no claim to art-historical expertise.

I. The term connoisseurship: a survey of usages and conceptions.

1. Art-historical connoisseurship. *Connoisseurship* in these pages refers primarily to the endeavor to identify artworks by time, culture and authorship. It is not restricted to any particular branch of this endeavor or to any particular means of identification. This contrasts with the usage that limits the term to connoisseurship of the eye as opposed to *scientific connoisseurship*, that is, physical testing to establish time or place of origin of the materials used. If there is a better term for the totality of the art-historical endeavor, I will be happy to embrace it. Until such a one appears, using *connoisseurship* in this comprehensive sense has merit. Given that the context is art history, all and only aspects of connoisseurship should be embraced by the term. The more limited modes of investigation within its purview are best designated by a qualifier, as in *connoisseurship of the eye* or *scientific connoisseurship*.[1] Insofar as iconography and social history can contribute to the authentication of works, one could speak with equal justice of iconographic connoisseurship or circumstantial connoisseurship, even though those usages do not currently exist, as far as I know.[2] The essential goal of art-historical connoisseurship is to establish so far as possible the work-identifying facts of production (who? when? where?). Other circumstances of production, including motive (why?), fall outside of, but may contribute evidence toward, the essential goal. Likewise assessment of the aesthetic or other values of works plays a merely supporting role, so far as the bottom line is concerned. Yet the support offered by appraisals of quality is often so important that it is easily mistaken for the main thing.

2. Aesthetic connoisseurship. In general usage the term *connoisseurship* commonly designates the cultivation of discriminating appreciation of works (and other things) in general, quite apart from the specifically art-historical authentication enterprise. Its essential target is the aesthetically good, not the art-historically authentic. The term *aesthetic connoisseurship* is appropriately used to refer to this appreciative enterprise. As just noted it plays a role in art-historical connoisseurship, but it may be carried on independently. Further, it need not be historical at all: one may adopt the aim of refined appreciation of styles and aesthetic effects (in art or anything else) wherever and whenever they appear. As philosophers love to point out, a fake may be aesthetically superior to its counterpart original. Anachronism need not be in itself an aesthetic demerit. Whether it is an artistic demerit arguably depends on the type of artistic project that gave birth to it.

3. Value-connoisseurship in general. In the world at large *connoisseurship* can refer to any refined practice of value discrimination, whether aesthetic or another value is in view. Thus there are connoisseurs of horse flesh. The practices here divide according to the specific sets of values: thoroughbreds are judged by speed and endurance, hacks by comfort of gait and manageability, hunters by strength, speed, endurance, courage and intelligence, quarter horses by speed, especially over short distances, agility, and intelligence. And so forth. No doubt aesthetic values play a part in the value sets relevant to these, but even when present they need not be dominant. The only limit on the term seems to be this, that the practice deals with things of notable value where the value in question admits of fine distinctions. Thus it would idiosyncratic to speak of a connoisseur of refrigerator stick-ons. Many collectibles are doubtful candidates for connoisseurship on grounds of insufficient (and insufficiently graduated) value. But the margins are definitely hazy. Where does philately fall? Can one be a value-connoisseur, as opposed to an authenticity connoisseur, of postage stamps?

4. Authenticity. Like many other terms for cognitive and moral value, *authentic* admits of a range of meaning. In some contexts the term is redundant, as are *true*, *real*, *actual*, and *genuine*. An authentic original is just an original, as a real thoroughbred is just a thoroughbred. The attributive merely highlights the substantive without adding anything of substance to it. But such qualifiers can also be used to raise the standard for the things referred to. A real man is a notable specimen, well above the average. A true friend is one whose friendship is deeply entrenched, emotionally engaged, and reliable. In art history *authentic* is used in both senses. (1) An authentic Raphael is just a Raphael; here the qualifier's function is rhetorical rather than substantively semantic. For there is no substantive difference for the qualifier to mark. A fake Raphael is no more a Raphael than a fake dollar bill is a dollar bill. It is this semantically empty sense that expresses the essential goal of art historical connoisseurship, since determining which works are authentically of an author, school, culture, or period is merely to determine which are of the author, school, culture, or period. (2) A work of art is also praised for being authentic when it meets high standards of creativity, personal expressiveness, or other prized artistic values. Since the prevailing wisdom is that copies by other hands, especially of different periods or cultures, never meet the standards set by originals deserving this appellation, authenticity in this sense is often taken as a reliable mark of authenticity in sense 1. On the negative side sense 2 allows one to say that an artist may occasionally copy herself rather than producing an authentic work. Some aesthetic rigorists are averse to inauthentic works counting as works of art at all.

5. Authentication. Unlike the adjective, the verb *to authenticate* is invariably semantically substantive. It means to establish that a work is of a certain author, culture, or period, in a context of initial uncertainty about these matters. In this context *establish* is not used always as an absolute; art-historical usage tolerates failed authentications, as when an art historian refers to the mistaken authentications of others. But of course the aim of the authentication enterprise is to reach conclusions that are both true and solidly grounded.

6. The scope of art-historical connoisseurship. Visual art comprises works of a considerable variety of types: unique or one-of-a-kind works (drawings, paintings, carved or modeled sculpture), multiples (prints, castings), and designs. Within each of these types one finds subtypes variously facilitating or limiting individual style or expressiveness, representational or thematic subtlety, or decorative splendor. Along a different dimension, the creative process may be solitary or collaborative, swift or protracted. Along another, the level of artistic accomplishment may vary widely. These differences must obviously be taken into consideration in the connoisseur's investigations, but none of the variations falls outside the scope of connoisseurship, which is as wide as are the who, where, when questions in the field of art broadly conceived.

Copies, forgeries, unauthorized reprintings or recastings, even reproductions, by whatever hand and under whatever pretensions of originality, fall within the connoisseur's purview, as do plagiarized or forged designs. But since authentication is labor intensive, priority is appropriately given to originals, and among them, to originals of significant artistic merit, except where the art-historical project to which authentication is relevant requires a different emphasis.[3]

II. Propositions concerning art-historical connoisseurship

1. Identifying properties. In attributing an artwork to an artist, culture, or time, any type of property or property-cluster may conceivably be of use, and even definitive. Style, subject matter, brushwork, materials, facture, labels, documents, and so on, may all enter into a reasoned case for a given attribution. No category of property is excluded a priori. The reason is simple. Uniqueness with regard to time, place, or author is a highly abstract relational property. It reduces to a negative, possessing some property not possessed by anything produced at other time or place, or by any other author. In the nature of the case there is no type of property that may not satisfy the uniqueness condition. For whether a property is unique to a given object O, or to a class of objects C, depends solely on what else there is. If the property is possessed only by O, or only by members of C, it identifies an individual as O or as a member of C. That is why uniqueness is a relational rather than an intrinsic property. For a property to identify a work as of an artist, culture, or time does not require the property to be aesthetically interesting or under the control of the artist or meet any condition other than being possessed exclusively by the relevant individual or class. Needless to say, unique properties typically are highly complex rather than simple, but in principle anything could suffice.

2. Recognizable identifiers. An identifying property may not, however, be demonstrably so. What art history needs are recognizable identifiers. There is no way a priori to know which these are. There is no a priori reason to believe that they constitute a single set for all artworks. A prudent connoisseur will therefore keep an open mind and welcome additions to the set of recognizable identifiers. This is simply a matter of making use of whatever valid clues come to light. The situation is essentially the same as in historical research in general. The fact that the objects of concern for connoisseurship are aesthetic products ought to exercise no constraint whatever. In particular, adventitious identifiers, ones that identify only sporadically and in an "accidental" fashion, ought not to be spurned. Much documentation is purely adventitious.

3. Generally applicable identifiers. Notwithstanding the previous caution, it is perfectly reasonable for connoisseurship to seek generally applicable identifiers. Even the ideal of an all-purpose identifier for given types of works is a rational goal. These desiderata are, after all, straightforward consequences of the basic aim, essential to any intellectual inquiry, to arrive at the simplest possible solution to the general problem at hand—that is, Occam's razor principle. Now it would be highly unrealistic to assume that such a condition can be met. For there is no reason a priori to think that any all-purpose identifier exists, comparable to the DNA identifier of individuals. But if, contrary to expectations, such a one is discovered for, say, Chinese paintings on paper or silk, then of course the connoisseurship problem for that class of objects would be considerably simplified.[4] And identifiers that are generally applicable to particular classes of works are not unreasonable to hope for. Giovanni Morelli is widely believed to have posited the existence of such identifiers for Italian Renaissance paintings. (See sections 27–28.)

4. Property-clusters. Typically, identifying properties are highly complex property-clusters. Logically these are conjunctive properties, where the property P = the conjunction (or intersection) of A, B, C.... The constituent properties taken together narrow the possibilities of origin to a given time, place, or author. They are the properties cited in an art historian's argument for a particular attribution. I will refer to the constituents of an identifying property as partial identifiers.

5. Partial identifiers. As in any inquiry into the identity of a thing, it is reasonable to begin with the partial identifiers that are suggested by such knowledge as we have of variables limiting the possible time, place, or authorship, and seek to refine our discernment of these features—always keeping our eyes open for other types of partial identifiers. Hence if we are sensitive to qualities of line, depicted form, tonality and color, texture, rendered atmosphere, spatial organization, and so on, it makes sense to draw upon these sensitivities, refining them to the nth degree and deploying them as systematically as possible. But there are compelling reasons why we should also explore other partial identifiers: physical evidence, iconographic evidence (in the broad sense that includes what Panofsky calls pre-iconographical subject matter),[5] evidence of manifest pictorial skill, documentation, evidence drawn from social history, and anything else that might conceivably be relevant. For in principle any partial identifier might complete the case for a given attribution. Equally, on the negative side, any partial identifier may demolish an otherwise plausible case for a given hypothesis. For until one has checked all the possible partial identifiers, one cannot in principle tell whether the work possesses a property incompatible with the identification seemingly supported by the others. Like all other empirical findings regarding distant states of affairs that, complex in themselves, also leave complex traces of many sorts, authentications can always, in principle, be falsified by new evidence.

6. The essential contextuality of evidence. No item is evidential of anything in the abstract, by itself, but only in the context of the total system of knowledge. It is easy to lose sight of this because the context tends to be taken for granted and attention given only to the item in question. Of course not everything in the context has much effect on the evidential force of a given item, but enough does to make it almost impossible to give a truly comprehensive account of it—that is, to construct an argument in which all contributors are given due credit. Thus a connoisseur confronting a work brings a complex set of posits from common and technical knowledge from many areas, in and beyond art and art making.[6] One result of this is that whole regions of possibilities of authorship, period, and culture are ruled out at a glance, since there will be massive incompatibilities between features of the work and large stretches of art history, both temporally and geographically. Coming to Raphael's *Alba Madonna*, for example, we see at a glance that its rendering of bodily form and circumambient atmosphere is too advanced for the Quattrocento, to say nothing of the Trecento. This perception narrows the possibilities within which all further investigation and argument take place. When one talks about one thing proving another, it must always be understood that the evidence has this or that degree of strength relative to the context of knowledge at that moment. Another consequence is that the soundness of an evidential argument will depend on the soundness of those parts of the background knowledge that are relevant to the kind of case under examination. Our immediate certainty about the *Alba Madonna* not belonging to the Trecento would collapse if our suppositions proved wrong about why Giotto painted as he did (to cite the merest tip of the iceberg).

7. The essentially eliminative force of evidence. Evidence in favor of authorship, period, or culture is always eliminative in the sense of ruling out possibilities, progressively narrowing down the unfalsified remainder, ideally until only one author, period, or culture is left. It is easy to overlook this when our belief flashes straight to the end result as if we directly perceived the goal: the authorship, time, or place. Taken in context some properties in an identifying cluster will summarily eliminate otherwise promising possibilities. Physical tests, for instance, are notorious for decisively defeating subtle intuitions of skilled connoisseurs of the eye. Stylistic properties may also strongly refute hypotheses based on documents, and vice versa. It is noteworthy that physical properties often testify to the impossibility of a work belonging to an artist, culture or time, whereas stylistic ones testify only to the improbability—for example, that any hand other than Raphael's or Su Shi's could have painted the work. Subject-matter properties sometimes raise the improbability close to the level of physical or psychological impossibility. A detailed, fully legible representation of a Stanley Steamer would be more than merely anachronistic in an otherwise apparently authentic sixteenth-century drawing, even one bearing all the stylistic marks of Leonardo.

8. Degrees of evidence. In certain cases the accumulation of evidence in favor of an attribution is so massive that for all practical purposes the attribution is absolutely certain. Some certainties (called "axioms" below, section 14) are in fact essential to the credibility of the practice of connoisseurship as a whole. But however diligent, industrious, and persistent the practice is, common caution forbids us to expect more than a modest degree of warrant for many, perhaps even a majority of attributions of authorship of known works. Inevitably the force of the evidence depends on the circumstances of the case. The natural and normal thing, given past practices of art making and conservation, is for there to be a wide range of attainable degrees of rational confidence, especially regarding authorship. Thus we must expect to encounter cases in which the yield obtained from further investigation will decrease without limit toward zero. There is no way to attain rock-hard certainty as to which these are, however, even after the zero point seems to have been reached. Art historians like police investigators depend heavily on totally unexpected and unearned revelations to crack hard cases. Absent such serendipities, refractory cases usually are never solved, partly because the passage of time progressively destroys whatever hidden evidence there was earlier. On the other hand, a revelation is never strictly impossible even after all the known trails of evidence have proven unproductive. Confessions are a paradigm case of unearned discovery, e.g., van Meegeren's, which was motivated by the need to defend himself against the charge of having sold Belgium's patrimony to the Nazis, and that of Israel Rouchemovski in the case of the Tiara of Siataphernes.[7]

9. Empirical observation. The security of an attribution depends heavily, directly or indirectly, on empirical observation of an ordinary sort, even in cases where the connoisseur's claim is backed only by arcane holistic qualities supposedly accessible only to the hypersensitive connoisseur. This is because rational confidence in the style or facture being authentically of the period or of a particular author rests upon generalizations about the probability of successful replication of known stylistic or facture properties. Such generalizations must be based on observation of the performance of painters of different skill levels who are trying to replicate the properties in question. Nothing short of such observation could validly underwrite claims to perceive the hand (spirit, personality) of the master as distinct from that of a copyist, in the work under scrutiny. Of course the evidence is almost always of a rather general sort, even when garnered from long experience, and it enters diffusely into the fabric of our knowledge. The result is that attributions on the basis of connoisseurship of the eye can enjoy a high degree of rational credibility only if documented by specifying the observable features that undergird the general impression and also reinforced by evidence of other kinds—documentation, physical tests of the age of materials, cultural history, and so on.

10. The effect of the medium on replication. Different media are variably difficult to replicate. Those that allow for preliminary drawing, gradual building up of opaque layers, and undetectable correction of slips of the hand are in general easier than those that make these preparations and revisions impossible. Chinese paintings on silk are a paradigm case of the latter. In such cases the possibility of a "perfect fake"—a copy literally indistinguishable from an original in side-by-side comparison—is excluded from the outset, although of course distinguishability does not reveal which is the original. Perhaps it is also more difficult to imitate exactly the hand of the master in such a work than it is in the case of an oil painting, for example. It is not easy to imagine a Chinese master standing in front of a copy and discoursing on his experience in helping to paint it as Giulio Romano is said to have done before Andrea del Sarto's copy of Raphael's *Pope Leo X and Two Cardinals*. Giulio's error is understandable because of the extraordinary likeness Andrea could achieve due to the revisability allowed by the medium.[8] The possibility of exact replication is of course also drastically affected by the character of the image. A twentieth-century non-figurative painting of the sort produced by Ellsworth Kelly is easily replicable at a level of effective indiscernibility, whereas no such possibility exists for one of Pollock's classic drip paintings. There can be no possibility of identifying Kelly's work by subtle stylistic discernment, whereas Pollock's work is made to order for that discernment.

11. The effect of the medium on physical tests. Media also divide with respect to their amenability to precise physical tests, given the cultural imperative to preserve the work. On this basis Chinese works on paper and silk are not well adapted to the tests currently available. Some of the difficulties are nicely explained in an article by John Promfret dealing with the career of the virtuoso connoisseur, painter, and forger Chang Dai-chien (Zhang Daqian) and the well-known controversy concerning his works in general and The Metropolitan Museum's *Riverbank* in particular.[9]

12. The effect of art-world practices. Social practices affecting the making, collecting, displaying, recording, and preserving of artworks have a large effect on the ease or difficulty of attributions. For they determine how much documentary evidence comes into the public domain regarding time, place, and authorship. Modern art-world practice has considerably expanded the available evidence, and this trend can be expected to continue, saving our descendants much labor regarding attribution. Mechanical reproduction is a major aid in this endeavor. The media frenzy of contemporary society ensures that every major artist's oeuvre is minutely documented. Still more sophisticated devices are available for use when and if the incentive exists, and technology will offer more and more unbeatable tags as time goes on. Where these safeguards are used from the time of production onward, attribution of the works thus secured will be far less of a problem. To be sure, technology also allows for more and more sophisticated ways of replicating works and of defeating safeguards—forging documentation, for example. But the overall trend will almost certainly be to diminish problems of attribution of new works.

13. Documentation. The term *documentation*, narrowly construed, refers to records directly pertaining to the work. Works for which no such records have been found are referred to as undocumented. In current art-historical practice, however, the term covers a somewhat larger body of records bearing directly or indirectly on the work without naming or describing it: records of artists' birth, death, marriage, family, travel, training, professional career, patrons, associates, and so forth.[10] Indeed if we rely on the general meaning of the term *documentation* the scope of the category could be extended over the entire body of background information relevant to a given authentication, since it can be brought to bear only if presented in some transmissible form, that is, by some form of documentation. But in the present context it seems best to adhere to the current usage, with two highly significant additions. It seems appropriate to add to documents in the usual sense, first, archeological evidence of the place and time of the work, sites offering geological documentation, so to speak, which is transmitted to art historians by documents in the normal sense; and second, evidence drawn from the physical character of the work concerning time and place, the materials documenting themselves and that record being revealed by physical tests. For these sources, like written documents concerning commissions or prices or ownership, are entirely independent of the intrinsic, artistic character of the works. Documents directly relevant to a given work are by no means restricted to those of the time or culture of origin. They need only intersect with the work at some stage of its career, including the present, as in the series of records establishing a provenance. Documents indirectly relevant to authorship, period, or culture are a rather sprawling lot without firm boundaries, but nothing is gained by trying to establish a firm threshold of relevance. Documents in the present sense include images as well as texts, for example the images obtained by X-ray examination of paintings and the now-ubiquitous photographic reproductions that vastly facilitate close comparison of works in distant places.

14. The epistemic priority of documentation; axioms; core oeuvres. The practice of authentication depends absolutely on documentation being sufficient to establish in a definitive way the authorship, period, or culture of some works, which serve as starting points, or axioms, of the entire authentication enterprise. The reason for documentation being (at this level) epistemically prior to, say, style or subject matter or facture is that it provides the only grounds anyone could conceivably have for thinking that stylistic or any other intrinsic likeness and difference can testify to time, culture, place, or authorship. At the most basic level direct observation of who makes what in what style grounds beliefs as to what similarities and differences of intrinsic properties are likely or unlikely in the work of individuals and groups in given cultures. On this documentation rest all the general hypotheses we apply to works of whose making we have no direct knowledge. This epistemic priority is greatly lessened once we have obtained credible (probabilistic) generalizations, or strong, widely based intuitions, concerning style and other intrinsic properties. Then likeness or difference of those properties may by itself testify convincingly in some cases. However, in principle the strongest sort of documentation always trumps the strongest possible stylistic and other intrinsic property clues as to authorship, period, or culture.[11] The epistemic priority of documentation should not be confused with objectivity or certainty. Some documentation is quite objective and quite certain (those two are not the same, either), and some is historiographically problematic. It is a commonplace that documents themselves call for documentation.

15. Widening the oeuvre. The process of reasoning involved in establishing an oeuvre (individual or collective) is centrifugal: one expands the oeuvre outward from the set of axiomatic works. Given a set of axioms, unbeatable documentary + physical + stylistic evidence can be assembled for a somewhat larger oeuvre. This can be called the *core oeuvre* of the artist, period, or culture. The core expands as more evidence is uncovered, but its integrity is compromised if the standards are lowered, since any inauthentic work accepted into a core oeuvre opens the door to others. Around the core can be grouped works less strongly attested by the total evidence but sufficiently warranted for practical historical purposes. The durability of axioms will depend on the survival of their documentation and the evidence relevant to its authenticity.

16. Oeuvres without axioms. Axioms need not obtain for all artists, since given credibly established core oeuvres, say those of Botticelli, Filippo, and Filippino Lippi, other oeuvres can conceivably be credibly projected consisting of "neighboring" works not furnished with axioms of their own. Whatever the merits of Berenson's particular argument, a case like the one he developed in favor of Amico di Sandro could conceivably have been prescient.[12] For circumstantial evidence might have accumulated sufficient to justify belief in some known artist hitherto without any securely documented works, say, Berto Linaiuolo, being the author of the works Berenson assigns to Amico—without there being "axiomatic proof" of any of these works, and therefore without the oeuvre enjoying as high a degree of rational assurance as axioms confer.[13]

A vast amount of art lacks the documentation required for axioms of authorship. Of course every work once had ample documentation—in the sense of transmissible evidence of authorship, time, and place, for instance, by those who witnessed its making. In the present day the basic "documentation" for Greek vase painting is limited mostly to the archaeological evidence of time and place of production, taken in conjunction with our knowledge of the culture at large. This, like physical tests of the work itself, never suffices to establish axioms of authorship, only axioms of time and place, which are more firmly grounded when stylistic variables cohere with the archaeological record. The occasional declaration of authorship found on a work itself may justify adding a name but only in a rather tentative way, since the surviving documents do not provide enough warrant for anything more decisive. Likeness of style may sometimes give credence to the attribution of a number of works to the same unknown author. But here again sparseness of documentation restricts the level of rational confidence.

17. Temporal asymmetry of possibilities. It is a truism that not everything in art is possible at every time. Artistic possibility is bounded by technical and aesthetic competences and preferences,[14] as well as by the opportunities afforded by the social context. These factors affect possibilities before and possibilities after. Thus, suppose we are confronted with the task of dating a work virtually identical in all major respects to a well-authenticated original work with a secure date of production. It is immediately apparent that the possible dates of production of the first work are unevenly distributed relative to the second. The work in question may be a copy by the same hand or by an associate of the artist. But equally it may be a forgery hundreds of years later. The possibilities before the fact are essentially nil, given the degree of similarity along all dimensions and given that the well-authenticated work is correctly authenticated.

Limitations of technical competence and aesthetic preference also govern the distribution of possible dates and authors where a work bears a lesser but still very substantial overall similarity to a securely attributed and dated original work. The work in question may be an earlier work by the same author or by a predecessor, or by an able contemporary who is drawn toward the style of the artist, or by a follower or a latter-day imitator. It will be judged a stage along the way to the latter, or a variation upon it, in homage or in rivalry. Here again, however, the distribution of possibilities is heavily weighted toward time after. The rarity of anticipations in comparison with reminiscences stands in rough proportion to the degree of overall similarity.

Only when the securely attributed and dated original work is itself consciously backward looking do the possibilities stretch out evenly in both directions or extend predominantly into the past. Nineteenth-century Nazarene homages to Quattrocento "primitives" are a case in point in Western painting,[15] and examples are legion in traditional Chinese art.

18. Technical competence. Technical expertise affects many aspects of works, material as well as depictive. Artistic effects often depend on technical virtuosity. Different artistic cultures develop different sorts and grades of competence for various classes of work. Since expertise is hard won, it emerges only when prized and persistently sought. Skilled practice is also expensive and therefore subject to the vagaries of patronage. When artists seek to develop new production techniques, as Leonardo did, they may venture into regions of incompetence with disastrous results.[16] Some great artists have been negligent of certain technical standards.[17] For all these reasons the sort and level of competence embodied in works differs greatly over time and with all manner of special circumstances. Its bearing on authentication is accordingly complex but quite substantial.

What a particular grade of a specific technical competence in a work shows as to the author, time, or culture can be determined only by particularizing art historical research, not by recourse to universally applicable principles. Nevertheless it is worth observing that the very concept of fine (high, serious, ambitious) art entails the aspiration to extend technical competences that have an artistic payoff. Hence in cultures embodying (even if not formulating) this "elitist" concept of art progressive refinement and diversification of competences is normal, even though there can also be dissenting practitioners who deliberately purvey technical crudities, as many twentieth century avant-garde artists did, or who deliberately eschew the higher levels of virtuosity in some respect, as certain Chinese scholar-amateur literati artists did in regard to depictive skill.[18] (Such willful deviation from the norm rarely occurs until the artistic tradition has attained a high level of technical mastery of the relevant sort.) In cultures not embodying the concept of fine-art fineness, development and diffusion of competences necessarily figure historically in the advent of the art and are at all times potentialities awaiting a motive.

Where the aspiration to a given form of technical mastery can be assumed, an original can often be distinguished from a copy by the level of mastery displayed. Accordingly, connoisseurs rightly examine works minutely for technical defects. The telling deficiency may be graphic or depictive. "Deficiency" like "mastery" is relative to the standard of expertise applicable to the work, however. A work is properly adjudged a later copy if the level of depictive competence exceeds the highest attainment for the documented time of the original.[19]

Sometimes specialized, easily recognized, graphic competences are extraordinarily difficult to replicate and therefore provide reliable marks of a masterful hand. An example of this, cited by Lo Ch'ing, is the extraordinary uniformity of wave-forms over a sizeable section of Wen Boren's painting *Lin-wu Cave of Tai Lake*, dated 1555. The difficulty resides in maintaining exact control of the forms and the flow of ink over hours of uninterrupted production.[20]

19. Are authentication arguments inherently circular? While there is no inevitable vicious circularity in connoisseurship, there is obviously a danger of it. For instance, where one attributes largely on the strength of a principle of stylistic likeness (this degree of likeness of works W and X making it probable that W is by the same hand as X), and then uses the class of works thus selected as a warrant for using the same likeness-principle in fresh cases (it worked in the last case so it is even more likely to work in this new one), and *then* claims that the extension retroactively confirms the initial posit. If the initial attribution is not independently confirmed by external evidence—by documents discovered, for example—then the process does not really give any grounds for greater confidence in that particular likeness-principle. In practice many fallacious "bootstrap" arguments of this sort are used. On the other hand, in many cases new, independent evidence is discovered and the circle broken.

20. Style-space. Since attributions derived by connoisseurship of the eye depend on perception of likeness and difference, the reliability of conclusions based on any such determination will be jeopardized by proliferation of examples done by close associates of the master. The difficulty here is one of the style-space cultivated by the master being close pressed and even infiltrated by the work of associates, or by copyists later on. Clearly it is possible for associates to infiltrate along many dimensions, even if it remains uncertain whether they can do so in all. The most admired masters are understandably the most attractive to imitators (bona fide or other) and their oeuvres therefore the most liable to corruption.

21. Social variables regarding authorship. Cultures and periods may place more or less importance on singularity of authorship. This will show itself both in (a) the process of creation, not just in overt autonomy or collaboration, but also in how publicly the artist works (there are famous cases in the Italian Renaissance of artists sealing off their workspace when engaged on an important commission); and in (b) the response of the public, particularly in the value placed by viewers on being able to recognize authorship. The same variation may occur with regard to the recognizability of the culture and time of origin of works. If a culture were entirely indifferent to all such recognizability, forgery and plagiarism would be conceptually impossible social practices, though of course copying would remain possible and would probably be an entirely acceptable, or even the normal, way to produce new works. While actual art cultures seem never to go that far, they do vary significantly with regard to stress on singularity. In those with well-developed fine-art practices singularity and recognizability tend to be highly valued and forgery a going enterprise.

22. "Autographic" works. In philosophical aesthetics the term *autographic* is used of symbols,[21] works counting as a variety of symbol, whose individual identity is defined by the full range of their properties, including the history of production. Hence in the field of visual art none but the unique physical object (painting, carving) can be the work. Even the perfect fake fails the strict identity test. The vast majority of artworks are in this technical sense autographic symbols. Much of the complexity and difficulty of connoisseurship is a direct consequence of this character. Proving concrete (spatiotemporal) particularity is harder than establishing visual similarity (or even indistinguishability). Autographic works need not be autonomously created. Collaborative works can be equally autographic. So can multiples conceived as a set of products uniquely resulting from the creator's activity, e.g., the authorized edition of a lithograph.[22]

23. Allographic works, in contrast, are ones that allow for significant diversity, both material and within limits stylistic, among the items that realize the work, as do correct performances of composed music or plays and correct editions of poems or novels. In the visual arts the clearest case of an allographic work is a design.[23] A true copy of a design, like a true copy of a poem, counts as a full instance of it regardless of when and by whom produced. The authentication of an instance of a design requires only a showing that it is a faithful and knowing realization of the creator's specifications, not that it was produced by the designer or at the designer's direction or within the designer's culture.[24] Hence, although allographic works are not merely general types but types created at a time and place by one or more creators, they cannot be forged. However, an existing design, like a poem, can be plagiarized, that is, claimed by someone other than the creator; and a design stylistically similar to the work of a known designer can be created and fraudulently ascribed to that designer. The latter is the only possibility of allographic forgery.

24. Autograph works. In art history "autograph"[25] refers most commonly to a work or part of a work produced by the hand of the artist as opposed to the hand of assistants or restorers. The usage seems to presume that the handwork is distinctive to the artist stylistically or expressively. Here the alternative is not allographic but simply non-autograph. The term refers not to a semiotic type but merely to production by the author. There are many degrees to which a painting can be autograph in this sense. A comprehensive authentication assessment would specify the degree of the artist's participation, somewhat along the following lines:

(a) fully autograph = painted exclusively by the author;

(b) autograph in all important respects = painted with only trifling assistance, for instance in the priming coat, varnishing, or stylistically insignificant in-painting;

(c) substantially autograph = painted in most significant respects by the author, but with assistants providing enough in-painting to provide a normally sufficient test of difference of hands.

(d) Selectively autograph = the author painting certain key parts, e.g., faces, and planning the rest, while the assistants paint enough for their style to be conspicuous in the work as a whole.

(e) Authorized studio work = assistants painting substantially the whole simulating the style of the master, who retouches the painting to bring it nearer his autograph standards and perhaps signs it.

(f) Unsupervised studio work = assistants painting the whole without supervision, without or without some initial contribution by the master, in the form of sketches or even a cartoon, or some preliminary underpainting, still within the ambit of the studio.

Since every part of a painting is the work of some hand, it follows that every part is "autograph" in relation to someone. But in practice the expression seems to be used almost wholly in reference to the master artist. Thus the portions of Raphael's *Transfiguration* painted by Penni are not typically referred to as autograph Penni. Exceptions are made in extraordinary cases, e.g., there is no oddity in Leonardo's angel in Verrocchio's *Baptism of Christ* being referred to as autograph Leonardo because his intervention is worthy of a master, revealing as it does a major emerging artistic personality different from that of his then master.

Justice requires us to acknowledge that the presumption of stylistic or expressive uniqueness of an artist's handwork must not be allowed to pass as a universal, let alone a necessary, truth. Rather it functions as an unstated background supposition on the strength of normal artistic practice. Thus autograph status would not be accorded to the handwork of the artist in a moment of entirely routine or mechanical activity. The term applies rather to the artist in the midst of focused artistic endeavor—the artist operating as such. Moreover, if an artist forcibly constrains her natural artistic impulses in order to imitate an alien style, the result will not qualify as autograph.[26] The reason is that such handwork is of scant artistic interest.

There is no way to boil all the diversity of autograph/non-autograph concepts down to a few, rigorously exclusive categories—and there is no reason for consternation at this irreducible diversity. A simpler set of concepts would be unfaithful to actual artistic practice, just as a simpler practice would not require so much conceptual diversity. In any case we can always say what we mean in clear terms, even if quite long phrases are required. Where the context makes clear what is meant, a simple term may suffice. Thus in reference to frescoes and paintings in oil and tempera, *autograph* refers to a range from (b) to (c); it does not require as much exclusivity as (a), which might be called *super-autograph*. But autograph western drawings and watercolors satisfy (a), as do Chinese calligraphy and painting on silk and paper. Works falling in (d) and below would be referred to as *studio* rather than autograph. But full elucidation of cases requires that the underlying particulars be set forth.

25. Establishing autograph status. Obviously it will be intrinsically harder to establish autograph status in sense (a) or (b), strictly construed, than it will to reach a more generalized conclusion, with one large exception. In cases where the medium and facture curtail collaboration of the master-assistant sort the default supposition is that the master's hand determines everything or nothing. Not always, of course, for it is often possible for a later hand to add something. Still, connoisseurship, especially connoisseurship of the eye, has a clearer field in which to exercise its sense of the artist's hand where the medium limits the possibility of revisions and collaborative handwork.

26. The legitimacy of authorship. Let me underscore that nothing in the above warrants saying that authorship is not a viable concept. The lesson is merely that there are many sorts of authorial contribution (hence the need for a variety of concepts). The sensible course here is to assimilate the complications into a better articulated conceptual scheme. If one rejects authorship on such grounds, one would have to reject all the interesting and useful concepts (green, woman, particle, light, apple, individual). The aim of connoisseurship is not to determine one and only one mode of "true" authorship, but to deal with the variety of cases in as specific (= informative) a way as possible.

27. Local or "measurable" properties. Most of the "measurable" properties of depicted form traditionally stressed by connoisseurship of the eye are not strictly measurable. Thus the width of the metacarpus, length of the index finger, bulbousness of the earlobe, curl of the lip, those notorious Morellian indices, are depicted properties, not graphic ones. That is, they are properties that the lines and shapes on the picture surface represent, not properties of the lines and shapes themselves. Hence one could take measurements of them only if the pictorial convention, as embodied in the work, permitted precise determination of depicted magnitudes or ratios.

But this is never the case in art; it is possible only in technical drawings that use strict parallel projection.

Thus most references to "measurable physical properties" are in fact references to more or less imprecise pictorial properties. The degree of imprecision is determined by how closely the pictorial convention (as employed by the artist) prescribes the absolute or relative magnitude. Thus if two viewers disagree about whether two depicted forms (two ears or noses) are depicted as being exactly the same or different, no procedure of exact measurement can settle the question. Rather, the determination must, in the end, be made by the (well-informed) eye, though measurements of marks on the picture plane are often helpful in refining the perceptiveness of that eye.

Typical references to these properties in fact involve another imprecision. For pictorial practices are quite imprecise, sometimes deliberately so, sometimes from incapacity to be more exact. Conventions for placing things in space, for color and lighting, and so on, are not sharp-edged enough for pictures to have a precise pictorial content. Vagueness and ambiguity abound, as does outright inconsistency, without necessarily frustrating artistic purposes. Indeed indeterminacy and inconsistency often facilitate these purposes, most obviously where the effect desired is that of a diffuse impression, a quick glance, or a mysterious world. They also facilitate the organization of the design on the picture plane, where unity can be achieved only by softening the effect of recession and protrusion.

28. Morellian properties. The local forms, e.g., of hands and ears, traditionally associated with Morelli,[27] need not be unique to a painter to serve as potent identifiers. They function always within a previously narrowed context. For example, where we deal with originals, not copies, the presence of period or school indicators makes it necessary to compare the "Morellian" features only within those boundaries. The features need be unique to the artist only within his period or school—or for that matter within a given stage of her career. More generally, the presence of a Filippo Lippi ear in a work could deceive only where the rest of the features are tolerably consistent with the work's being a Filippo Lippi.

It is not necessary for an artist always to render a local feature in the same way, even during a period of her career, for it to help identify. For (a), even if an artist uses a variety of ear forms, the set may still be unique to her. And (b) deviations need not obscure authorship if they can be explained by special circumstances, e.g., where too much uniformity would be conspicuous, as in a row of figures like those in the Brancacci Chapel fresco cited by Wollheim.[28] (c) Occasional deviations do not keep the typical form from being unique to that artist. The typical form can still identify wherever the artist uses it. Thus there is no need to claim, as Morelli once did in a moment of exuberance, that an artist's characteristic forms never deviate at a given career stage. One must only avoid summarily rejecting a work that deviates. (d) Since in any given work there are many such local forms, deviation in one need not prevent the others from providing sufficient evidence of authorship.

29. Holistic properties. Many of the properties important in connoisseurship are "regional" or holistic rather than local. Regional properties are relational properties that arise from (are "supervenient" upon) local properties distributed in a pattern. The color or curve of an earlobe is a local property, the overall color or tone of a work a holistic one (witness Berenson on Filippo Lippi's Naples *Madonna and Child*: "the golden flesh, the golden red hair, and the mauve of the Child's tunic produce an effect of light tone never paralleled in Botticelli").[29] Some holistic properties are as "measurable" (accurately discernible) as most local ones are, for instance an overall effect of golden light. But frequently they consist of somewhat elusive impressions based on distributions of local properties that seem beyond our capacity to pin down. Still, they are crucial for artistic purposes. Artists aim to embody them, art lovers delight to perceive them. Refinement of our capacity to discriminate different degrees (strictly different rank orderings) of holistic properties is practically a definition of aesthetic refinement of our faculties. Aesthetic production and reception is largely a venture in sensitizing oneself to these, in achieving intensifications and attenuations of them in works, and in discerning and relishing them in works viewed. Connoisseurs rightly insist that many of these properties can be sensed in a very precise way. The "spirit" of a work or oeuvre or period is just an extreme case of a holistic property. Chinese connoisseurship famously proceeds largely by reference to such diffuse properties: "vital force," and so on.

30. Consistency and inconsistency. Among the holistic properties of oeuvres or their subsets is the property of consistency (continuity, regularity). Even more interestingly, so is the property of creative inconsistency. This is not the complement of consistency—not just any violation of consistency will do. Rather it is a departure from an achieved, therefore now "easy," consistency that conveys an effect of freshness (= good novelty), a sense of creative power in reserve showing itself in a departure that could be the basis for a new sort of valuable consistency. Such inconsistency is thus a new, looser sort of consistency (continuity, regularity). There is no real paradox here, merely a complication of just the sort intrinsic to the notion of fine-artistic fineness.

31. Intuitive discernment. Although the perception of subtle holistic properties is "intuitive," a point much stressed by writers on connoisseurship,[30] it is essential not to construe this discernment in a mystical way. It is solidly rooted in features of line, design and facture (chiefly brushstroke) that are individually perceptible without use of aesthetic sensitivity. The "mystery" of the quality consists in two things: first, the elusiveness of the pattern of relationships among those basic features, a pattern that enables them to produce the overall effect; and second, the "metaphorical" character of the effect itself. Thus "vital force" is rooted in base features that collectively produce the aesthetic effect; and that effect is a perceived (or felt) likeness between the pattern of features and experiences of vitality of body and spirit. Further, the likeness is cross-categorial, that is, it cannot in principle be increased to the point of exact likeness or indistinguishability. The experience of a line cannot be exactly like the experience of animal or spiritual vitality. Given these sources of the effect, whenever a question arises about whether work W has more vital force than work X, the issue can be negotiated rationally by the disputants pointing out as completely as possible the features on which their perception is grounded and the likenesses that operate in that perception. There is no reason to suppose that a good faith effort to reach agreement must fail.[31] That is, potentially these perceptions are intersubjectively valid, even universally so. The possibility of well-founded connoisseurship of the eye rests absolutely upon this potentiality being realized.

32. Intersubjectivity. Two intersubjectivities need to be achieved in relation to the holistic properties just referred to. One intersubjectivity concerns the properties themselves. The other relates to their description, which often seems subjective in the sense of "poetic" or idiosyncratic to a given writer. As just indicated, the descriptions are typically metaphorical. Despite their reputation for being "subjective," closer inspection will reveal that there is no sharp difference between them and literal descriptions in point of vagueness or variability from speaker to speaker in a close-knit linguistic community such as the community of art-historical scholarship. When Sydney Freedberg says that in Titian's *St. George* (ca. 1509) "The armour of the Saint is taken as occasion for a turbulence of light,"[32] the description gains specificity from the metaphor. All the controls listed below can be exercised as rigorously upon metaphorical as upon literal descriptions. There is therefore no special problem of describing artworks stemming from the indispensability of metaphor. As with literal descriptions, the problem is simply (!) one of achieving the needed level of accuracy and clarity.

33. The role of ostension. In this regard a distinction has often been noted between descriptions standing by themselves, capable of serving satisfactorily in absence of their referent, and descriptions whose full utility is dependent on the presence of the referent or an adequate surrogate. When the painting (or reproduction) is present, descriptions may use "ostension," that is, direct reference to, that is, pointing to, the work that manifests the property. Thus descriptions such as "spatially incoherent" or "quasi-cubist" (said of a Chinese landscape) or "foreground figures plastically realized while background figures are reduced to heads with doubtful bodies plugged into the openings left by the former" have a quite specific sense. There may be no need to work up a more self-sufficient formulation, and it may be counterproductive to try. Such reliance on ostension is not essentially different from a botanist speaking of different sorts of foliage forms by terms that require the referent to be displayed before it is well understood. All this is natural and normal, by no means unique to aesthetic descriptions. Descriptions normally get their specificity from known comparison cases, or points of reference, which establish standards (of slimness or corpulence, of brightness or dullness, of heaviness or lightness, slowness or alacrity, and so on). It is necessary to have a suitable comparison case in mind, if not always before one's eyes. Where the property described is unfamiliar and subtle, however, it may be essential to surround it with relevant comparison cases; or where it is complex and metaphorical, as is frequently the case in connoisseurship.

Given that an individual connoisseur's intuitive perception is sufficiently stable and important to weigh heavily in her mind regarding an attribution, there is reason to expect that intensive, protracted, freely experimental, collegial effort by the connoisseur and others will develop a descriptive practice (aided by ostension) sufficient both to convey the property the connoisseur discerns and to reveal at least many of the local features on which it depends. The working assumption should be that no such property will forever resist all efforts at comprehension. No *je ne sais quoi* should be accepted as the final word.

34. Verbal formulation. Verbal descriptions of stylistic and facture properties (the latter referring to brushwork and other properties of the physical "make" of the work) cannot be either perfectly comprehensive or perfectly specific. They cannot encapsulate the full individual character of their subject, whether this be a part or the whole of a work. This limitation is not unique to descriptions of artworks or things of aesthetic interest, or cultural as opposed to natural things, or to any category as opposed to another. It is a truism that descriptions are in some measure general and selective. Indeed, their normal purpose requires that they be so—that they not give more information than is relevant. From this truism, however, it is wrong to conclude that descriptions have some particular ceiling of specificity or comprehensiveness. Descriptions can be made increasingly subtle and comprehensive without known limit. The utility of descriptions is not in general dependent on any particular level being attained in either of these dimensions, but only on the level being appropriate to the need.

Most of the hurtful imprecision in describing artworks comes not from any intrinsic limitation of description as such, but from the describer not knowing enough about the subject of description or from the art world at large not having developed a sufficient common understanding of the subject and sufficient descriptive resources to provide an adequate description for the purpose at hand; for instance, to articulate what in the work is truly distinctive to an artist, school or period or what properties of the work justify a particular assessment of its quality.

35. Seeing differently. It is often said that everyone "sees differently," as if subjective differences excluded objectivity across the board. But while it is true that no one sees everything at all times identically to anyone else, it is quite false that no one sees anything at any time to have identically the same property as is seen by another. A large part of our cognitive career is taken up with learning how to see the same properties as others do, and we succeed for a considerable range of cases. The range has no detectable boundary, and we are constantly extending it in some directions by improved methods, just as we are constantly losing ground in other directions from falling out of practice, e.g., skill in following faint spore through the bush or in cutting complex angles in wooden beams by sight. It is clear that refining perception requires persistent effort. The lesson is obvious, and it runs directly counter to the skeptical conclusions drawn from commonplaces about the utter and irredeemable uniqueness of each individual's perception, conclusions whose power to persuade is rooted in ideology, not in research.

The correct application of those commonplaces to connoisseurship is not dogmatic skepticism but rational caution. Prudent connoisseurs freely concede that subtle recognitions of likeness and difference depend upon constant practice where that practice is subject to correction in light of (a) fixed benchmarks, for example undoubted originals and undoubted copies; (b) the judgments of colleagues; and (c) the entire body of external evidence bearing on the cases at hand. This sort of intuitive perceptiveness is to that extent "constructed" by an ongoing process, but the process is subject to painstaking intersubjective criteria. Intuitive perceptions, that is to say, are only credible to the extent that those criteria are met. The life of the conscientious connoisseur is a constant exercise in confirming and correcting her intuitive perceptions at all levels, local and global.

36. Acknowledging uncertainty. Wherever an attribution question is impossible to resolve in a reasonably decisive way, using strictly valid methods and standards, the uncertainty should be acknowledged. A fine balance must be maintained between overeagerness and excessive caution. The first is endemic among proprietors, private and institutional. The second is a subtler temptation for those whose chief claim to fame is critical discernment and who therefore hate to be wrong.

37. Aesthetic quality. The ultimate in intuitive discernment is reached in perceptions of the aesthetic quality of a work, since such intuitions necessarily depend on appreciation of the relevant local and holistic qualities, which are precisely what is aesthetically good about the work. That a work is aesthetically good is simply and solely a matter of the aesthetic goodness of its relevant qualities. Where the value intuition concerns the work as a whole, virtually all of its properties that are meant to be perceived or understood are relevant. Accordingly the connoisseur's study must be searching, unhurried, and renewed after intermissions. On the other hand any aspect of the work that is subject to artistic management, the structural design, the depicted spatiality, atmosphere, light and shadow; the figuration, the color harmonies, the emotional expressiveness, or the presentation of narrative and thematic content, may be the subject of a separate aesthetic evaluation.[33] Similarly parts can be assessed separately from the whole. Since aesthetic quality (of parts, aspects, and the whole) is a prime aspiration in art of all sorts, at all times and in all cultures—nothing is more central to the concept as well as the practice of art[34]—it is bound to feature prominently in connoisseurship. Artists are ranked by the aesthetic quality of their work, even though that is not by any means the only measure of their significance. Aesthetic quality is also the default measure of the work of masters as opposed to that of students or copyists—defeasible though that measure be. The stages of an artist's career must also be understood in part by reference to aesthetic quality (of aspect or whole) gained or lost, for that is the artist's own measure of success or failure.

Naturally skeptics suspect that intuitions of aesthetic quality are incorrigibly subjective. But in fact there is wide agreement within artistic traditions and among those connoisseurs who make the most finely differentiated distinctions within given ranges of works. Few philosophical skeptics make the grade—or even try to. Connoisseurs when challenged sometimes find it convenient to plead *nolo contendere* and go right on with their useful, indeed indispensable, evaluative practice. In my view the success of their collective practice is the most reliable indication of how much intersubjective warrant aesthetic value-intuitions can acquire. Merely theoretical doubts, or doubts based on unseasoned perceptions, are too circumstantial to carry much weight.[35]

38. Autograph worship. Connoisseurship is haunted by the glamour of the true original, the artist's hand, and so on. Consignment of a work to workshop or school status casts it out of the stellar into the lunar sphere or worse, even when in point of artistic quality the work may be as good as or even better than some members of the select circle. While there are good reasons for favoring autograph works in certain respects, the distorting effects of autograph worship should be recognized and resisted. Among these distortions are the tendencies (a) to assign more artistic value to autographs just because they are autographs and (b) to give works autograph status just because they are artistically good enough to be such.

39. The aesthetic rationale of connoisseurship of the eye. Part of the legitimate appeal of connoisseurship of the eye consists in the enhanced cultivation of our aesthetic powers that it promotes. This should be taken as a consolation where the use of these powers for identification in a given case is refuted by scientific evidence. Equally it should be a sufficient reason for continuing to try to discern the artist's hand and personality even in the (extremely) unlikely event that scientific methods entirely supersede connoisseurship of the eye for purposes of attribution. The aesthetic experiences of intuitive connoisseurs, so eloquently and appealingly expressed in the literature, play a central part in the refined enjoyment of art. They deserve respect independently of their objective reliability since they rank among the highest and most essential consummations of the entire artistic enterprise. It seems likely that this high value, taken together with the concentration of energies needed to attain it, explains the hyperbolic claims made by traditional connoisseurs for the authority of their intuitions of authenticity.

40. Interplay of connoisseurship and other art-historical specialisms. As already indicated, connoisseurship in the sense used here is foundational for art history, in that art-historical accounts of style or content or fabrication or training or institutions or social relations or any other art-historical project depend absolutely on knowing what works are authentically of the relevant time, culture, or author. Until one has a fairly firmly established period or cultural oeuvre to deal with, no iconographical or social or any other kind of history of that art can be written. At the same time it is equally evident that connoisseurship draws evidence from the findings of these other specialisms. All contribute in one way or another to authentication projects. The interdependence of all parts of art history should by right override and expunge the spirit of rivalry that has often existed within the field of art history as a whole, connoisseurs in the West pitted against iconographers and, more recently, social historians and those who cultivate "visual studies" against all their forebears; and in China advocates of the textual approach resisting the intrusion of the visual approach. Every specialism has its role to play, none can stand by itself. Reflection on the epistemology of connoisseurship may help to bring home the obvious lesson: collegiality is as axiomatic to method as truth is to aim.[36]

Notes

A brief version of this essay was presented at the 2003 Summer Institute of Connoisseurship of Chinese Calligraphy and Painting at the University of Maryland.

[1] Jerome Silbergeld, "Chinese Painting Studies in the West," *Journal of Asian Studies* 41 (November 1987): 849–97, speaks of "brush-oriented connoisseurship" and "structural connoisseurship" in Chinese art studies. Both are varieties within what in the West is called *connoisseurship of the eye*.

[2] A reason against thinking of any of these specialized practices or schools as sorts of connoisseurship is that none of them deals with all the evidence manifestly relevant to a given authentication. It seems better to regard them as lines of inquiry within connoisseurship.

[3] The importance of the roles of various copying practices in the Chinese artistic tradition demands that copies be carefully studied. Thus exhibits such as *Seeing Double: Copies and Copying in the Arts of China*, The Art Museum, Princeton University, 2001, are not just appropriate but necessary. Cary Y. Liu, "Seeing Double: Copies and Copying in the Arts of China," *Orientations* 32 (March 2001): 3.

[4] However, a form of connoisseurship of the eye would still be highly relevant to art history. See infra, section 39.

[5] Erwin Panofsky, *Meaning in the Visual Arts: Papers in and on Art History* (Garden City, N.Y.: Doubleday, 1955), 28ff.

[6] An indication of the breadth of the evidence presupposed by connoisseurship of the eye can be gleaned from what is said about the education and training needed by the aspiring connoisseur: general cultural knowledge, extensive knowledge of art history, protracted training in discriminating shades of stylistic difference, observation of and hands-on experience in the making of art, and so forth. For connoisseurship as a whole, to this can be added the knowledge and skills serving the connoisseur's purposes coming from other fields: paleography, epigraphy, archaeology, physics, chemistry, radiology, anthropology, ethnology, history of costume, classics, theology, and on and on. The global reach of the evidence is now widely acknowledged (e.g., Marilyn and Shen Fu, *Studies in Conniosseurship: Chinese Paintings from the Arthur M. Sackler Collection in New York and Princeton* [Princeton: Princeton University Press, 1973], 18–19). Of course it is not supposed that any single person can be the master of all types of evidence.

[7] Kathryn C. Johnson, *Fakes and Forgeries* (Minneapolis: Minneapolis Institute of Arts, 1973), entry 1.

[8] Giorgio Vasari, *Lives of the Most Eminent Painters, Sculptors, and Architects*, trans. Mrs. Jonathan Foster (London: George Bell, 1878) 3:216ff.; also in the trans. by Gaston du C. de Vere (New York: Harry Abrams, 1979), 2:1031–32 (text), 898 (illustration). A mark had to be made on the back of the copy to indicate which was which for the benefit of those who arranged the deception. Vasari convinced Giulio of his error only by showing him this device. Sarto's copy is discussed in John Shearman, *Andrea del Sarto* (Oxford: Clarendon Press, 1965), 2:265–66 and illustrated in black and white, 1:136a; another discussion and a full color illustration appears in Antonio Natali, *Andrea del Sarto: Maestro del "maniera moderna"* (Milan, Leonardo Arte, 1998), 154–56.

[9] John Pomfret, "The Master Forger," *The Washington Post Magazine* (Jan. 19, 1999), 14ff, esp. 18. The scholarly treatment of the *Riverbank*, from which many lessons can be learned, is found in Judith C. Smith and Wen C. Fong, eds., *Issues of Authenticity in Chinese Painting* (New York: The Metropolitan Museum of Art, 1999).

[10] Documentation so conceived will include what Berenson calls "tradition." Bernard Berenson, *Study and Criticism of Italian Art*, 2nd ser. (1902; repr. London: G. Bell, 1931), 116–19.

[11] Particularly telling in support of the power of documentation is the documentary evidence of ghost painters employed by many famous Chinese masters as well as high court amateurs. See James Cahill, *The Painter's Practice: How Artists Lived and Worked in Traditional China* (New York: Columbia University Press, 1994), 136ff. Equally instructive is the corrupting effect of false documentation, which can be corrected only by research uncovering

more reliable documents. An outstanding example in recent Chinese art studies concerns "the degree to which standard accounts of Chinese artists are idealized and untrue to their realities," faults which can be corrected by collecting "letters, diaries, jottings, untypically revealing inscriptions" (ibid., 5).

[12] Bernard Berenson's original argument is set forth in *The Study and Criticism of Italian Art*, 1st ser. (1903; repr. London: G. Bell, 1930), 46–69. His confidence in the reality of Amico had waned by 1932, when he reattributed some of Amico's works to Filippino Lippi (*Italian Pictures of the Renaissance* [1932; repr. London: Phaidon, 1952]). In 1938 he disowned Amico ("this delightful, if mythical personality") altogether. He had, he said, "returned to the subject with a better eye, a better method, and greater knowledge...." He proceeds to discuss in detail the reasons relating to the drawings in the hypothetical oeuvre (Bernard Berenson, *The Drawings of the Florentine Painters*, amplified ed. [Chicago: University of Chicago Press, 1938], app. VI). In the meantime Amico di Sandro had been adopted by at least two art historians of note, Raimond Van Marle, *The Development of the Italian Schools of Painting* (1923–38; repr. New York: Hacker Art Books, 1971), 12:245–66; and Catherine Bishop Neilson, *Filippino Lippi* (1938; repr. Westport, Conn.: Greenwood Press, 1972), 20–37.

[13] Such has occasionally happened, as in the identification of Berenson's "Alunno di Domenico" with Bartolomeo di Giovanni. See David Allen Brown, *Berenson and the Connoisseurship of Italian Painting* (Washington, D.C., National Gallery of Art, 1979), 42, 59 n. 123.

[14] By "aesthetic competence" I mean the judgment involved in attaining a convincing unity of effect as opposed to a pastiche whose elements do not fully go together. By "aesthetic preferences" I mean to include both deliberate and unwitting aesthetic choices, the latter covering those that arise from the prevailing taste of the painter's period in defiance of his intention to remain true to the period he intends to replicate. These are often cited in exposés of forgeries.

[15] Examples may be found in Keith Andrews, *The Nazarenes: A Brotherhood of German Painters in Rome* (Oxford: Clarendon Press, 1964).

[16] Most notably in the utter failure of his large wall painting, *The Battle of Anghiari*, to adhere to the wall in the Palazzo Vecchio, but also in the early deterioration of the *Last Supper*.

[17] The materials of Delacroix's paintings were notoriously unstable because he often disregarded good advice for the sake of immediate gratification: "It was above all a question of whether he liked the grain of the canvas, the nuances of color. If so, any objections you could make to his using them in a work were useless" (Frederic Villot, quoted by Barthélémy Jobert, *Delacroix* [Paris: Gallimard, 1997], trans. Terry Grabar and Alexandra

Bonfante-Warren [Princeton: Princeton University Press, 1998], 9). Joachim Gasquet reports Cézanne saying of the *Entry of the Crusaders into Constantinople* that he saw it "die, fade, go away" (ibid.).

[18] Cahill, *Painter's Practice* (see n. 11), 124ff. Part of the motivation was to distinguish oneself from artisan painters. Another was to concentrate on certain expressive qualities of brushwork rather than on pictorial verisimilitude.

[19] Similarly, a level of competence exceeding what is likely for the purported author may testify to production by an anonymous "ghost painter" in the Chinese tradition. Ibid.,136.

[20] Lo Ch'ing expatiated upon this in the 2001 Summer Institute of Connoisseurship of Chinese Calligraphy and Painting at the University of Maryland directed by Jason Kuo. The image is published by Lo Ch'ing in *Juemiao haohua* (Taipei: Xiongshi tushu, 1998–99), 1:50. Such distinct and continuous wave-patterns seem comparatively rare. An accessible Song example in the "fishnet" pattern is cited by Sherman Lee in his contribution to Smith and Fong, *Issues in Authenticity* (see n. 9), 82. A Yuan example is illustrated at p. 84. In Wen Fong's *Images of the Mind* (Princeton, N.J.: The Art Museum, Princeton University, 1984) one finds on p. 358 a detail from a scroll by Chü Chieh (ca. 1531–1585) with a looser patterning. Xu Yang's *The Qianlong emperor's southern inspection tour*, scroll 4, *The confluence of the Huai and Yellow Rivers*, 1770 (Dillon Collection 1984.6 in the Metropolitan Museum of Art in New York), provides a heroically extended example of wave forms (again, not in the fishnet pattern).

[21] Nelson Goodman, *Languages of Art*, 2nd ed. (Indianapolis: Hackett, 1976), section III.

[22] There are daunting complications in working out precisely what in the history of production defines the autographic status of multiples, e.g., what distinguishes a full-fledged autograph print from one drawn from the original plate without the artist's consent.

[23] Some philosophers have argued that one-of-a-kind works are at a deep level merely designs, with the result that an exactly similar copy, like a correct performance of a musical composition, counts as the same work. That is, they have contended that all artworks are ontologically allographic. The "original," that is, the artist's physical work, serves merely as an illustrative instantiation of the properties of that design (Gregory Currie, *An Ontology of Art* [London: Macmillan, 1989]). Needless to say this view is not likely to appeal to connoisseurs of art.

[24] By this standard, an exactly similar design created entirely independently of an existing design would be a different work.

[25] "Autographic" is also sometimes used in this sense. In the present context the adjectival usage of "autograph" has the advantage of distinguishing itself from "autographic" in the semiotic sense.

[26] Such a view is congenial to a philosophy of art such as that of R. G. Collingwood, *Principles of Art* (1938; repr. Oxford: Oxford University Press 1958), in which the uniqueness of expression in genuine art is carried to the limit. For him all so-called art that fails this test is mere "craft."

[27] Morelli (Giovanni Morelli, *Italian Painters: Critical Studies of their Works*, trans. Constance J. Ffoulkes [London: John Murray, 1892–93]) has been poorly treated by most commentators, who exaggerate the importance he accords to a narrow class of local features. A careful reading of his texts shows that (a) all local features, whether of the body or anything else (he specifically mentions landscape backgrounds), are to be minutely studied; and (b) this aspect of the work forms only part of the connoisseur's evidence of authorship or school. The holistic qualities discussed below are equally evidential. In my opinion Morelli's appreciation of the total relevant evidence is virtually faultless, given that the scientific tests now available did not exist in his day. The true Morellian method—the one he advocated as well as the one he practiced—is admirably comprehensive.

[28] Richard Wollheim, "Giovanni Morelli and the Origins of Scientific Connoisseurship," *On Art and the Mind* (Cambridge, Mass.: Harvard University Press, 1974), 196.

[29] Berenson, *Study and Criticism*, 1st ser. (see n. 12), 49. Ironically for Berenson's claim, the painting is now in the Norton Simon Museum where it is ascribed to Botticelli and entitled *Madonna and Child with Adoring Angel.*

[30] E.g., by Fu and Fu, *Studies in Conniosseurship* (see n. 6), 17.

[31] An interesting problem arises from a long-established tradition of putative recognition of properties such as "spirit resonance" in a class of especially admired works (H. C. Chang, "Inscriptions, Stylistic Analysis, and Traditional Judgment in Yuan, Ming, and Ch'ing Painting," *Asia Major* 7 [1959]). That tradition, conveyed by declarations contained in the surviving literature, does seem sufficient to attest to the works having some property to which the "airy language" (ibid., 21) is appropriate. The key questions are, first, is it one and the same property that all the traditional voices are reporting? And second, if so, what property is it? The concurrence of many sensitive connoisseurs suffices to establish artistic quality of eminent degree in the works cited. But that does not identify the holistic property or properties on which the evaluative agreement is grounded. Only a concerted effort to gain a better articulated understanding of the property or properties can create the basis needed for "the traditional judgment contained in such writ ten records...[to] provide the clue to the style of certain masters" (ibid., 2).

[32] Sydney Freedberg, *Painting in Italy, 1500 to 1600* (Baltimore: Penguin, 1971), 136.

[33] This obviously presupposes that aesthetic quality is not to be construed narrowly, e.g., à la Bell's significant form (Clive Bell, *Art* [London: Chatto and

Windus, 1914; New York: Frederick A. Stokes, 1920]).

[34] Whether the art be high, low, or somewhere in between.

[35] Philosophical skepticism is based more on thought experiments concerning possible worlds than on the realities of actual practice. Connoisseurship need only concern the latter. Empirical skeptics, as we might call them, cite actual disagreements in evaluation, but without due attention to the manifestly imperfect conditions under which they arise. The practical realist about aesthetic value need not blanch at the spectacle of aesthetic disagreement. First, it does not affect gross differences of value, where there is virtual unanimity; second, the residual disagreement concerns subtler distinctions. Here the question is whether more intensive study and negotiation can produce non-coerced agreement among those who are maximally (and consistently) discriminating as to the aesthetic value of parts, aspects, and wholes.

[36] Let me here disclaim any intention of advocating connoisseurship (or any other special area) as the main or most essential art-historical field. This canard keeps surfacing when anyone defends the legitimate role of connoisseurship in art history, though a stake should long since have been driven through its heart.

6

Afterword: Chinese Brushwork and the Well-Informed Eye

Karen Lang

> Despair. One imagines that once the other person is made to see the significant differences, no doubt could remain about which is original and which copy; but evidently it isn't so.
>
> *James Cahill in a letter to Maxwell Hearn, 1995*[1]

Li Anzhong's *Landscape* of 1117 (figs. 1 and 2), an album leaf, ink and light colors on silk, is an instance of what James Cahill calls poetic painting in China, "an idea and a practice" that began "in the Northern Sung period in the eleventh century, with a cluster of interrelated developments."[2] Arising from the recognition by Northern Sung literati "that poetry and painting can be virtually interchangeable in their content," poetic painting describes "a lyric journey" of the subject—a scholar, a poet, a retired official—from a life secluded in nature to "travels that expose him to sensory experiences that nourish his spirit," to the contemplation of arresting views and sounds, to a return "to the security of his thatched house."[3] If

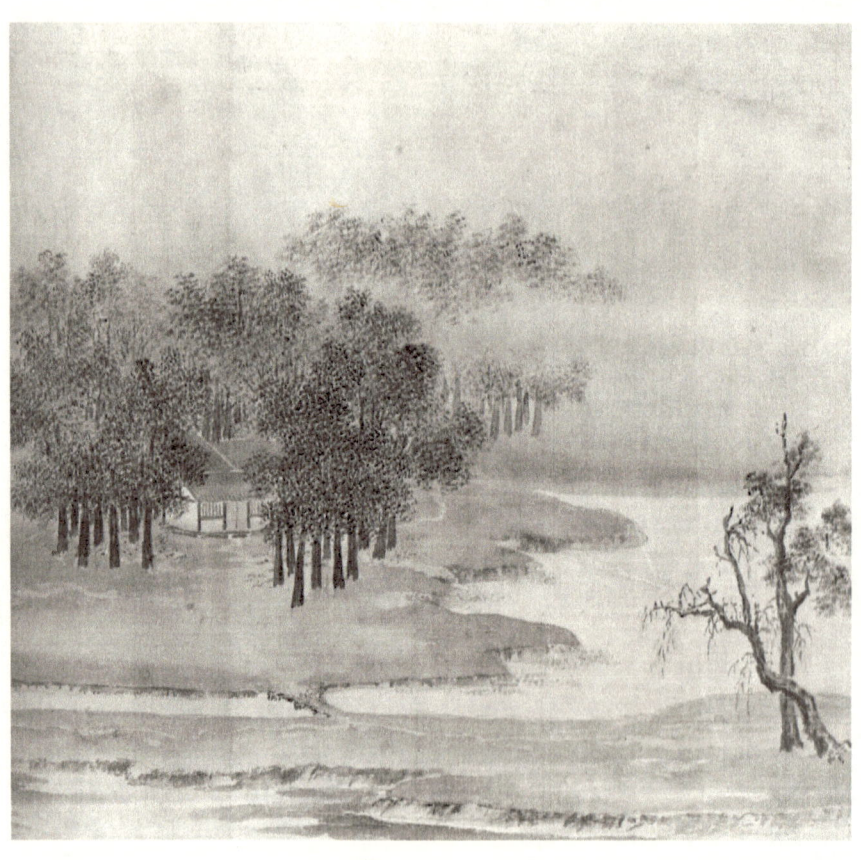

Figure 1. Li Anzhong, *Landscape*. Dated 1117. Album leaf, ink and light colors on silk, 24.2 × 26.3 cm. Cleveland Museum of Art (63.588).

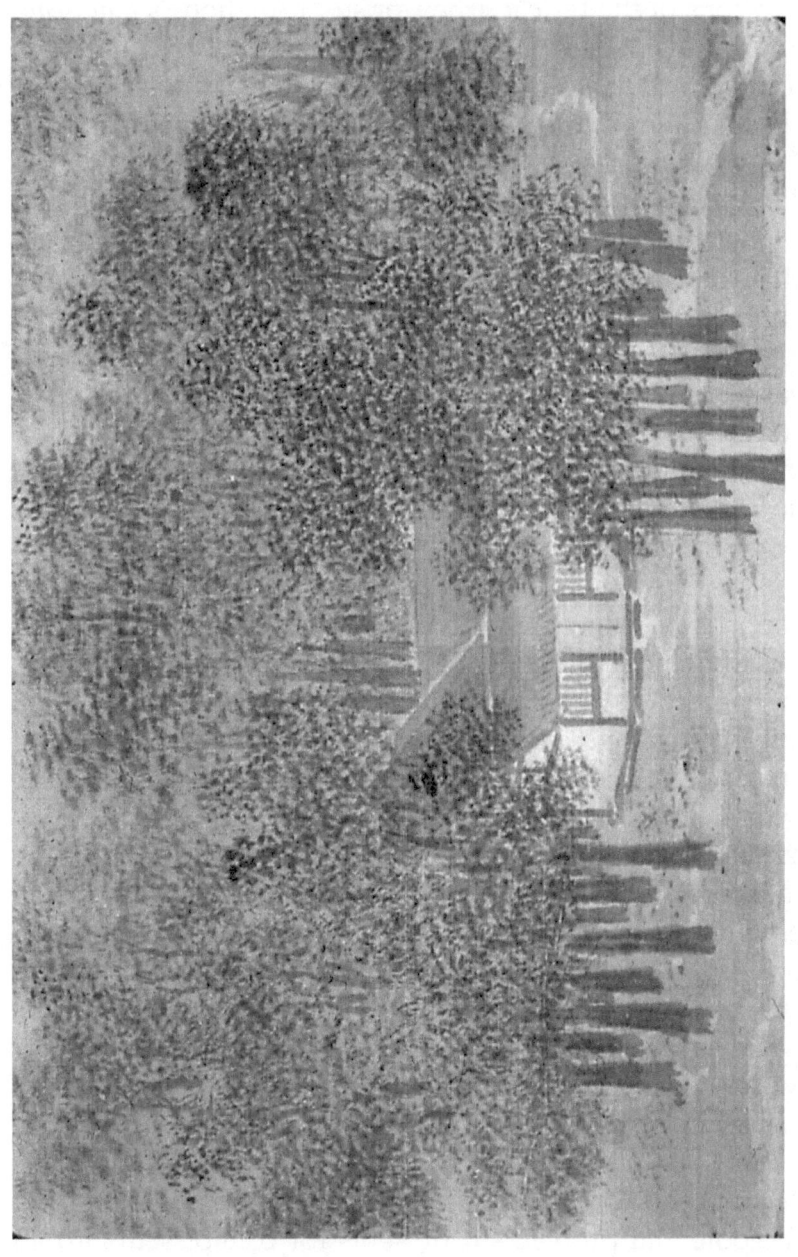

Figure 2. Detail of Li Anzhong, *Landscape.*

poetry and painting can be interchangeable, so too might be the stations of the lyric journey, or so Li Anzhong's *Landscape* might lead us to believe.

Landscape is devoid of human figures. Instead of employing the human figure to open out a narrative and our relation to it, Li Anzhong draws us into the painting's space without making explicit the relation between point of view and meaning: has the subject of the lyric journey left the safety of this thatched house to begin his travels; has he stopped to contemplate the landscape before him, a scene rendered indeterminate by fog's grip; or has he reached the final stretch toward home, destination in sight, at last? Without explicit documentary evidence, there is no clear answer. More to the point, so-called poetic painting, like poetry itself, does not issue forth from absolutes but achieves its intended effects through evocation.

Just as Li Anzhong's *Landscape* offers "no one there to see," so too are the poet-painter and the viewer "both there only as disembodied presences. Nor," Cahill continues, "is the scenery at which they gaze fully revealed: it is partially hidden in fog, which opens to disclose only selected passages of landscape or 'small scenes.'" The author vividly describes the way the brushwork technique of "self-effacing" artists like Li Anzhong "permitted them to create images that seem to have been impressed by nature itself onto the silk, without human intervention."[4] Invited for a closer look at a work that appears to posit itself in our reality, the vaguer its forms, shapes, and details become. Whether we take up the vantage of what the Austrian art historian Alois Riegl termed the distant or the near view, we cannot "see" the forest *or* the trees.[5] Along with what it teaches us about the characteristics of poetic painting of the Northern Sung period, Li Anzhong's album leaf introduces us to the central role of brushwork in Chinese painting and to the potential problems it presents for connoisseurship. Li Anzhong's *Landscape* underlines, as well, the fact that one intervenes in a work of art in order to observe it. As Jerome Silbergeld had learned from a geophysicist colleague about the inner workings of the atom, here we might say that "only our observation—our intrusive observation—makes things seem to resolve one way or the other."[6]

Like Chinese poetic painting, the connoisseurship of Chinese painting abounds in irresolution. Nonetheless, connoisseurship is indispensable to the field of Chinese art history. In the words of Wen C. Fong, since "the history of Chinese painting is fraught with imitations and forgeries, connoisseurship remains the only means we have with which to determine the authenticity and significance of an individual work as evidence of historical inquiry."[7] Yet brushwork, style, documentary evidence and scientific measurements are not failsafe guides for attribution and authenticity. Just as one intervenes in a painting in order to observe it, so does what Silbergeld calls "the rule book"— the book of materials and techniques (signatures, seals, and so forth); stylistic history (genre and style); and social content and context—affect connoisseurial judgment.[8] That said, "there can be no real understanding of an individual work, either as art or as material object, without our first ascertaining, as accurately as possible, the date and circumstances of its production."[9] The history of Chinese painting, a relatively new field of inquiry, should continue to move beyond its objects toward questions of context and meaning. The essays in this volume demonstrate, however, that not all questions are possible at all times—in order to be valid, historical and theoretical questions must arise from an understanding of the time and circumstances of an object's making.

Painterly brushwork plays a key role in the connoisseurship of the Chinese "fine arts" of painting and calligraphy.[10] At the same time, painterly brushwork creates special challenges for both scientific connoisseurship and connoisseurship of the eye. That even early writings on Chinese painting "are full of references to fakes and forgeries" attests to the slipperiness of brushwork as a benchmark for attribution and authenticity.[11] In a study of the semantic tides of the term *pittoresco* in seventeenth- and eighteenth-century Italy, Philip Sohm notes the way painterly brushwork "may describe recognizable objects, yet simultaneously it forms ornamental patterns that are...'artificial touches' indicating the artist's gesture as much as the object represented."[12] The use of painterly brushwork to both depict form and render "touch" begs the question of how it might be employed as a criterion for attribution and authenticity. Should emphasis be placed on brushwork's relation to learning, tradition, or what Cahill calls "pictorial integrity," or should it be considered a sign of the artist's hand—and by extension, the artist's character and imagination? Historically speaking, conflating the artist's hand with his particular qualities was an easy slide, as Sohm demonstrates: Since character and imagination "are peculiar to the artist, distinguishing him from all others, so too was his brushwork individual."[13]

The history of Chinese painting has favored both uses of the brush. In regard to the Song period, Cahill writes that "getting the image 'right' was a major criterion...for identifying the best artists and pictures." One the other hand, literati or scholar-amateur paintings like the "old, twisted tree" attributed to Su Shi or Su Dongpo (1036–1101) "was read as a visible manifestation of his personal qualities and feelings; the trees and the rocks in it were (in the words of his friend Mi Fu) 'queerly tangled like sorrows coiled up in his breast.'"[14] To further complicate matters we have cases like Li Anzhong's *Landscape*, where painterly brushwork has all but penetrated into the painting's support. Brushwork might be a primary tool in the connoisseurship of Chinese painting, but as a benchmark for attribution and authenticity, brushwork, we might say, is fast and loose.

The theory of Chinese painting asks us to pay heed to the brush as a sign or metaphor of the artist's character and imagination. Applied to art theory, the word *zhen* and its various compound forms denote "the idea of self-expression through the traces of one's hand, which," Cahill notes, "were read as the imprints of one's mind, comparable to verbal expressions in poetry. Traces reliably from the hands of persons of a certain moral stature and spiritual attainment, then, were authentic in both senses."[15] Silbergeld reminds us that Confucius makes a related point in his *Analects*: "The gentleman is not an implement.'"[16] And, we might presume, neither is the gentleman-artist's brush. The history of Chinese painting attests to the primacy given to "the artist's touch" and to the brush as the primary means of self expression.

Conflations, like these, between the artist's hand and his character and imagination have led Silbergeld and others to consider spontaneous creativity an index of attribution and authenticity. Laying emphasis on brushwork as the marker of imagination and originality leads questions of attribution and authenticity back onto the figure of the artist. But it also makes murky categories like imagination, temperament, and feeling the basis for evaluation.[17] What is more, forgeries call the equation between painterly brushwork and the "artist's hand" into question.[18] Nonetheless, Silbergeld is right to draw our attention to the roles intuition and aesthetic quality play in connoisseurship and, in the case of Chinese painting, to brushwork as "the intuitionist's ultimate criterion."[19] Giovanni Morelli, employing his well-known method of "scientific" connoisseurship toward the end of the nineteenth century, enjoyed remarkable success at reattribution. Yet surely nobody "learns how to be a connoisseur simply by applying the rules."[20] Certain factors such as intuition, which cannot be measured quantitatively, play a steady role in making the conjectural leap from brushwork to attribution, from part to whole.

Using statements on Chinese connoisseurship from the fourteenth century, Silbergeld shows that connoisseurs "in their writing as in their thinking, indulge heavily in such aesthetic and vaguely spiritual terms as *shenhui*, 'spiritual communion,' or *qiyun*, 'life-breath,' to distinguish good works from bad... and they spend their time looking for *zhenji*, 'authentic traces.'"[21] While *shenhui*, *qiyun*, and *zhenji* are as murky, scientifically speaking, as imagination, temperament and feeling, the use of these words and the cluster of ideas related to them underline the key role in connoisseurship of aesthetic quality.[22] In *Rudiments of Connoisseurship*, Bernard Berenson distinguishes between scientific connoisseurship and "the Sense of Quality," a sense that "does not fall under the category of demonstrable things." Here is Berenson (the emphasis is his own): "*The greater the artist, the more weight falls on the question of quality in the consideration of a work attributed to him.*"[23] Berenson's remark raises the specter of another qualitative value, artistic genius: when considered as signs of a deeper (or even a transcendental) quality, the characteristic forms of the artist, including painterly brushwork, may be said to express a sense of artistic genius that is a priori—an indemonstrable sense of genius that does not exist independently of the work of art but is necessary for the artwork to be what it is.

"Naturally," John H. Brown argues, "skeptics suspect that intuitions of aesthetic quality are incorrigibly subjective. But in fact there is wide agreement within artistic traditions and among those connoisseurs who make the most finely differentiated distinctions within a given range of works." Claiming a work of art has aesthetic quality is one thing, and more easily agreed upon; determining date and attribution are other things, and often much more contentious. Nonetheless, like the date of the work itself, the qualitative and potentially loaded notion of aesthetic quality is a necessary starting point in any attribution. After all, one would not spend their connoisseurial energies on a work not deemed fit to the task. Brown makes the important distinction between aesthetic connoisseurship, "the cultivation of discriminating appreciation of works (and other things in general)," and "the specifically art-historical authentication enterprise," while he urges us, rightly, not to mistake aesthetic connoisseurship for "the main thing."[24]

Just as the existence of forgeries calls "the artist's hand" into question, the distinction between original and copy is itself fluid. Brown notes that "*authentic* admits of a range of meaning," while Silbergeld provides evidence for this claim when his recounts the "many [Chinese] words and shades of meaning" for copywork: "*mo*, an exact copy; or *lin*, a freehand copy or close approximation; as *fang*, inspired creativity, freely done in the manner of someone else; as *zao*, an outright original; or as a *daibi*, literally a 'substitute brush,' following the dictates of, and standing in for, a fellow artist." The Chinese, then, have long been concerned with issues of authenticity. For Cahill, Chinese painting presents "the most interesting authenticity problems" because "fooling the foreigners [and the Chinese themselves] has always been regarded in China as a perfectly honorable enterprise," one that has brought with it "no moral opprobrium." This state of affairs has resulted in a history of Chinese painting shot through with what Richard Spear terms "originality problems."

Clearly, originality problems would not exist if originality, and related notions related like the artist's hand, artistic genius and so forth, were not accorded such high cultural and economic value. But who determines the value of originality? Like Silbergeld's "many words and shades of meaning" for copywork, Cahill's reminder of "the common Chinese practice of replicating or forging (the distinction isn't always clear)," should give us pause: perhaps the field of Chinese art history—along with the museum, the gallery and the collector—demand an irrefragable definition of originality that is out of tune with the historical practices of Chinese painting itself.

Spear informs us that in regard to pictures, "originality" itself has two meanings—first, an autograph work versus a copy, an imitation or a reproduction; second, "the uniqueness of design and style in the creative sense." He reminds us that connoisseurship "depends directly not just on the recognition of individual styles, but on a concept of value residing in distinguishable artistic personalities." As the recent case of the Metropolitan Museum of Art's *Riverbank* shows, the connoisseurship of Chinese painting is directed toward works that are original in both senses of the word— paintings, in other words, that can be attributed to a specific artist who is himself recognized for "the uniqueness of [his] design and style." According emphasis to both meanings of "originality," including the underlining value associated with a distinguishable "artistic personality," raises the stakes for authenticity and attribution in the connoisseurship of Chinese painting, a point I shall return to below.

Akin to notions of the artist's hand and aesthetic quality, originality brings us back to the artist's imagination, temperament and feeling, even as it manifests itself in the work of art. Advocating for "pictorial integrity" and structural accuracy as useful criteria for the authenticity of Chinese painting, Cahill turns the attention from "the painting as the product of a particular master's hand" to "the painting as a picture, which can have its own integrity, as if apart from the identity and character of the artist." His method of gauging "pictorial integrity" brings to mind Morelli's focus on earlobes, fingernails and the like in old Master paintings: "A copyist, attempting to replicate some painted form, will misunderstand and garble it; recognizing such pictorial misunderstandings…should enable us to decide with some finality which is which." For Cahill, the difference between an authentic work and a copy is the difference "between an artist depicting some object in the world around him, and one who is attempting to copy a form from a painting, without necessarily having firsthand knowledge of the thing it was meant to portray, or even being clear on what it is." Looking closely at several pairs of paintings, he points to what he terms pictorial blunders, inaccuracies or lapses of attention that, according to him, are giveaways to a painting's inauthentic status.

In his 1996 book *The Lyric Journey: Poetic Painting in China and Japan*, Cahill noted the way brushwork operated in the Song period to render feeling or mood. In his essay for this volume, he makes a plea for "pictorial integrity" based on the assumption that "getting the image 'right' was a major criterion" in the Song period "for identifying the best artists and pictures."[25] If along with the author we now disregard the use of the brush to render feeling or mood, then we could say that the authentic painting "will always be the one in which the brushstrokes, lines, and so on best perform their descriptive function. That," Cahill asserts, "has proven true for me so consistently, that I'm ready to make a rule of it."[26] At the same time as Cahill would like to make a rule of the objective representation of nature; he concedes to the limits of pictorial integrity as a method: "the elements of landscape [and here we might note the prominent role of landscape in Chinese painting], less fixed in form than figures and artifacts, are," he writes, "less susceptible to 'wrong' representation."[27] On this point Brown's words apply well to Chinese landscape painting. When "the effect desired is that of a diffuse impression, a quick glance, or a mysterious world," indeterminacy and inconsistency of depiction can often facilitate an artist's pictorial aims.[28] As for the other side of the coin, namely those cases where artists might desire to render as faithfully as possible a scene before them, Ernst Gombrich demonstrates that even their pictures will display significant differences, since artists "represent what they see in ways that reflect their individual artistic personalities and their training."[29]

As a method, pictorial integrity draws upon the comparison of artworks and a concept of period style. If Gombrich's anecdote underlines the inevitable individuality of style, Heinrich Wöfflin's *Principles of Art History* rests on the concept of a shared period style. Here is Wölfflin: "Every artist finds certain visual possibilities before him, to which he is bound. Not everything is possible at all times. Vision itself has its history, and the revelation of these visual strata must be regarded as the primary task of history."[30] Chinese art historians have argued for the necessity of period style to organize and render comprehensible the objects and anomalies of the field. In this sense, they agree with Wölfflin that primacy should be given to the recognition of "visual strata," and much energy has been accorded to this endeavor.

As general tools of connoisseurship, dating and period style are useful places to begin one's inquiry. When period style is considered a priori, or employed too restrictedly, it can do more harm than good, however. Following Wölfflin, Ludwig Bachhofer rendered the history of Chinese art into a series of periods and stylistic categories Western art historians could understand.[31] Doing so, he employed the concept of style as a procrustean bed, as "an *a priori* framework to which works of art in evolutionary progression are made to fit."[32] The case of Bachofer is extreme. Nonetheless, it reminds us that the concept of period style requires some hewing of the evidence.

Dating and period style, moreover, set us into the trap of circular reasoning. In the foreword to *Issues of Authenticity in Chinese Painting*, Judith G. Smith and Wen C. Fong put the matter succinctly. "The dating of early Chinese paintings proceeds in a circular fashion: individual works are dated according to our conception of a period style, which in turn must be expanded and refined on the basis of specific paintings. As more key monuments are placed one by one into their proper stylistic and historical contexts, individual works become evidence for documenting other attributed works." Dating and period style rely on smooth interactions between the specific and the general, or known and unknown works of art. Since the production of knowledge proceeds by relating the unknown to the known through comparison, hypothesis, and the formation and use of concepts, the trap of circular reasoning is not something from which we can ever hope to escape, entirely.[33] That said, it is useful to remember that what we begin with—and continue to use—is what is available to us in the historical record. As the general and the specific interact in the connoisseurship of Chinese painting (and in the study of Chinese art history) to produce knowledge, certain artists and artworks become exemplary, the standard by which unknown works of art are measured.

Writing in the early years of the twentieth century, Erwin Panofsky recognized that the transformation of the object from aesthetic phenomenon to historical work of art required one to connect images with their history, a process that can be achieved through dating and attribution. As he indicates, relating these historical objects to each other is then a matter of finding the uniformities among them and of forming classes or types of objects based on certain common attributes—a process generally known as finding the category and "style" of the work of art. Thus related, heterogeneous objects become homogeneous series of objects organized according to certain sets of structural relations.[34] Charting what I call the transformation of the artwork from aesthetic object to historical work of art, to object of "knowledge," Panofsky outlines the way a unified field of inquiry is created from an aggregate of original works of art. Like all historical sciences, Chinese art history operates as a unified field of inquiry, a disciplinary space wherein questions are posed and contested, where objects are studied and introduced.

Dating and period style are tremendously useful yet flawed tools for the connoisseurship of Chinese painting. On the one hand, Panofsky articulated the way dating and period style enable us to connect artworks with their history and in so doing to transform an aggregate of individual objects into a unified field of inquiry. On the other hand, Bachhofer offers a strong example of the way period style functions as a procrustean bed. Consider the rub: for artworks to become meaningful, we have to be able to relate them to concepts—artist, date, style, and so forth; at the same time, concepts determine and constrain what we might "know" about works of art. Cahill echoes Wölfflin when he remarks that "in painting style, not everything is possible at any given time."[35] True enough, and period style functions as a schema, a category of attributes of the possible at a spatiotemporal moment. Yet period style is established by the evidence available in the historical record.

What to make of works of art that do not fit? Copies and forgeries are often sorted out since copyists and forgers, attempting to render as accurately as possible the visual schemata of the past, can never entirely break free from the schemata of their own present. But what of those works of art that "somehow depart from the common practice, whether in subject or style." Those works that, to use Cahill's eloquent phasing, represent "some direction not followed up, or not preserved because it failed to fit within the tastes of collectors as these were conditioned and partly formed by the influential arbiters." As we find ourselves, along with Cahill, "regretting what has been lost, even as we continue to admire and enjoy the riches of what has come down to us," we might also note the way both past and present inhibit our ability to know the historical record completely.[36] If what survives shapes our knowledge of the past in the present, so do the concepts and categories we use in the present determine and constrain our knowledge of the past.

Art historians, then, are also subject to the schemata of their time.[37] These include not only the methodological toolkit of the field, within which we find general connoisseural tools like dating and attribution, but also the norms and expectations of the art historian's time. The development of the field of Chinese art history is coterminous with the cult of the artist as creative genius, an idea that bloomed with Romanticism and prospered with the ever-increasing link among artists, artworks, and the avenues of the art market—the gallery, the museum, and the collector. It should come as no surprise to discover that Chinese art history, as a field of inquiry, has been engaged in the discovery its own "art stars," the very artists and works of art that have become the standards by which unknown artists and artworks are measured.[38] While this process has been necessary for the organization and development of the field, it has also raised the stakes for attribution. As Silbergeld put it recently in relation to the Metropolitan Museum's *Riverbank*, attributing the painting to Dong Yuan is "a glamorous prospect."[39] In terms of the marketplace and idea of cultural heritage, doing so would dramatically increase the economic and cultural value of the painting; in terms of art history, doing so would rewrite the historical record of Chinese painting.

Finally, documents and connoisseurs can lie. When faced with an unknown work of art, art historians and connoisseurs often turn to documents to solve questions of date and attribution. Yet works of art might not have supporting historical evidence, or documentary evidence and the work of art it documents might be forgeries. Whether lured by the "glamorous prospect" of making history by attributing a painting to a well-known artist, or by the cash such attributions can garner, connoisseurs can also fall prey to the cult of the artist and the currency of the art market. The Berenson scandal is a case in point.

Using dealer's records and other correspondence, Colin Simpson chronicles Berenson's Faustian pact with the American art dealer Joseph Duveen: for a 25 percent cut of the profits, Berenson used his inestimable reputation to certify the authenticity of Italian Renaissance paintings of dubious provenance. The scheme served both sides rather well— Simpson makes clear that Berenson and Duveen became rich while several American magnates (the likes of Mrs. Horace E. Dodge, Mr. and Mrs. Henry Huntington, Samuel Kress, and Andrew Mellon), bilked of large sums of money, were none the wiser. In fact, according to Berenson and Duveen, these Americans were simply thrilled to be adding painted masterworks to their cultural capital.[40] Even as the Berenson scandal reveals the interest at the heart of one connoisseur's masquerade of disinterest, it demonstrates the constitution of the connoisseur's authority. Connoisseurship presupposes a kind of neutral, authoritative view, a view wherein the visual gives authority.

This last point is rather wonderfully illustrated in a suite of photographs of Berenson at work in the Villa I Tatti, studying photographs of Italian Renaissance paintings sent to him by his American customers. By this time, Berenson's eye had acquired such authority that he no longer needed to be present in front of the original work of art. By putting his name to the photograph, Berenson attests to having "seen" the painting as well as to its correct attribution. The signature "Berenson" signifies the historical person and the impersonal agent. By signing the photograph, Berenson registers the move from authorial presence to connoisseurial authority, as his signature, his testament to the authenticity of the painting represented in the photograph, moves the image into the precincts of the supposedly true and the factual.

Berenson was certainly not exercising objectivity in the attributions he made in cahoots with Duveen. Nor, as Thomas Nagel and others have taught us, is absolute objectivity ever possible in the human sciences.[41] More than registering the impossibility of objectivity, the Berenson scandal—the way his attributions moved paintings from the category of the unknown to the known; the way his signature garnered authority—demonstrates the power of attribution in the making of reputation and history. "Empirical skeptics," as we might call them with Brown, "cite actual disagreements in evaluation, but without due attention to the manifestly imperfect conditions under which they arise." Inevitably, he argues convincingly, "the force of the evidence depends on the circumstances of the case."[42]

Even when exercised ethically and judiciously, connoisseurship is not a science in the Gallilean sense. It is more a protocol or, in Silbergeld's terms, a set of rules.[43] When faced with an unknown work of art, Chinese art history commences with the general connoisseurial tools of dating and attribution. As for ascertaining date and attribution, the field seems to rely on brushwork and some version of Cahill's "pictorial integrity," that is, a judgment about whether the techniques and visual schemata—the marks, forms, and structures—of the painting are convincing as a picture. Writing his "Thoughts on Painting" in the first decades of the seventeenth century, Guilio Mancini's words presage Cahill's lament in the epigraph to this afterword, and they ring true for the connoisseurship of Chinese painting today. "Despite all these observations on how to distinguish a copy from an original, nevertheless it happens that sometimes the copy is so well made that it fools us anyway, even if both the artist and the buyer are intelligent. And what is more, having both the original and copy, sometimes it happens that you cannot tell which is which."[44] To the general connoisseurial tools of dating and attribution, we must add the inevitability of interpretation. This is especially true for the connoisseurship of Chinese painting, since the Chinese "fine arts" of painting and calligraphy have their basis in brushwork—a pliant brush that both depicts form and renders "touch."

Even as brushwork is a sign of the "artist's hand," that hand might be forged; even as brushwork is the Chinese artist's primary artistic means, brushwork might penetrate into the painting's support, as it does in Li Anzhong's *Landscape,* thereby rendering it extremely difficult to "see." To quote Silbergeld, in terms of the connoisseurship of Chinese painting, "we can deny uncertainty but we cannot escape it."[45] Turning from despair, we can agree that connoisseurship is not a Galilean science but a necessary and very helpful methodological tool, especially for study of Chinese painting. A Chinese painter, Fong tell us, "links his pictorial representation through calligraphic brushwork to his own physical self."[46] Whether relying on a notion of the "artist's hand" or forming hypotheses based on the visual and technical evidence of the artwork, the field of Chinese art history depends on the connoisseur's well-informed eye to attribute a painting to that self. Since the history of Chinese painting abounds in fakes and forgeries, since Chinese forgers suffer "no moral opprobrium," then— for better or worse—the field of Chinese art history will continue to depend on the connoisseur's craft.

Notes

[1] Richard M. Barnhart, James Cahill, Maxwell K. Hearn, and Stephen Little, "The Tu Chin [Du Jin] Correspondence, 1994–1995," *Kaikodo Journal* 5 (Autumn 1997): 13.

[2] James Cahill, *The Lyric Journey: Poetic Painting in China and Japan* (Cambridge, Mass.: Harvard University Press, 1996), 7. This book is based on the Edwin O. Reischauer Lectures Cahill delivered at Harvard in 1993.

[3] Ibid. 8 and 58. Cahill (62–64) notes similarities between Chinese "poetic painting" and the art of the German romantic painters, particularly Caspar David Friedrich. To these we might add the striking similarity between the stations of the subject in the "lyric journey" and those of the subject in German romanticism, especially in Goethe's poetry. See L.

A. Willoughby, "The Image of the 'Wanderer' and the 'Hut' in Goethe's Poetry," *Études Germaniques* 6, nos. 3–4 (July–December 1951): 207–19.

[4] Cahill, *Lyric Journey*, 9, 20, and 64.

[5] Alois Riegl, *Spätrömische Kunstindustrie*, 2nd ed. (Vienna: Der Österreichische Staatsdruckerie, 1927), 43–44. I examine Riegl's near, normal, and distant viewing in my book, *Chaos and Cosmos: On the Image in Aesthetics and Art History* (Ithaca: Cornell University Press, 2006), 153–57.

[6] See Silbergeld in this volume.

[7] Wen C. Fong, "*Riverbank*: From Connoisseurship to Art History," in *Issues of Authenticity in Chinese Painting*, ed. Judith G. Smith and Wen C. Fong (New York: The Metropolitan Museum of Art, 1999), 260.

[8] Jerome Silbergeld, "The Referee Must Have a Rule Book: Modern Rules for an Ancient Art," in *Issues of Authenticity in Chinese Painting*, 155.

[9] Fong, "*Riverbank*," 260. Francis Haskell elaborates on this point: "For before the historian can try to make valid use of a visual source, however undemanding, however simple, he has to know what he is looking at, whether it is authentic, when and for what purpose it was made, even whether it was considered to be beautiful. He also has to have some awareness of the circumstances, conventions and constraints that always govern what can be represented in art at any given time and of the technical means that are available to the figurative [or abstract] artist for expressing his vision." Francis Haskell, *History and Its Images: Art and the Interpretation of the Past* (New Haven: Yale University Press, 1993), 2.

[10] In the words of Silbergeld (in this volume): "Calligraphy and painting, among all other media were considered to reveal a distinctive 'hand,' associated with individual personality, defined in terms of originality, and regarded as 'high art' (in modern Chinese, *meishu* as opposed to *gongyi*, or craft)."

[11] The controversy over the authenticity of the Metropolitan Museum of Art's *Riverbank* demonstrates that brushwork is a primary criterion for the connoisseurship of Chinese painting, and that even scientific connoisseurship does not provide definitive answers to questions of date and attribution. Listen to Maxwell K. Hearn, curator of the Department of Asian Art at the Met as he concludes his essay on the physical analysis of *Riverbank*: "The physical attributes of the weave structure, coloration, condition, manner of restoration, and seal impressions on *Riverbank* all support an early date for the painting.... While such a physical examination cannot settle the question of *Riverbank*'s authorship or period of execution, it nonetheless makes it impossible to argue convincingly that it is of modern manufacture." ("A Comparative Physical Analysis of *Riverbank* and Two Zhang Daqian Forgeries," in *Issues of Authenticity in Chinese Painting*, 112.)

In his essays for the Met volume and this book, Cahill, on the other hand, argues against an early date for the painting.

[12] Philip Sohm, *Pittoresco: Marco Boschini, His Critics, and Their Critiques of Painterly Brushwork in Seventeenth- and Eighteenth-Century Italy* (New York: Cambridge University Press, 1991), 21.

[13] Ibid., 22.

[14] See Cahill in this volume.

[15] See Cahill in this volume. According to Fong (*"Riverbank,"* 287), "this connection with morality served as the artist's personal confirmation of selfhood during a time of trouble. Unlike in the Western tradition, as Gombrich has described, in which painting has been pursued as a science, Chinese painters attempted to grasp the expressive nature of the image." (Fong cites Ernst Gombrich's *Art and Illusion: A Study in the Psychology of Pictorial Representation* [Washington, D.C: Pantheon Books, 1960], 320–21. This book is based on the A. W. Mellon Lectures in the Fine Arts Gombrich presented in 1956.)

[16] See Silbergeld in this volume.

[17] In the early years of the twentieth-century, Erwin Panofsky argued against Heinrich Wölfflin's double root of style (by which Wölfflin meant an "expressive, interpretative capacity for meaningful content" on the one hand, and a "psychologically meaningless form of seeing" on the other) by claiming that the eye could never be an organic, unpsychological instrument, as Wölfflin claimed. For Panofsky, the cluster of concepts that denote seeing—the act of seeing, the eye, and the optical—remained mechanistic and empty of connotation when these were understood only literally. Stressing the role of the psyche (*Seele*), or the inner dimension that provides the "empty container" of the eye with the capacity for content and meaningful expression, Panofsky demonstrated the combined role of representation and expression in perceptual experience. Yet even as Panofsky presumes the a priori nature of his most critical term, *Seele*, he fails to determine this term critically. Panofsky's efforts provide a cautionary tale: though in our time we accept it as a given that seeing and expression are intertwined, perhaps we can still do no better than Panofsky in determining why this is the case, other than to resort to "imagination," "temperament," or "feeling." See Erwin Panofsky, "Das Problem des Stils in der bildenden Kunst," *Zeitschrift für Ästhetik und allgemeine Kunstwissenschaft* 10 (1915): 460–67; and Karen Lang, "Points of View in Panofsky's Early Theoretical Essays," in *Chaos and Cosmos*, 12–40 (as above, n. 5).

[18] To make his point, Cahill (in this volume) cites the example of the "brilliant and versatile" forger Zhang Daqian (1899–1983).

[19] See Silbergeld in this volume.

[20] Carol Ginzburg, "Clues: Morelli, Freud and Sherlock Holmes," in *The Sign of Three: Dupin, Holmes, Pierce*, ed. Umberto Eco and Thomas Sebeok (Bloomington: Indiana University Press, 1988), 110.

[21] See Silbergeld in this volume.

[22] "Since aesthetic quality (of parts, aspects, and the whole) is a prime aspiration of art of all sorts, at all times and in all cultures…it is bound to feature prominently in connoisseurship." See Silbergeld in this volume.

[23] Bernard Berenson, *Rudiments of Connoisseurship: Study and Criticism of Italian Art* (New York: Schocken, 1962), 147.

[24] Quotations from Brown, Silbergeld, and Cahill here and in the next four paragraphs are drawn from their essays in this volume.

[25] See Cahill in this volume.

[26] "The Tu Chin [Du Jin] Correspondence," 8; cited by Silbergeld in this volume.

[27] See Cahill in this volume. The depiction of water is prominent in Chinese landscape painting; it has been judged according to the standards of naturalism and pictorial integrity by Cahill and Sherman Lee. See Sherman Lee, "*Riverbank*: A Recent Effort in a Long Tradition," in *Issues of Authenticity in Chinese Painting*, 81–82.

[28] See Brown in this volume. He continues: "They also facilitate the organization of the design on the picture plane, where unity can be achieved only by softening the effect of recession and protrusion."

[29] Robert E. Harrist, Jr., "Connoisseurship: Seeing and Believing," in *Issues of Authenticity in Chinese Painting*, 294. Harrist cites Gombrich's *Art and Illusion* (Princeton: Princeton University Press, 1969), 63.

[30] Heinrich Wölfflin, *Principles of Art History* (New York: Dover Publications, 1950), trans. M. D. Hottinger, 11. At the same time as Gombrich employs a well-known anecdote to underline the inevitable individuality of style, it should be said, as Harrist rightly notes ("Connoisseurship: Seeing and Believing," 294) that "applied diachronically to the history of art, this same principle explains, in Gombrich's famous theory, how painters of different periods and places have employed historically and culturally determined schemata in order to render images of the three-dimensional world on a two-dimensional surface."

[31] Ludwig Bachhofer, *A Short History of Chinese Art* (New York: Pantheon Books, 1946).

[32] Benjamin Rowland, Jr., book review of Bachhofer's *A Short History of Chinese Art*, *The Art Bulletin* 24 (1949): 139–41. Rowland continues: "Style [for Bachhofer] is a kind of sinister autonomous force which in all ages and in all climes inexorably induces artists to produce works of art in a certain preordained fashion." Cited in Fong, "*Riverbank*," 264.

[33] See Lang, *Chaos and Cosmos*, 12–40, for a more thorough treatment of these ideas.

[34] See Erwin Panofsky, "The Concept of Artistic Volition," trans. Kenneth J. Northcott and Joel Snyder, *Critical Inquiry* 8, no. 1 (Autumn 1981): 18; and Lang, *Chaos and Cosmos*, 21.

[35] James Cahill, "The Case Against *Riverbank*: An Indictment in Fourteen Counts," in *Issues of Authenticity in Chinese Painting*, 16.

[36] Cahill, *The Lyric Journey*, 2. Cahill continues: "Sometimes it was whole movements or genres of painting that were stunted and virtually discontinued, largely as a result of critical disapproval; this is especially true of varieties of painting that did not survive, or scarcely survived, that great turning point between early and later Chinese painting that is customarily located around the end of the Sung dynasty."

[37] Silbergeld elaborates on this point in his essay "Referee," 163–65 (as above, n. 8).

[38] Cahill (in this volume) makes a similar point when he remarks that connoisseurship "based heavily on brushwork and professing to ignore readable imagery as a criterion of value belongs mostly to a later period and to the world of prestigious name-artist collecting."

[39] Silbergeld, "Referee," 166.

[40] Colin Simpson, *Artful Partners: Bernard Berenson and Joseph Duveen* (New York: Macmillan, 1986). On the use, publicity, and reception of "scientific" connoisseurship in America see Flaminia Gennari Santori, *The Melancholy of Masterpieces: Old Master Paintings in America, 1900–1914* (Milan: Continents Editions, 2003).

[41] See for example, in order of appearance, Karl Popper, *Objective Knowledge: An Evolutionary Approach* (Oxford: Clarendon, 1972); Thomas Nagel, *The View from Nowhere* (New York: Oxford University Press, 1986); David Carrier, "Erwin Panofsky, Leo Steinberg, David Carrier: The Problem of Objectivity in Art Historical Interpretation," *Journal of Aesthetics and Art Criticism* 47, no. 4 (Fall 1989): 333–47; Lorraine Daston and Peter Galison, "The Image of Objectivity," *Representations* 49 (1992): 81–128; and Allan Megill, ed., *Rethinking Objectivity* (Durham: Duke University Press, 1994).

[42] See Brown in this volume.

[43] Silbergeld, "Referee" (as above, n. 8) and in this volume.

[44] Guilio Mancini, from his "Considerazioni sulla pittura," trans. Robert Enggass in *Italy and Spain 1600–1750: Sources and Documents*, ed. Robert Enggass and Jonathan Brown (Englewood Cliffs, N.J.: Prentice-Hall, 1970), 35.

[45] Silbergeld, "Referee," 165.

[46] Fong, "*Riverbank*," 287 (as above, n. 7).

Select Bibliography

N.B. Only select works in Western languages are listed here. For works in Chinese, please consult the notes to essays in this volume.

I. General Studies on Connoisseurship

Beck, James H. *From Duccio to Raphael: Connoisseurship in Crisis*. Florence: European Press Academic Publishing, 2006.

Berenson, Bernard. *Rudiments of Connoisseurship: Study and Criticism of Italian Art*. New York: Schocken Books, 1962. See pp. 111–48.

Bowden, Ross. "What Is Wrong with an Art Forgery? An Anthropological Perspective." *Journal of Aesthetics and Art Criticism* 57, no. 3 (Summer 1999): 333–43.

Dutton, Denis, ed. *The Forger's Art: Forgery and the Philosophy of Art*. Berkeley: University of California Press, 1983.

Ebitz, David. "Connoisseurship as Practice." *Artibus et Historiae* 9, no. 18 (1988): 207–12.

Hebborn, Eric. *The Art Forger's Handbook*. Woodstock, N.Y: The Overlook Press, 1996.

Jones, Mark, ed. *Fake? The Art of Deception*. With PaulCraddock and Nicolas Barker. Berkeley: University of California Press, 1990.

_____, ed. *Why Fakes Matter: Essays on Problems of Authenticity*. London: British Museum Press, 1992.

Maginnis, Hayden B. J. "The Role of Perceptual Learning in Connoisseurship: Morelli, Berenson, and Beyond." *Art History* 8 (1990): 104–17.

Morelli, Giovanni. *Italian Painters: Critical Studies of Their Works*. London: John Murray, 1900. See pp. 41–49, 72–82.

Neill, Alex, and Aaron Ridley, eds. *Arguing about Art: Contemporary Philosophical Debates*, second edition. London: Routledge, 2002.

Philips, David. *Don't Trust the Label: An Exhibition of Fakes, Imitations and the Real Thing*. London: Arts Council of Great Britain, 1986.

Stalnaker, Nan. "Fakes and Forgeries." In *The Routledge Companion to Aesthetics*, edited by Berys Gut and Dominic McIver Lopes, 395–407. London: Rouledge, 2001.

Wollheim, Richard. "Giovanni Morelli and the Origins of Scientific Connoisseurship." In *On Art and the Mind*, 177–201. Cambridge, Mass.: Harvard University Press, 1974.

Zerner, Henri. "Editor's Statement: The Crisis in the Discipline." *Art Journal* 42, no. 4 (Winter 1982): 279.

II. Connoisseurship of Chinese Calligraphy and Painting

Barnhart, Richard M. "*Fishing in an Autumn River:* A Handscroll in the Freer Gallery of Art (Back to the Problem of Li Tang?)" *Ars Orientalis* 25 (1995): 87–96.

_____. "An Imaginary Exhibition of Chinese Paintings from the Freer Gallery." *Orientations* 24 (March 1993): 32–41.

_____. "Li T'ang (c. 1050–1130) and the Koto-in Landscape." *Burlington Magazine* 114 (May 1972): 305–14.

_____. "On Dating the Paintings of Ch'en Chia-yen." *Yale University Art Gallery Bulletin* 40, no. 1 (Spring 1987): 47–51.

_____. "The 'Snowscape' Attributed to Chü-jan." *Archives of Asian Art* 24 (1970): 6–22.

_____. "*Streams and Hills under Fresh Snow*, Attributed to Kao K'o-ming." In *Words and Images: Chinese Poetry, Calligraphy, and Painting*, edited by Afreda Murck and Wen C. Fong, 223–46. New York: The Metropolitan Museum of Art, 1991.

_____. "Yao Yen-ch'ing, T'ing-mei, of Wu-Hsing." *Artibus Asiae* 39 (1977): 105–23.

Barnhart, Richard M., et al. *Painters of the Great Ming: The Imperial Court and the Zhe School.* Dallas: Dallas Museum of Art, 1993.

Cahill, James. "Ch'ien Hsüan and His Figure Painting." *Archives of the Chinese Society of America* 12 (1958): 11–29.

Chang, Joseph. "A Study of *Large Emerging from Small* in the Collection of the National Palace Museum, Taipei." Ph.D. dissertation, University of Kansas, 1995.

Chang, Joseph, et al. *In Pursuit of Heavenly Harmony: Paintings on Calligraphy by Bada Shanren from the Estate of Wang Fangyu and Sum Wai.* Washington, D.C.: Freer Gallery of Art, 2003.

Chou, Ju-hsi. "Are We Ready for Shih-t'ao?" *Phoeus* 2 (1979): 75–87.

_____. "The Methodology of Reversal in the Study of Wen Cheng-ming." In *Essays in Commemoration of the Golden Jubilee of the Fung Ping Shan*

Library (1932–1982), edited by Chan Ping-leung et al., 29–437. Hong Kong: The Fung Ping Shan Library, 1982.

Edwards, Richard. *Li Ti*. Washington, D.C.: Freer Gallery of Art, 1967.

Fong, Wen C. *The Lohans and a Bridge to Heaven*. Washington, D.C.: Freer Gallery of Art, 1958.

———. *Masterpieces of Chinese and Japanese Art: Freer Gallery of Art Handbook*. Washington, DC: Freer Gallery of Art, 1976.

———. "The Problem of Forgeries in Chinese Painting." *Artibus Asiae* 25 (1962): 95–140.

Freer Gallery of Art. *Eugene and Agnes E. Meyer Memorial Exhibition*. Washington, D.C.: Freer Gallery of Art, 1971.

Fu, Shen C. Y. "An Aspect of Mid-Seventeenth Century Chinese Painting: The Dry Linear Style and the Early Works of Tao-chi." In *Proceedings of the Symposium on Paintings and Calligraphy by Ming I-min*, 579–617. Hong Kong: Institute of Chinese Studies, University of Hong Kong, 1976.

———. "Chang Dai-chien's 'The Three Worthies' and His Practice of Forging Ancient Art." Translated by Jan Stuart. *Orientations* 20, no. 9 (September 1989): 56–72.

———. "A Further Note on Chiang Shen." *National Palace Museum Bulletin* 1, no. 6 (Jan. 1967): 1–9.

———. "Huang Binhong's Shanghai Period Landscape Paintings and His Late Floral Works in the Arthur M. Sackler Gallery." *Orientations* 18, no. 9 (September 1987): 66–78.

———. "*Little Hermitage in the Autumn Woods:* A Late Ming Painting by Xiang Dexin Misattributed to Tao Fuchu of the Yuan." *Ars Orientalis* 25 (1995): 109–18.

———. "Notes on Chiang Shen." *National Palace Museum Bulletin* 1, no. 3 (July 1966): 1–11.

———. "Two Anonymous Sung Dynasty Paintings and the Lu Shan Problem." *National Palace Museum Bulletin* 2, no. 6 (Jan.–Feb. 1968): 1–16; 3, no. 1 (Mar.–Apr. 1968): 6–10.

———. "Yang Wei-chen." *National Palace Museum Bulletin* 7, no. 4 (Sep.–Oct. 1973): 1–12.

Fu, Shen C. Y., and Marilyn W. Fu, *Studies in Connoisseurship: Chinese Paintings from the Arthur M. Sackler Collection in New York and Princeton*. Princeton: Art Museum, Princeton University, 1973.

Fu, Shen C. Y., in collaboration with Marilyn W. Fu, Mary G. Neill, and Mary Jane Clark. *Traces of the Brush: Studies in Chinese Calligraphy*. New Haven: Yale University Art Gallery, 1977.

Fu, Shen C. Y., et al. *From Concept to Context: Approaches to Asian and Islamic Calligraphy*. Washington, D.C.: Freer Gallery of Art, 1986.

Gulik, Robert H. van. *Chinese Pictorial Art as Viewed by the Connoisseur.* Roma: Istituto Italiano per Medio ed Estremo Oriente, 1958.

Kuo, Chi-sheng [Jason C.]. "Space in Late Yüan and Early Ming Painting." *National Palace Museum Bulletin* 16, nos. 1–2 (Apr.–June, 1984): 1–11.

_____. "Towards Understanding a 'Snowscape' Attributed to Hsia Kuei." *National Palace Museum Bulletin* 16, no. 5 (Nov.–Dec. 1981): 3–17.

Kuo, Jason C. "Word and Image in 'Watching the Waterfall at Mt. Lu' by Shih-t'ao." *National Palace Museum Bulletin* 28, no. 5 (Nov.–Dec. 1993): 1–13.

Laing, Ellen Johnston. "'Suzhou Pian' and Other Dubious Paintings in the Received 'Oeuvres' of Qiu Ying." *Artibus Asiae* 59, nos. 3–4 (2000): 265–95.

Lawton, Thomas. *Freer Gallery of Art Fiftieth Anniversary Exhibition.* Vol. 2, *Chinese Figure Painting.* Washington, D.C.: Smithsonian Institution, 1973.

_____. "Notes on Five Paintings from a Ch'ing Dynasty Collection." *Ars Orientalis* 8 (1970): 191–215.

_____. "Notes on Keng Chao-chung." *Renditions* 6 (Spring 1976): 144–51.

_____. "The Sixtieth Paintings: An Ancient Theme Re-Identified." *The National Palace Museum Quarterly* 11, no. 1 (Autumn 1976): 17–36.

Li, Chu-tsing. "The Freer *Sheep and Goat* and Chao Meng-fu's Horse Painting." *Artibus Asiae* 30 (1968): 279–346.

Li, Lin-ts'an. "The *Ch'iu-shih hai-t'ang-t'u.*" *National Palace Museum Bulletin* 6, no. 3 (July–Aug. 1971): 1–5.

_____. "The Double Portrait of Ch'ien-lung and a Sung Figure Painting." *National Palace Museum Bulletin* 7, no. 5 (Nov.–Dec. 1972): 1–6.

_____. "Fan K'uan's *Fishing on a Snow-bound River.*" *National Palace Museum Bulletin* 5, no. 5 (Nov.–Dec. 1970): 6–12.

_____. "The Five Old Man at Sui-yang." *National Palace Museum Bulletin* 8, no. 5 (Nov.–Dec. 1973): 1–21.

_____. "Huang Kung-wang's *Chiu-chu feng-ts'ui* and *T'ieh-yai-t'u.*" *National Palace Museum Bulletin* 7, no. 6 (Jan.–Feb. 1973): 1–9.

Lovell, Hin-cheung. "Wang Hui's 'Dwelling in the Fu-ch'un Mountains': A Classical Theme, Its Origin and Variations." *Ars Orientalis* 8 (1970): 217–42.

Luce, H. Christopher. *A Literati Life in the Twentieth-Century: Wang Fangyu — Artist, Scholar, and Connoisseur.* New York: China Institute in America, 1999.

Maeda, Robert J. "The Chao Ta-nien Tradition." *Ars Orientalis* 8 (1970): 243–53.

Robinson, James. "Postscript to an Exhibition: A Discovery of a Collaborative Work." *Ars Orientalis* 25 (1995): 143–48.

Rowley, George A. "A Chinese Scroll of the Ming Dynasty: 'Ming Huang and Yang Kuei-fei Listening to Music'." *Artibus Asiae* 31, no. 1 (1969): 5–31.

Smith, Judith G. and Wen C. Fong, eds. *Issues of Authenticity in Chinese Painting.* New York: The Metropolitan Museum of Art, 1999.

Stanley-Baker, Joan. "Forgeries in Chinese Painting." *Oriental Art,* n.s., 32, no. 1 (Spring 1986): 54–66.

_____. "Identifying Shen Zhou (1427–1509): Methodological Problems in Authentication." *Oriental Art,* n.s., 55, no. 3 (March 2006): 48–60.

_____. *Old Masters Repainted: Wu Zhen (1280–1354), Prime Objects and Accretions.* Hong Kong: Hong Kong University Press, 1995.

Stuart, Jan. "Calling Back the Ancestor's Shadow: Chinese Ritual and Commemorative Portraits in the Arthur M. Sackler Gallery." *Oriental Art* 43, no. 3 (Autumn 1997): 8–17.

Wenley, A. G. "*A Spray of Bamboo* by Wu Chen." *Archives of the Chinese Art Society of America* 8 (1954): 7–9.

III. Basic Reference Works

Cahill, James. *An Index of Early Chinese Painters and Paintings: T'ang, Sung, and Yüan,* Berkeley: University of California Press, 1980.

Lovell, Hin-cheung. *An Annotated Bibliography of Chinese Painting Catalogues and Related Texts.* Ann Arbor: Center for Chinese Studies, University of Michigan, 1973.

Wilkinson, Endymion. *Chinese History: A Manual.* Revised and enlarged edition. Cambridge, Mass.: Harvard University Asia Center, 2000.

IV. Works on Seal and Cursive Scripts

Kuo, Jason. *Word as Image: The Art of Chinese Seal Engraving.* New York: China Institute in America, 1992.

Wang, Fangyü. *Introduction to Chinese Cursive Script.* New Haven: Far Eastern Publications, Yale University, 1958.

Wieger, Léon. *Chinese Characters: Their Origin, Etymology, History, Classification and Signification; A Thorough Study from Chinese Documents.* Translated by L. Davrout. New York: Dover Publications, 1965.

About the Editor

Jason C. Kuo is Professor of Art History and Archaeology at the University of Maryland and has taught at the National Taiwan University, Williams College, and Yale University. He is the author of *Wang Yüan-ch'i's Art of Landscape Painting* (Taipei: National Palace Museum, 1981), *Trapping Heaven and Earth in the Cage of Form* (Taipei: Shih-pao wen-hua Publishing, 1986), *Innovation within Tradition: The Painting of Huang Pin-hung* (Williamstown: Williams College Museum of Art, 1989), *The Austere Landscape: The Paintings of Hung-jen* (Taiwan and Seattle: SMC Publishing in cooperation with University of Washington Press, 1991), *Word as Image: The Art of Chinese Seal Engraving* (New York: China Institute in America; distributed by University of Washington Press, 1992), *Chen Chikwan* (Taipei: Chin-hsiu Publishing, 1995), *Rethinking Art History and Art Criticism* (Taipei: National Museum of History, 1996), *Practicing Art History and Art Criticism* (Taipei: National Museum of History, 2002), and *Transforming Traditions in Modern Chinese Painting: Huang Pin-hung's Late Work* (Bern and New York: Peter Lang, 2004). He is the editor of several books and exhibition catalogs, including *Heirs to a Great Tradition: Modern Chinese Painting from the Tsien-hsiang-chai Collection* (distributed by University of Washington Press, 1993), *Discovering Chinese Painting:*

Dialogues with American Art Historians (Dubuque: Kendall/ Hunt, 2000), *Understanding Asian Art* (Dubuque: Kendall/ Hunt Publishing, 2001), *Discovering Chinese Painting: Dialogues with Art Historians* (Dubuque: Kendall/Hunt, 2006), and *Visual Culture in Shanghai, 1850s–1930s* (Washington, D.C.: New Academia, 2007). His writings have appeared in numerous journals, including *Art Journal, Asian Culture Quarterly, Chinese Culture Quarterly, Chinese Studies, Bulletin of the National Palace Museum, Orientations, China Quarterly, Journal of Asian Studies, Journal of Asian and African Studies,* and *Ars Orientalis*. He has received an Andrew W. Mellon Foundation Fellowship, a grant from the National Endowment for the Humanities, two Stoddard Fellowships in Asian Art at the Detroit Institute of Arts, two fellowships from the J.D. Rockefeller III Fund, and many other scholastic honors. In 1991–1992, he received the Lilly Fellowship for teaching excellence at the University of Maryland. In 1992–1993 he organized and directed a National Endowment for the Humanities Summer Institute for College Teachers on "The Art of Imperial China." From 1993 to 1998, he undertook the study of the nineteenth- and twentieth-century art of Shanghai, a research project funded by the Henry Luce Foundation that combined the work of six scholars from China and six from the United States. He directed the Summer Institute of Connoisseurship in Chinese Calligraphy and Painting from 2001 to 2003, also funded by the Luce Foundation. He was a Fulbright Scholar in Taipei in 2001–2002.

About the Authors

James Cahill
In the field of Chinese painting, Cahill (Professor Emeritus of the History of Art, University of California at Berkeley) is generally regarded in the United States as its most important art historian, even though his stature is not unchallenged or unrivaled. In 1978–1979, he delivered the Charles Eliot Norton Lectures at Harvard University; since its establishment in 1925, the Norton Eliot Professorship of Poetry has become one of the nation's most illustrious guest lectureships, with past incumbents such as Luciano Berio, Leonard Bernstein, Harold Bloom, Jorge Luis Borges, John Cage, Carlos Chávez, Aaron Copland, e. e. cummings, Umberto Eco, T. S. Eliot, Robert Frost, Dame Helen Gardner, Paul Hindemith, Roger Sessions, Leo Steinberg, Frank Stella, Igor Stravinsky, Lionel Trilling, and Thornton Wilder. Cahill's lectures were published in 1982 as *The Compelling Image: Nature and Style in Seventeenth-Century Chinese Painting* (Cambridge: Harvard University Press, 1982). The book was awarded the College Art Association's Morey Prize for the best art history book of 1982. The College Art Association, recognizing that this is "a time of great methodological shifts in the field" and that the profession must foster a "dialogue within and among the different generations of art historians," saluted him as the Distinguished Scholar at its annual convention in 2004. In 2007, he received the Distinguished Lifetime Achievement Award for Writing on Art from the College Art Association.

His 1991 Bampton Lectures at Columbia University appeared in 1994 as *The Painter's Practice: How Artists Lived and Worked in Traditional China* (New York: Columbia University Press, 1994). He gave the Reischauer Lectures at Harvard University in 1993; these lectures appeared as a book in 1996 under the title *The Lyric Journey: Poetic Panting in China and Japan* (Cambridge: Harvard University Press, 1996). His Getty Lectures, given at the University of Southern California in 1994, will appear as a book to be titled *The Flower and the Mirror: Representations of Women in Late Chinese Painting*. Another book, *Pictures for Use and Pleasure: Urban Studio Artists in High Qing China*, is in press. A study of paintings done for women in the Ming-Qing period, given as a lecture at several places, is being prepared for publication.

His other publications include *An Index of Early Chinese Painters and Painting: T'ang, Sung, and Yuan* (Berkeley: University of California Press, 1980), *Hills Beyond a River: Chinese Painting of the Yuan Dynasty, 1279–1368* (New York: Weatherhill, 1976), *Parting at the Shore: Chinese Painting of the Early and Middle Ming Dynasty, 1368–1580* (New York: Weatherhill, 1978), *The Distant Mountains: Chinese Painting of the Late Ming Dynasty, 1570–1644* (New York: Weatherhill, 1978), and *Three Alternative Histories of Chinese Painting* (Lawrence: Spencer Museum of Art, University of Kansas, 1988).

Before his appointment at Berkeley, he was Curator of Chinese Art at the Freer Gallery of Art in Washington, D.C. Among U.S.-resident art historians of Chinese painting, Professor Cahill is perhaps the best known in China, in part because several of his books have been translated into Chinese, in part because he frequently traveled to and lectured at institutions of higher learning in China. For instance, he was Chair of the Chinese Painting Delegation to China in 1977. His writings on Chinese painting have generated much enthusiasm, as well as opposition and anger, among Chinese scholars, exactly because they differ from the standard versions of Chinese painting history, raise new issues, and make challenging arguments. An anthology of his essential writings will be published in Chinese soon.

Professor Cahill now lives in Vancouver with his wife Hsing-yuan Tsao, who teaches at the University of British Columbia, and their twelve-year-old twin sons Benedict and Julian.

Jerome Silbergeld

Jerome Silbergeld is the P. Y. and Kinmay W. Tang Professor of Chinese Art History at Princeton University and Director of Princeton's Tang Center for East Asian Art. He was previously the Chair of Art History and Director of the School of Art at the University of Washington at Seattle. He teaches and publishes research on the topics of traditional and contemporary Chinese painting, cinema, architecture, and gardens. Among his publications are *Chinese Painting Style: Media, Methods, and Principles* (Seattle: University of Washington Press, 1982), *Mind Landscape: The Paintings of C. C. Wang* (Seattle: Henry Art Gallery, University of Washington and University of Washington Press, 1987), *Contradictions: Artistic Life, the Socialist State, and the Chinese Painter Li Huasheng* (Seattle: University of Washington Press, 1993), *China into Film: Frames of Reference in Contemporary Chinese Cinema* (London: Reaktion Books, 1999), and *Hitchcock with a Chinese Face: Cinematic Doubles, Oedipal Triangles, and China's Moral Voice* (Seattle: University of Washington Press, 2004). He coedited (with Dora C. Y. Ching) *Persistence/Transformation: Text as Image in the Art of Xu Bing* (Princeton: Princeton University Press, 2006).

Richard Spear

Richard Spear is Visiting Professor in the Department of Art History and Archaeology at the University of Maryland, College Park. Prior to his appointment at Maryland, he taught at Oberlin College, where he also directed the Allen Memorial

Art Museum. He has served as Editor-in-Chief of *The Art Bulletin* and is the recipient of numerous awards, including grants from the American Council of Learned Societies, the National Endowments for the Humanities, the Center for Advanced Study in the Visual Arts of the National Gallery of Art, the National Humanities Center, and the Guggenheim and Rockefeller Foundations. His many publications have focused on Caravaggio and his followers and the school of the Carracci, particularly Domenichino and Guido Reni. His books include *Domenichino* (New Haven: Yale University Press, 1982) and *The "Divine" Guido: Religion, Sex, and Art in the World of Guido Reni* (New Haven: Yale University Press, 1997). His current research focuses on the economic lives of painters in seventeenth-century Rome.

John H. Brown
John H. Brown has been a member of the Philosophy Department at the University of Maryland at College Park since 1963, specializing in aesthetics and philosophy of art, including philosophy of art history. His publications include the articles "Beauty" and "Abstract Art" in the *Routledge Encyclopedia of Philosophy* (New York and London: Routledge, 1998). His recent works include projects that use digital technology to analyze space in visual art. These and other works can be accessed on his website, http://www.philosophy.umd.edu/Faculty/jhbrown.

Karen Lang
Karen Lang is Associate Professor of Art History at the University of Southern California. Her research focus is modern German art and aesthetic theory. Her book, *Chaos and Cosmos: On the Image in Aesthetics and Art History* (Ithaca: Cornell University Press, 2006), examines the conceptual foundations of the discipline of the history of art. In addition to her scholarship on art history as a field of study and the

ways we situate, address, and explain works of art, she has written on the concept of the monument and the monument's relation to German national identity in the late nineteenth and early twentieth centuries; Alexander Pope's garden and grotto; the grotto as "escape space," from the eighteenth century to Rem Koolhaas's Y2K House of 2000; and Kantian philosophy. Her second book project, *Max Beckmann's Inconceivable Modernism*, studies the artist's work in relation to an emerging canon of modern European art. Focusing on Beckmann's visual art, manifestos, plays, letters, and diaries, this book explores the ways works of art are translated and categorized into systems of knowledge such as "Modernism," or are rendered inconceivable within the parameters set up by these categories. Professor Lang teaches undergraduate courses on European modernism, visual culture, and critical approaches to modern art. Titles of her graduate seminars include "Theories and Methods of Art History," "The Sublime in Aesthetics and Visual Culture," "Style: Problems and Prospects in Art History and Aesthetics," and "New Books and the Book Review." Whenever possible, Professor Lang teaches with original works of art. Her seminar on German Expressionism focused on prints and drawings in three local collections; her fall 2006 seminar coincided with an exhibition at the Getty Museum titled "From Caspar David Friedrich to Gerhard Richter: German Paintings from Dresden." Her essays include "Encountering the Object," in *The Lure of the Object*, ed. Stephen Melville (New Haven: Yale University Press, 2005), 135–36; "The Hamburg Bismarck as City Crown and National Monument," in *Modernism and the Spirit of the City*, ed. Iain Boyd Whyte (New York: Routledge, 2003), 119–45; "The Far in the Near," *Art Bulletin* 89, no. 1 (2007): 26 34; "The Dialectics of Decay: Rereading the Kantian Subject," *Art Bulletin* 79, no. 3 (1997): 413–39; "Monumental Unease: Monuments and the Making of National Identity in Germany," in *Imagining Modern German Culture: 1889–1910*, ed. Francoise Forster-

Hahn (Washington, D.C.: National Gallery of Art, 1998), 274–99; "Reason and Remainders: Kantian Performativity in the History of Art," in *Performing the Body/Performing the Text*, ed. Amelia Jones and Andrew Stephenson (New York: Routledge, 1999), 11–27.

Index

www.ingramcontent.com/pod-product-compliance
Lightning Source LLC
Chambersburg PA
CBHW021647210526
45160CB00013B/38/J